TERMITES AND SOILS

TERMITES AND SOILS

K. E. LEE and T. G. WOOD

*C.S.I.R.O., Division of Soils,
Adelaide, South Australia*

1971
ACADEMIC PRESS
LONDON AND NEW YORK

ACADEMIC PRESS INC. (LONDON) LTD
Berkeley Square House
Berkeley Square
London, W1X 6BA

U.S. Edition published by
ACADEMIC PRESS INC.
111 Fifth Avenue
New York, New York 10003

Library of Congress Catalog Card Number: 76-153527
ISBN: 0-12-440850-8

Printed in Great Britain by The Whitefriars Press Ltd
London and Tonbridge

Foreword

Many books have been written on the chemistry and physics of the soil, on the mineralogy and colloids of the soil, on the geographical distribution of soils and on the morphological characteristics and classifications by which they can be described. Few have been devoted to the biology of soils.

Yet the one feature which distinguishes what we call soil from the decomposing rock fragments which are its precursors is the presence of living organisms.

The role that these organisms, the flora and fauna of the soil, play in the transformation of soil organic matter, in amending the conditions in which the mineral particles exist, and in altering the manner in which the ultimate physical particles are organized into structures is only just being appreciated. In some ways this is surprising, for it is more than a hundred years since Darwin first drew attention to the effect of earthworms on soils of temperate England. In Australia, where the earthworm population is restricted, termites appear likely to play an important role, and in many parts of the tropics the castellated architecture of their dwellings literally thrusts their activities on our attention.

When I asked Dr. Lee to come to Australia to set up the Soil Zoology Section of the Division of Soils, it seemed logical that he should make the first assignment of his group the study of the effect of termites on soils. It was first necessary to summarize what was known about this in the world at large, and this book represents a synthesis from the world's literature on termites and the early work that Drs. Lee and Wood have been able to undertake.

It appears that the role of termites in soils differs markedly from that of earthworms in temperate lands. However, it is still far from clear whether termites have a beneficial effect in our soils, or whether they are a luxury that mankind can not afford, but the work of the next few years in this field promises to be of great interest, in pedology no less than in agriculture. It may give a clue to the extent to which the two animal groups which possess the most highly organized social structures, man and the termites, can cohabit the Tropics.

E. G. HALLSWORTH

Chief, C.S.I.R.O.
Division of Soils
Adelaide
January, 1971

Acknowledgements

We gratefully acknowledge the assistance of the following members of staff of C.S.I.R.O., Division of Soils: our technical assistants, Messrs J. C. Buckerfield and R. W. George, who have helped us with field and laboratory work throughout our investigations; Mr. A. R. P. Clarke, for advice on chemical analyses, Dr. J. N. Ladd, for advice on biochemical analyses, Mr. J. Pickering, for determining the clay minerals in our samples of termite structures and soil samples, and Dr. R. Brewer and Mr. J. R. Sleeman for their assistance in preparing and interpreting thin sections of samples from mounds and other structures built by termites. Mr. F. J. Gay and Dr. J. A. L. Watson, C.S.I.R.O., Division of Entomology, have helped us with identification of Australian termite species, and given us much useful advice, while Dr. D. E. Bland, C.S.I.R.O., Division of Forest Products, determined the lignin content of samples of carton, and their help is gratefully acknowledged.

We are also indebted to Mr. P. H. Nye, University of Oxford, Mr. W. A. Sands, Termite Research Unit, British Museum (Natural History), Mr. F. J. Gay and Dr. J. A. L. Watson, C.S.I.R.O., Division of Entomology, and Dr. C. Noirot, Faculty of Science, University of Dijon, for their helpful criticism of the manuscript. We particularly thank Mr. W. A. Sands for his assistance in bringing the nomenclature of *Macrotermes* spp. into line with the recent revision of the genus by Ruelle (1970).

Preface

The aim of this book is to assess the role of termites as soil animals, bringing together for the first time the widely scattered observations and experimental data on the subject, and attempting to integrate biological and pedological knowledge relating to a most important, but previously rather neglected, component of the soil fauna.

Current knowledge of soil zoology derives very largely from work in the cool temperate zones of the world, where termites are usually rare and often absent, and comparatively little is known of soil animals in the warm temperate and tropical zones, where termites are numerous and commonly dominate the soil fauna. There is a vast literature on termites. Snyder (1956, 1961, 1968) listed 5809 publications in his annotated bibliographies of termites, which cover publications up to 1965, and the total may now be 8000 or more. However, the majority of papers concern taxonomy, biology, and control of termites as pests, and comparatively few have any direct bearing on the significance of termites as soil animals.

All termites except Kalotermitidae and some Termopsinae live in the soil or maintain some connection between their nests and the soil. Their principal effects on soils derive from their burrowing and nest building behaviour, and their digestive capabilities, especially their ability to decompose structural plant polysaccharides and to use these materials as their main source of energy. Few soil animals have the ability to digest structural polysaccharides, and studies of the significance of the fauna in soils lacking termites emphasize the importance of fungi and micro-organisms in the decomposition of plant tissue, with the major contribution of soil animals being the comminution of plant debris and its incorporation in the soil.

Earthworms usually dominate (in terms of biomass) the soils of cool temperate regions, and their effects on soil formation and litter decomposition have received much attention from soil zoologists and pedologists. The contributions to litter decomposition of enchytraeid worms, mites, Collembola, millipedes and many other groups of soil animals common in temperate regions have also been studied in detail. Frequent references to termites as soil animals are found in accounts of tropical soils, and it has often been presumed that they are the analogues in tropical soils of earthworms in soils of temperate regions, as was first suggested by Drummond (1886). There is some truth in this analogy, but it has tended to obscure the very great differences between these two groups of animals, especially in their effects on the distribution of organic matter in the soil and its decomposition.

Substantial contributions to understanding of the significance of termites in soils have been made, especially by French zoologists working in western Africa and English zoologists in eastern Africa. We have worked in Australia, where we have been fortunate in taking up the study of relationships between termites and soils at a time when basic taxonomic studies of the Australian termites and scientific studies of Australian soils have reached a high standard. This has enabled us to integrate the results of our work into a framework provided by others, to an extent that soil zoologists elsewhere have rarely been able to attain. We have frequently used our findings as a basis for comparison of results of termite investigations made elsewhere, but have tried not to put too much emphasis on Australian work. Much of the results of our work appear for the first time in this book, but more detailed accounts of some aspects of our studies have been published elsewhere (Lee and Wood, 1968; Wood and Lee, in press; Lee and Wood, in press).

The subject is treated under two principal headings; first (Chapters 1-4) some aspects of the biology, distribution, ecology, behaviour, and abundance of termites that are particularly relevant to their role as soil animals, and secondly (Chapters 5-9) the effects of the activities of termites on the physical and chemical constitution of soils, soil profile morphology, vegetation, and agricultural practices.

In a concluding chapter we attempt to summarize the significance of termites in the soil/plant ecosystem and compare their influence on the soil with the influence of other soil animals, especially earthworms. Techniques for sampling populations of termites in soils are discussed in an appendix. Authorities for termite names are listed in a glossary at the end of the book. Authorities for species other than termites appear in the text.

Many questions remain unanswered, and it has been our aim to draw attention to them in the hope that others will be stimulated to contribute to their solution.

K. E. LEE
T. G. WOOD

C.S.I.R.O.
Division of Soils
Adelaide
January, 1971

Contents

CHAPTER 1

Termite Classification, Biology and Geographical Distribution

The recently published "Biology of Termites" (Krishna and Weesner, Vol. I, 1969; Vol. II, 1970) draws together a vast amount of literature on various aspects of termite biology. However, with the notable exception of Bouillon's (1970) paper on the Ethiopian fauna in Volume II, the ecology of termites receives scant attention. The theme of our book is primarily an ecological one, but we must necessarily present a brief, general account of termites before considering relationships between termites and soils. For details of termite classification, biology, and distribution, interested readers are referred to the above-mentioned book and to the works of Hegh (1922), Grassé (1949), Ratcliffe *et al.* (1952), Skaife (1955), Weesner (1960), and Harris (1961). Detailed bibliographies to literature on termites have been compiled by Snyder (1956, 1961, 1968).

I. Classification

Insects of the order Isoptera are usually known as termites or "white ants", the latter being an unfortunate term as the insects are more closely related to cockroaches (Blattaria: Dictyoptera) than to the true ants (Formicoidea: Hymenoptera). Approximately 1900 living and fossil species of termites have been described, the vast majority being found within the tropics. We have followed the classification of Krishna (1969) which is largely based on the works of Snyder (1949) and Emerson (1955). This classification recognizes the following families and sub-families:

1. Mastotermitidae
2. Kalotermitidae
3. Hodotermitidae
   Termopsinae
   Stolotermitinae
   Porotermitinae
   Cretatermitinae (fossil)
   Hodotermitinae

   4. Rhinotermitidae
         Psammotermitinae
         Heterotermitinae
         Stylotermitinae
         Coptotermitinae
         Termitogetoninae
         Rhinotermitinae
   5. Serritermitidae
   6. Termitidae
         Amitermitinae
         Termitinae
         Macrotermitinae
         Nasutitermitinae

The first five families are known collectively as the lower termites and the sixth family (Termitidae), which includes approximately 75% of the known species, as the higher termites.

II. Biology

Termites are polymorphic, social insects which live in nests (termitaria) of their own construction. The termitaria, discussed in more detail in Chapter 2, serve to house and protect the colony, store food and maintain an optimum environment. Together with the social behaviour of the termites themselves, the termitaria tend to produce a condition of homeostasis by the self-regulation of optimal conditions for development, maintenance and reproduction of the society (Emerson, 1956). There appears to exist, within the society, a continual exchange of substances (trophallaxis) which guide the reciprocal behaviour of individuals (Stuart, 1967). Trophallaxis includes in addition to the exchange of nutrients, which is the "strict" meaning of the term, recognition of colony mates, inter-individual communication, distribution of pheromones involved in caste differentiation and caste elimination (by cannibalism), and transfer of cellulose-digesting protozoa in those families (lower termites) harbouring them (McMahan, 1969). The functioning of the society is based on this self-regulated behaviour of individuals and division of labour among the different groups (castes) within the colony.

   Detailed treatment of various aspects of the biology of termites can be found in the works cited at the beginning of this chapter. Aspects we consider to be significant to the theme of this book are discussed below.

A. Castes

The individuals comprising a colony of termites consist of several castes which are morphologically and functionally distinct. Newly hatched individuals (larvae) are capable of developing into any caste depending upon the requirements of the colony. The direction of differentiation is acquired before the first moult and appears to depend upon pheromones given off by members of the reproductive and soldier castes, although the problem is complex and is by no means fully understood. Further control of the proportions of different castes is achieved by selective cannibalism of soldiers or reproductives on the part of the workers.

1. Reproductive castes

The reproductive castes consist of primary and secondary reproductives. Primary reproductives (also known as first form reproductives, winged imagines or alates) consist of males (kings) and females (queens). They leave the nest at certain times of the year (the well-known phenomenon of swarming), shed their wings and attempt to mate and establish a new colony. In those pairs (only a fraction of the total) that succeed in establishing a new colony the king shows little change during the rest of his life and his sole task is to fertilize the queen. In contrast, the queen undergoes several internal changes manifested externally by the abdomen increasing in size as the ovaries enlarge and egg-laying capacity increases. In the primitive Kalotermitidae, which have small colonies, the queen's abdomen is only slightly enlarged, whereas in many termites, notably the Macrotermitinae, with extremely large colonies the queen is physogastric and may be 12 cm in length. Such queens are more or less immobile and often spend their lives in a specially constructed portion of the nest (the royal chamber). The queen is attended by the king, soldiers and workers. Alates develop through a series of nymphal instars. Alates produced within a colony have no function within that colony (with the exception of adultoids noted below) although they may occasionally be dealated within the nest with subsequent atrophy of their reproductive organs and assumption of the role of workers.

The supplementary reproductives develop functional reproductive organs without leaving the parent colony and are of three types. Adultoid reproductives, developed from imagines, are found only in certain Termitidae. Other supplementary reproductives are neotenics and develop functional reproductive organs without becoming alates. Brachypterous neotenics (also known as second form reproductives or nymphoids) possess wing buds and develop from juveniles (nymphs) that have already developed wing buds. Apterous neotenics (also known as third form reproductives or ergatoids) do not possess wing buds and develop from juveniles (larvae) that have not developed wing buds. The function of supplementary reproductives is to act as substitutes for the king or queen should either or both of these die, or to supplement the egg-laying capacity of the queen should this fall below the level necessary to maintain the colony. As they are not as fecund as the queen several, sometimes hundreds, are found within a single colony. Their development is regulated according to the requirements of the colony; it can be accelerated, retarded or, should there be a shortage of workers or soldiers, even reversed. Most species of termites are capable of producing neotenics, although certain species such as *Nasutitermes exitiosus* in Australia (Ratcliffe *et al.*, 1952) appear to have lost the faculty.

2. *Sterile castes*

The most important sterile castes are the workers and the soldiers, which are apterous individuals in which the development of sexual organs is suppressed or the organs are atrophied. The workers are by far the most numerous caste in the termite colony. In the Termitidae they are preceded by two larval instars, except in the Macrotermitinae which have three larval instars. In this family the workers consist of "stable" individuals which have achieved their final development and also other individuals which are capable of further moulting, either whilst remaining as workers or by transformation to soldiers. With the possible exception of Rhinotermitidae and possibly some species of Hodotermitidae, there are no "stable" workers in the lower termites and the so-called workers are pseudergates ("false workers"). Pseudergates retain the potential of caste differentiation and of developing into soldiers or sexuals; they develop either by regression from nymphal stages by moults that reduce or eliminate wing buds or from larvae by "stationary" non-differentiating moults. Workers may be dimorphic, consisting of major (large) and minor (small) forms which may be males or females depending upon the species concerned. The true workers take no part in reproduction and "workers" (including pseudergates) seldom take part in defence of the colony. However, they are responsible for all foraging activity and they care for the eggs, larvae and queen. The larvae, soldiers and queen are incapable of feeding themselves and rely for their nourishment on the workers. In the Macrotermitinae the workers are also responsible for maintaining the "fungus gardens".

Soldiers are, like the workers, wingless and sterile. They are distinguished by their modified mouth parts and strongly chitinized heads, which are usually pigmented and often larger than the heads of other castes. Two well-defined types of soldiers can be distinguished, the mandibulate type with large, prominent and often grotesquely-shaped mandibles and the nasute type in which the rostrum is prolonged into a "snout" and the mandibles are small or vestigial. In most species soldiers are of one sex, either male or female, depending upon the species. Dimorphism, with the existence of major and minor forms as in the workers, is common and some species have trimorphic soldiers. Soldiers are a "stable" caste incapable of moulting. They are always preceded by a "white soldier" stage (pre-soldier, soldier-nymph) which in the lower termites develops from a larva, pseudergate or nymph, but in the Termitidae develops from a larva or a worker. The function of soldiers is to defend the colony within the precincts of the nest and also to defend workers which may be foraging at some distance from the nest. Their powerful mandibles are effective against certain predators, such as some of the ants, but certain species have adopted chemical warfare as a means of defence. The nature of some of these defensive secretions has been discussed by Moore (1969). The Rhinotermitidae have mandibulate soldiers but some species, such as members of the genera *Rhinotermes* and *Coptotermes,* can secrete a viscous, white fluid from the frontal pore on the anterior margin of the head. Nasute soldiers of the Nasutitermitinae rely entirely upon this method for defence and their secretions appear to be highly irritating not only to ants, the principal enemies of termites, but also to vertebrates. The heads of soldiers of certain species are particularly enlarged and in *Cryptotermes* the shape is such that the head is used effectively to plug tunnels and entrance holes to the nest.

In addition to soldiers and workers there are other sterile castes of minor importance. Intercastes are individuals which are morphologically intermediate between soldiers and sexuals or soldiers and workers. Achrestogonimes are alate imagines which remain in the nest after swarming, lose their wings and suffer atrophy of their gonads, are capable of feeding themselves but play no useful role in the maintenance of the colony.

B. Food

Two types of food can be distinguished: that provided by the workers to the dependent castes and that obtained by the workers. Larvae, nymphs of some families and reproductives are incapable of feeding themselves and are fed by the workers with either stomodeal or proctodeal food. Stomodeal food may be a clear liquid (presumed to be saliva), which is the sole nourishment of the functional reproductives, or regurgitated food. Soldiers are fed largely on the latter but in certain Termitidae they have an exclusively liquid diet. Proctodeal feeding is practised only in the lower termites which have a protozoan intestinal fauna. Proctodeal food consists of liquid excretions from the rectal pouches and is excreted in response to tactile stimuli from other termites; in Kalotermitidae it is quite distinct from the dry, solid pellets excreted from the rectum (Grassé, 1949). By this means larvae fed on proctodeal food acquire the protozoa essential for digestion (see p. 125). The food collected by the workers, both for their own use and for the dependent castes, is the basic energy resource of the colony. It consists of plant material, either living, dead, partially or almost entirely decomposed. The source and subsequent decomposition of food has far reaching implications in relationships between termites and soils, as by their feeding activities and subsequent transformation of the food by digestion (see

Chapter 6), termites affect the cycling of organic matter and nutrients. In addition the concentration of food and waste products of digestion in termitaria influences the disposition of organic matter and nutrients in the ecosystem. The different types of food of the worker termites are considered below.

1. Wood

Grassé and Noirot (1959b) regarded a xylophagous diet as primitive. This diet is retained, not only in the majority of the lower termites, but also by many Termitidae. The condition of the wood appears to be important in determining whether or not it is suitable for a particular species.

Living wood appears to be attacked by relatively few species (Adamson, 1943). In Australia and Malaya members of the genus *Coptotermes* habitually feed on living trees, but with the exception of a few species belonging to genera such as *Schedorhinotermes, Heterotermes, Zootermopsis* and *Reticulitermes,* termites feeding on living wood are largely members of the Kalotermitidae (and, in Australia, Mastotermitidae). Very few Termitidae appear to feed on living wood. *Sound dead wood* is the chief diet of Kalotermitidae, Rhinotermitidae and certain members of the Hodotermitidae and Termitidae. Among the higher termites, many of the Macrotermitinae and Nasutitermitinae feed on this substrate. *Rotten* or *decaying wood* is the principal food of many Hodotermitidae (all sub-families except the Hodotermitinae), Rhinotermitidae, certain members of the Termitidae but few Kalotermitidae. Many species will feed only after the wood is in an advanced state of decomposition and it is possible that fungi are an important constituent in the diet of these species. In addition fungi may also render the wood more digestible and decompose repellent or toxic substances. Williams (1965) showed that the heartwood of *Pinus caribaea* Morelet was both toxic and repellent to *Coptotermes niger* due to its content of resin and turpentine, but when these substances were broken down by a brown-rot fungus (*Lentinus pallidus* Berk. and Curt.) the rotten heartwood was readily attacked by the termite. The fungus also appeared to have some nutritional value to the termites as they survived longer on a diet of rotten heartwood than on sound heartwood from which the repellent and toxic substances had been removed by solvents. Sands (1969) has reviewed the relationships between termites and fungi. Several termites appear to be nutritionally dependent on certain wood-rotting fungi. Others, although not dependent on fungi, benefit from their presence and many species (including some of the typically sound, dead wood-feeders, such as Kalotermitidae) have shown a positive response to wood infected with fungi or to fungal extracts; some species have shown a negative response. It has been suggested (Grassé, 1949 and others) that such fungi provide vitamins and "growth factors" but this has not been demonstrated.

Little is known of the feeding preferences of wood-feeding termites. Noirot and Noirot-Timothée (1969) suggested that there appeared to be little specificity or preference for certain types of vegetation. This may be true for many species of termites but some species do exhibit distinct likes or dislikes for certain timbers. In Tanzania, Bouillon (1970) noted that on the coastal plains *Bifiditermes durbanensis* occurs commonly in *Brachystegia* and other trees but never in *Acacia*, while in other areas on higher ground it is found in a particular species of *Acacia*. Ratcliffe *et al.* (1952) pointed out that several Australian trees were very resistant to attack by termites. Jarrah (*Eucalyptus marginata* Donn ex Sm.) is very resistant to attack by *Coptotermes* but is somewhat susceptible to *Nasutitermes exitiosus*, whereas hoop pine (*Araucaria cunninghamii* Ait. ex D. Don.) is susceptible to *Coptotermes* but resistant to *N. exitiosus*. The work of Moore (1965) has indicated that substances present in certain trees may influence the behaviour of termites. The "alarm" pheromone of *Nasutitermes exitiosus* is largely composed of α- and β-pinenes which are present in the essential oils of many species of plants and occur in large quantities in most pine (*Pinus* spp.) trees. It is known (Ratcliffe *et al.*, 1952) that where native *Eucalyptus* forest has been cleared and the ground planted with pines, colonies of *N. exitiosus* do not persist for very long even though there may be plenty of *Eucalyptus* timber available. In contrast, *Coptotermes lacteus*, which does not have these compounds in its pheromones, readily attacks pine wood. Even within a given piece of wood termites may select certain portions in preference to others. For instance, Snyder (1948) noted that *Reticulitermes* ate the larger-celled, faster-growing tissue and left the smaller-celled, denser wood untouched. Bouillon (1970) also noted that whereas *Coptotermes* attacks only the spring wood of rubber trees, *Cryptotermes* attacks both spring and autumn woods, and *Macrotermes bellicosus* attacks bark, cambium and wood equally. Rudman and Gay (1963, 1967a, b) investigated some of the factors responsible for the natural resistance of certain trees to attack by termites. They concluded that chemical substances in the wood were the principal factor involved in resistance of certain species (e.g. *Eucalyptus microcorys* F. Muell.) and in differences in susceptibility of different regions (e.g. inner and outer heartwood of *Eucalyptus marginata*) of the one species.

Some of the wood-eating termites tend to be polyphagous and consume not only wood but a wide variety of living plants, plant debris, dung and a variety of stored products and materials used by man. These polyphagous species are major pests in many areas (Snyder, 1948; Ratcliffe *et al.*, 1952; Harris, 1961). One species worth noting here is the sand termite, *Psammotermes hybostoma* (Rhinotermitidae), of the Sahara desert. Harris (1970, quoting Bernard) stated that in some areas it appears to exist on wind-blown accumulations of vegetable debris and animal droppings. In areas of complete desert it may exist on exposures of subfossil relics of a humid Pleistocene flora. In less arid areas all types of plant are attacked, even those which are highly poisonous to mammals.

2. Grass, herbs and plant litter

Foraging or harvester termites include species which forage on the surface and cut down standing grass and herbs (the true harvesters) and also those that collect leaves, twigs, seeds and other plant litter lying on the soil surface. It would be preferable to regard the latter group as scavengers, rather than harvesters, but there is no clear-cut distinction between the two groups. Species such as *Hodotermes mossambicus* in South Africa (Coaton, 1954) and *Drepanotermes* spp. in Australia (Watson and Perry, in prep.), which are predominantly harvesters, also collect various types of plant debris lying on the surface. On the other hand, *Amitermes neogermanus* which is predominantly a scavenger, often attacks the aerial parts of grasses (Ratcliffe *et at.*, 1952). At the other end of the scavenger range are those species feeding on well-decomposed plant material, dung or similar substrates. It is quite likely that these species ingest soil, more or less incidentally, whilst feeding and are therefore akin to those species feeding on "humus". However, it is preferable to include in the latter category only those species whose principal food is soil rich in organic matter (see below).

The true harvesters are the Hodotermitinae (*Hodotermes* of Africa, *Microhodotermes* of northern Africa and *Anacanthotermes* of northern Africa and the arid belt of Asia); some Amitermitinae (such as *Drepanotermes* in Australia); and some Nasutitermitinae (such as certain *Nasutitermes* and *Tumulitermes* in Australia, *Trinervitermes* in Africa and Indo-Malaya, and *Syntermes* in South America). These species invariably store harvested material in their nests, sometimes in exceedingly large quantities (Fig. 1; see also p. 58).

The size of fragments of harvested material stored in nests varies with the species concerned. We (Wood and Lee, in press) studied three grass-harvesting species in an area of savanna woodland in northern Australia; the mean length (mm) of stored grass-fragments was 8.61 ± 0.51 for *Nasutitermes triodiae,* 7.71 ± 0.25 for *Drepanotermes rubriceps* and 6.50 ± 0.23 for *Drepanotermes* sp. (Fig. 2).

We had no information on the species of grasses or other plant material harvested by these three species but more detailed investigations (Watson and Perry, in prep.) of the material stored in nests of *Drepanotermes* spp. indicate that there are seasonal and regional variations in the type of material collected. In addition *D. rubriceps* is principally a grass-harvester whereas *Drepanotermes* sp., in addition to harvesting grass, also stores a considerable proportion of chopped-up leaves of non-graminaceous plants and also seeds and small twigs which it probably collects from the ground-surface. Sands' (1961) studies of three sympatric grass-harvesting species of *Trinervitermes* in northern Nigeria

Fig. 1. Outer galleries of a mound of *Nasutitermes triodiae*, near Mareeba, Queensland, showing harvested grass stored for food, and probably also serving as insulation.

showed that *T. geminatus* stored longer fragments (mean length 6.26 mm) than *T. trinervius* (3.76 mm) and *T. togoensis* (3.97 mm). The food preferences of *T. geminatus* and *T. trinervius* were very similar, both consuming a wide range of species. The smaller, fine-leaved grasses were preferred to larger, coarser-leaved grasses and both species showed little inclination to eat *Aristida kerstingii* Pilger, a particularly tough and resistant species, or *Cymbopogon citratus* (Hochst.) which is reputed to be repellent to insects. There is thus little information available on the feeding habits and food preferences of the harvester termites. There is, however, a distinct need for information of this nature as, in addition to their more obvious effects on denudation and erosion (see p. 171), these species may have some effect on the composition of the vegetation itself. In this connection it is interesting to note that in the savanna where Sands (1961) studied *Trinervitermes* the smaller fine grasses (the preferred food of the termites) were comparatively scarce compared with the larger grasses which were less palatable to the termites.

Even less is known about the habits and food preferences of scavenging termites feeding on freshly fallen plant litter, decaying plant remains, dung and similar substrates. With very few exceptions, scavenging termites belong to the

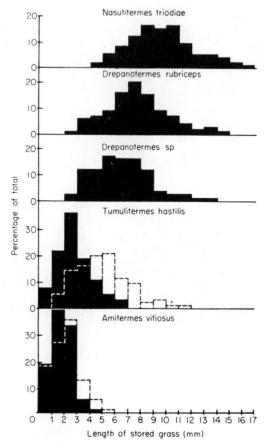

Fig. 2. Lengths of stored grass in termite mounds. Continuous lines for five species of termites near Larrimah, N.T., Australia. Broken lines for mounds at Tennant Creek, N.T., where *Drepanotermes* was rare and *Nasutitermes triodiae* was absent. (After Wood and Lee, in press.)

Termitidae, and lower termites with these habits are often polyphagous. Some of the harvester termites, such as *Anacanthotermes* in North Africa (Harris, 1970), tend to be polyphagus, consuming a wide variety of plant debris, such as dry grass, straw and trash from date palms, dung and occasionally wood. We have summarized (Table 1) the feeding habits of those Australian termites listed by Gay and Calaby (1970) and only two of the lower termites, *Mastotermes darwiniensis* and *Schedorhinotermes intermedius,* which have been occasionally found in dung, fall into the category of scavengers. Among the Termitidae there are many species known to be scavengers. In the genus *Amitermes,* there are seven species known to feed on dung, eight feeding on various types of plant debris (litter) and five feeding on grass; some of this last group possibly combine the harvesting habit with scavenging. In the genus *Nasutitermes* there are four litter-feeding species and four species feeding on grass, although at least two of the latter, *N. triodiae* and *N. magnus*, are harvesters, not scavengers. In the genus *Tumulitermes* there are five litter-feeding species and seven species feeding on grass, although at least one of the latter, *T. pastinator*, is probably a harvester, not a scavenger. Some of these scavenging species store food in their nests. The stored material is often, as in the case of *Tumulitermes tumuli*, so finely comminuted that its origin is not obvious. In some species, such as *Amitermes vitiosus*, *Tumulitermes hastilis* (Fig. 2) and *A. laurensis* the stored portions of material are of sufficient dimensions that they can be recognized; in the case of these three species grass appears to constitute a large proportion of the diet. However, food-storage is probably the exception, rather than the rule, among scavenging termites. This appears to be true at least for the Australian fauna where the majority of scavengers, such as the many species of *Amitermes*, live a subterranean existence in small colonies. Two of the five species of *Trinervitermes* studied by Sands (1961) in northern Nigeria, *T. oeconomus* and *T. occidentalis*, are scavengers and browsers and, in contrast to the three other species which are harvesters, they do not store food in their nests.

Closer examination of the habits and food preferences of scavenging termites will probably indicate that although a wide variety of plants, in various stages of decomposition, are eaten, many species will have distinct preferences. As a result of extensive feeding trials, Skaife (1955) concluded that *Amitermes hastatus* showed a distinct preference for partially decomposed stems of reed-like plants belonging to the family Restionaceae. The degree of decomposition appeared to be of some significance, the preferred state being soft stems still retaining their original form. The termites also fed on moist, rotten wood, and in the absence of their preferred foods also consumed dung. They rejected a wide range of natural foods including "leaf mould" and "humus". As we have already noted, in discussion of the wood-feeding termites, the preferences of species feeding on partially decomposed plant material are likely to be influenced by the growth of fungi and other micro-organisms on these substrates.

Ferrar and Watson (1970) examined records of dung-feeding termites in Australia and their findings are summarized in Table 2. The collections were strongly biased towards bovine dung which was the food of all but five of the 46 dung-feeding species and sub-species. The relatively low incidence of species in the dung of native animals is probably a reflection of the low incidence of collecting rather than a preference for the dung of introduced animals. The majority of the species also fed on wood, some fed on various forms of plant debris and grass, while a few (principally *Mastotermes* and the Rhinotermitidae) also attacked crops and various forms of manufactured plant products. Only six species, all relatively rare, were found solely in dung. Termites attack both moist

TABLE 1

The Food Habits of Australasian Termites (Information Taken from Gay and Calaby, 1970)

Genus	Number of species in genus	Number of species considered	Wood Living	Wood Sound dead	Wood Rotten dead	Grass	Various plant debris	Living herbaceous and woody plants	Dung	"Carton" in occupied termitaria
Mastotermitidae										
Mastotermes	1	1	1	1				1	1	1
Kalotermitidae										
Neotermes	1	1		1	1					
Kalotermes	7	6	3	6	1					
Ceratokalotermes	1	1	1	1						
Glyptotermes	5	3	3	3						
Bifiditermes	1	1	1	1						
Cryptotermes	3	1	1	1						
Hodotermitidae										
Stolotermitinae										
Stolotermes	5	4		1	4					
Porotermitinae										
Porotermes	1	1	1	1	1					
Rhinotermitidae										
Rhinotermitinae										

Taxon									
Coptotermitinae									
Coptotermes	6	6	4	6	1	5	8	2	
Termitidae									
Amitermitinae									
Amitermes	57	19	12		5	5	8	1	1	7
*Drepanotermes**	2	1				1				3
Ahamitermes	3	3								1
Incolitermes	1	1			1					
Microcerotermes	11	6	6		1		1	1		
Termitinae									
Protocapritermes	1	1	1	1						
Paracapritermes	2	1	1	1			1			
Termes	19	3	3	3						
Nasutitermitinae									
Nasutitermes	19	10	7	1	4	4	4			
Tumulitermes	17	7	2	1	1	7	5			
Occasitermes	1	1	1	1						
Occulitermes	1	1								
Australitermes	1									
Macrosubulitermes	2									

} Feeding habits unknown

*A revision of this genus (Watson and Perry, in prep.) recognizes several species.

TABLE 2

The Feeding Habits of Termites Recorded from Dung in Australia
(Adapted from Ferrar and Watson, 1970)

Dung—native: 1 (Emu), 2 (Kangaroo/Wallaby), 3 (Wombat)
Dung—exotic: 1 (Camel), 2 (Cattle), 3 (Horse), 4 (Sheep)
Wood: 1 (Living), 2 (Dead—dry), 3 (Dead—decaying)

Species	Dung		Various plant debris	Grass	Crops	Wood	Manu-factured plant products
	Native	Exotic					
Mastotermitidae							
Mastotermes							
darwiniensis		2	+		+	1,2	+
Rhinotermitidae							
Heterotermes							
ferox		2,3				2	+
Heterotermes							
p. paradoxus		2			+	2,3	+
H. p. intermedius		2,3				2	+
Schedorhino-							
termes							
intermedius		2			+	1,2	+
S. seclusus		3			+	1,2	
Termitidae—							
Amitermitinae							
Amitermes							
abruptus	2	2,3,4		+		2	
A. agrilis		2		+		2	
A. boreus		2,3		+		2	
A. colonus		3,4				2	
A. darwini		2,3,4	+			2	
A. dentosus		2,3,4				2	
A. deplanatus		3				2	
A. eucalypti		2				2	
A. exilis		2,3				2	+
A. germanus		2,3				2	
A. gracilis		2					
A. hartmeyeri	2	2,3				2	
A. herbertensis		2			+	2,3	
A. heterognathus		2	+			2	
A. lanceolatus		2,3				2,3	
A. latidens		2			+	1,2	
A. lativentris		2				2,3	
A. laurensis		2	+	+			
A. modicus		2		+		2	
A. neogermanus		1,2,3		+		2	

Table 2–*cont.*

Species	Dung		Various plant debris	Grass	Crops	Wood	Manufactured plant products
	Native	Exotic					
Termitidae							
Amitermitinae— *cont.*							
A. obtusidens		2,3			+	2	
A. parvus*		2					
A. peramatus	1	2		+		2	
A. vitiosus		2,3	+	+		2	
A. westraliensis		2		+		2,3	
A. xylophagus	3					2,3	
A. sp. nr. *colonus*		2		+			
A. sp. nr. *dentosus*		2					
A. sp. nr. *eucalypti*		2					
A. sp. nr. *obtusidens*		2					
A. sp. no close affinities		2		+			
Microcerotermes cavus		2				2	
M. distinctus		2				2,3	+
M. nervosus		2				2	
M. serratus		2,3			+	2	
Nasutitermitinae							
Nasutitermes eucalypti		2				2,3	
N. kimberleyensis		2				2	
N. longipennis		2		+		2,3	
N. torresi		2,3					
Tumulitermes comatus		2	+	+		2,3	
T. dalbiensis		3	+	+			

*Doubtful record.

(i.e. fresh) and dry (i.e. old) dung. There was little information regarding feeding on moist dung, partly due to under-collecting, but the termites may possibly be seeking moisture, rather than food, in wet dung. The majority of the records were from old dung and apparently, in northern Queensland, an average sized bovine dung pad is disintegrated in approximately three months.

3. Humus

There has been a certain amount of confusion over the term "humus-feeding" as applied to termites and in addition to the well-known, soil-ingesting groups (such as *Cubitermes*), species feeding on substrates such as dung and plant litter in various stages of decomposition have been described as humivores (see MacGregor, 1950). However, as noted above, it is preferable to regard humivores as those species which habitually ingest appreciable quantities of mineral soil. This habit was noted by Fuller (1918) who suggested that *Cubitermes bilobatus* fed on soil containing much humus (i.e. organic matter). Kalshoven (1941) stated that *Capritermes* spp. appeared to feed entirely on humus. Adamson (1943) examined the gut contents of various termites from Trinidad and showed that in the following species they consisted largely of soil, apparently swallowed indiscriminately without selection of organic particles: *Anoplotermes* spp., *Labiotermes labralis*, *Cavitermes tuberosus* and *Crepititermes verruculosus*; soil also appeared to be an important, though less conspicuous, part of the diet of *Armitermes holmgreni*, *Termes hispaniolae*, *Neocapritermes angusticeps* and some species of *Subulitermes*. Thus, there is sufficient evidence that humus-feeding is a habit more or less distinct from scavenging. It is most unlikely that soil is ingested indiscriminately but that there is selection, as there is in earthworms, of certain organic-rich components. However, this is an aspect of termite-feeding about which nothing is known.

Recent investigations have established a correlation between humus-feeding and morphology of the mouth parts. Sands (1965c) stated that "... the most characteristic adaptation of soil-humus feeding termites is the loss of transverse grinding ridges on the molar plates (of the workers), particularly the right one, and their transformation to crushing cusps by the development of rounded flanges on both sides. This occurs convergently in the sub-families Termitinae, Amitermitinae and Nasutitermitinae and in the latter is the distinguishing feature (in the Ethiopian fauna) of the *Paracornitermes* branch". Deligne (1966) studied the gut contents and mouth parts of a wide range of species and concluded that the humivorous diet was correlated with a similar modification of the molar plate. Among the species studied by Deligne, the Nasutitermitinae included two Neotropical genera and three of the six Ethiopian genera included in Sands' *Paracornitermes* branch; the Amitermitinae included one humivorous genus (*Anoplotermes*); most of the humus-feeders were in the Termitinae (16 genera, which included all those examined except *Termes* and *Neocapritermes*). In addition to these genera, the humivorous diet has been attributed to species within the genera *Labiotermes, Subulitermes* and *Armitermes* (Nasutitermitinae) by Adamson (1943); *Termes* (Adamson, 1943; Corbett and Miller, 1936), *Neocapritermes, Crepititermes* (Adamson, 1943) and *Capritermes* (Kalshoven, 1941) (Termitinae); *Eurytermes, Speculitermes, Euhamitermes, Firmitermes, Pseudhamitermes, Eburnitermes* and others (Amitermitinae) by Noirot and Noirot-Timothée (1969).

These proven and suspected humivorous species appear to be widely distributed throughout the Neotropical, Ethiopian and Oriental regions (Araujo, 1970; Bouillon, 1970; Roonwall, 1970). However, of the genera discussed above only *Termes* occurs in the Australasian region and the species in this genus appear to be largely wood-feeders and scavengers (Hill, 1942; Gay and Calaby, 1970). There is, as yet, no evidence that any Australasian species are humivores.

4. Fungi

We have already noted the importance of fungi to many of the termites feeding on rotten wood and also the likelihood that fungi are of some significance to scavengers and humivores. Kalshoven (1958) noted that the "black termites", *Hospitalitermes* spp. (Nasutitermitinae), of Indo-Malaya fed largely on lichens growing on tree trunks and other structures, but it is not known whether fungi or algae are the more important resource.

Association between termites and fungi has reached its highest degree of specialization in the Macrotermitinae. Sands (1969) has summarized the literature, which includes several conflicting opinions, on this subject. These termites construct special structures, known as "fungus combs", in their nests. Sands believes that they are constructed primarily from faecal material (but see p. 143). They support a growth of various fungi belonging to the genus *Termitomyces*. Their function appears to be partly nutritional and partly concerned with environmental control within the nest (see also pp. 59, 64). The fungus combs are not static structures but are continually being eaten by the termites and replaced with fresh faecal material. However, the fungus combs constitute only a small proportion of the diet and although the fungus probably breaks down lignin (see p. 143), its primary nutritional function may be to provide nitrogenous materials and vitamins. It is not known for certain that the fungus combs are an essential part of the diet of Macrotermitinae; Grassé (1959b) has kept a colony of *Macrotermes* alive for 18 months on rotten wood alone, but Sands (1956) showed that the survival of *Odontotermes badius* in the absence of viable fungus comb did not differ from its survival under conditions of starvation.

5. *Special diets*

Kaiser (1953) reported on the specialized root-feeding habits of *Anoplotermes pacificus* in South America. It is a humus-feeder and its nests are invaded by a dense mat of plant roots. The termites eat the roots, showing preference for the apices of young roots which are in the process of invading the termitaria. Small, bulbous swellings appear at the tips of attacked roots and these swellings are also eaten by the termites. Thus, the termites appear to be practising "root culture". The relationship appears to be a symbiotic one, as in abandoned termitaria the roots are dead.

The consumption of "carton", the faecal material used by many termites to construct portions of their nests (see p. 139), is a normal process among certain species that enlarge their nests by a process of reorganization (see p. 29). However, in Australia there are two genera, *Ahamitermes* and *Incolitermes*, which are obligate inquilines in nests of *Coptotermes* (Gay and Calaby, 1970) and their food consists entirely of the carton produced by their hosts. We have found (p. 36) that the carton of *Coptotermes acinaciformis* and *C. lacteus* is unusual in containing much undigested wood, and this may explain the association of the two genera with nests of *Coptotermes*.

6. *Cannibalism and oophagy*

Grassé (1949) noted that in the early stages of colony foundation the king and queen often consume considerable quantities of eggs. We have already noted that workers may control the proportions of various castes by selective cannibalism. In addition, the workers also consume unhealthy and wounded individuals, corpses and exuviae and Gay and Calaby (1970) noted that *Amitermes laurensis* often stored large numbers of dead termites in the outer galleries of its mounds, probably for food purposes.

Cannibalism appears to be a response to protein starvation under certain circumstances. Cook and Scott (1933) and Hendee (1934) observed a high incidence of cannibalism in laboratory cultures of *Zootermopsis angusticollis* fed on a diet of pure carbohydrate or fungus-free wood. However, as pointed out by Ratcliffe *et al.* (1952), there is no information on the incidence of cannibalism under natural conditions. Its primary function is probably that of nest-sanitation as in relatively few species can dead termites be found in the nest. Protein conservation may be only of secondary importance but may occasionally contribute towards survival of the colony.

C. ALIMENTARY SYSTEM OF THE WORKERS

Noirot and Noirot-Timothée (1969) have discussed the anatomy and functions of the alimentary system in some detail. Basically the alimentary canal consists of a *fore-gut* comprising oesophagus, crop and gizzard, a *mid-gut* which is usually a simple tube, and a hind-gut consisting of five segments, the segment preceding the enteric valve, the enteric valve, paunch, colon and rectum. The lower termites, which are largely wood-feeders and have a protozoan intestinal fauna located in the paunch, have an alimentary canal of fairly constant anatomy. In the Termitidae, the Macrotermitinae have an alimentary canal similar to that of the lower termites, whereas the other sub-families exhibit variations, which, surprisingly, are only poorly correlated with feeding habits. For instance, humus-feeders have a particularly well-developed hind-gut but possess both of the two types of alimentary system recognized by Noirot and Noirot-Timothée (1969) in the Termitinae. These authors also recognized two types of alimentary system in the Nasutitermitinae with nasute soldiers. One type is found in the *Subulitermes* group, which are largely humus-feeders, and the other in the *Nasutitermes* group which include wood-feeders, grass-feeders and scavengers.

The digestive processes of termites will be considered later in relation to the processes of transformation of organic matter (Chapter 6).

III. Geographical Distribution

The distribution of termites has recently been discussed by a number of authors in the second volume of "Biology of Termites" (Krishna and Weesner, 1970), and it is not our intention to discuss the subject in detail.

The great majority of termites live in tropical and subtropical regions, but they extend into the temperate zone to about 45°N (Harris, 1970) or 48°N (Emerson, 1955), and about 45°S (Araujo, 1970). Between these latitudes lie about two-thirds of the earth's land surface.

Of the 41 species known from the Palaearctic region, 34 belong to the lower termite families Kalotermitidae, Hodotermitidae and Rhinotermitidae, while seven are included in the typically tropical and supposedly more recent family Termitidae (Harris, 1970). Gay and Calaby (1970) similarly note that of 172 Australian species there are about equal numbers of species north and south of the Tropic of Capricorn, but there is a preponderance of Termitidae to the north and of lower termites to the south of the Tropic. Only four species, two Kalotermitidae and two Hodotermitidae are known from Tasmania.

About 1900 living and fossil species have been described (Krishna, 1969). The greatest number of species is in the Ethiopian region where Bouillon (1970) recognized 570 species, of 89 genera. Within the tropics, many species in Africa and South America are found in rain forests. This is not so in Australia, where only four species (two Hodotermitidae, two Rhinotermitidae) are known to be restricted to tropical rain forest, and the majority are found in the sclerophyll forests, woodlands and savannas (Gay and Calaby, 1970). Similarly in Madagascar (Paulian, 1970) most species are found in the semi-arid to arid regions with xerophytic vegetation, and few species are found in the rain forest areas of the north. Tropical rain forest in Australia is confined to small areas on the east coast of Queensland and covers a very small proportion of the total area of tropical Australia. However, the present arid phase of Australian climate is a recent phenomenon. Burbidge (1960) considered there to have been since late Pleistocene times at least two pluvial phases separated by an arid phase and followed by another arid phase which is still in progress; the tropical vegetation of the north and east has retreated with increasing drought and advanced with increasing rainfall. It is therefore surprising that there is not a rich fauna of relict species with Papuan and Indo-Malayan affinities in the small contemporary areas of tropical rain forest. The absence of such a group of termites led Gay and Calaby (1970) to conclude, in contrast to Burbidge (1960), that tropical rain forest may never have been an important Australian vegetation type. Their conclusion receives some support from the observation of Paulian (1970) that the semi-arid to arid southern region of Madagascar has probably had a fairly constant climate since at least the late Tertiary; like the Australian semi-arid to arid regions termite species are most numerous there.

In Australia, termites are particularly common in tropical savannas. Figure 3 shows a typical concentration of mounds of *Amitermes vitiosus* and

Fig. 3. Concentration of mounds of *Amitermes vitiosus* and *Tumulitermes hastilis* in tropical savanna woodland near Larrimah, N.T., Australia.

Tumulitermes hastilis in tropical savanna woodland; also present at this site were mound-building *Nasutitermes triodiae, Drepanotermes rubriceps, Drepanotermes* sp. and the log-inhabiting species *Termes sunteri* and *Schedorhinotermes intermedius actuosus*. High population densities are found even in savanna woodlands that adjoin tropical rain forests with their impoverished termite fauna (e.g. on the Atherton Tableland in northern Queensland).

Arid regions have few termites, but some are apparently confined to such regions. Emerson (1955) stated that all species of the genera *Anacanthotermes* and *Psammotermes* are so confined. There are no Australian genera whose species are all confined to arid regions. *Tumulitermes tumuli* is essentially a termite of arid areas, and its mounds are usually built in the shade of low bushes. Various species of *Drepanotermes* (Watson and Perry, in prep.), *Amitermes*, and *Tumulitermes* are widespread in semi-arid and arid areas of Australia.

CHAPTER 2

Nests, Mounds and Galleries

All termites are social insects and live in communities, large or small, within the limits of a nest-system. The nest and associated structures, such as mounds, subterranean galleries and covered runways, comprise a closed system largely isolated from the external environment but allowing for the egress of foraging parties and flight of alates. Harris (1961) attributed the success of termites, particularly in the tropics, largely to the possession of a nest-system within which the micro-climate can be controlled within certain limits, food can be stored, and which provides a large measure of protection from enemies.

I. The Nest System

Grassé (1949) divided the nest and associated structures into four regions. The *endoecie* consists of chambers where the royal pair live, where eggs are deposited and the brood is raised and, in some species, where food is stored and fungus combs are cultivated. Often, particularly in epigeal mounds, there is a distinct innermost region, which has been called the nursery (Hill, 1942; Ratcliffe *et al.*, 1952), habitacle (Noirot, 1970) or hive (Bouillon, 1970), surrounded by peripheral galleries and chambers. The nursery houses the royal pair, the brood and attendant workers and soldiers, while the peripheral chambers, which are populated largely by workers and soldiers, serve as a protective barrier around the nursery. In turn, the peripheral chambers may be surrounded by a protective wall which varies in thickness from a few centimetres to over 1 m and which is part of the periecie. A protective wall may also be found surrounding subterranean nests. The *periecie* is the network of peripheral galleries communicating with sources of food and building materials and includes subterranean galleries, galleries within sources of food, such as logs, and epigeal covered runways and sheets. The *exoecie* consists of a system of cavities situated externally to the *endoecie* and *periecie*. These cavities open to the exterior but there is no permanent connection to the endoecie or periecie. They are found only in certain Macrotermitinae and their function is obscure. The *paraecie* is an open space frequently found between subterranean nests and the surrounding soil. In epigeal nests there is often a space between the outer wall and nursery or peripheral chambers which Noirot (1970) regarded as being homologous with the *paraecie*. These regions are illustrated in Fig. 4 (see also Fig. 21, p. 59).

The variety of nest-systems constructed by different groups of termites has been discussed at length by Emerson (1938), Grassé (1949), Bouillon and Mathot (1965) and Noirot (1970). *Mastotermes darwiniensis,* the only living representative of the primitive Mastotermitidae, builds nests under the ground or within trees or tree stumps and has a vast *periecie* of subterranean galleries, covered runways or galleries within wood. The Kalotermitidae, which live in dry wood, and the Termopsinae, which live in damp wood, have a small, diffuse nest with no distinct *endoecie* or *periecie*. The Hodotermitinae construct subterranean nests consisting of a number of interconnected, partitioned chambers from which galleries lead to the surface. Some chambers are used as "granaries" for storing food. The Rhinotermitidae have a variety of nesting habits. Some, such as the Heterotermitinae, live in small colonies in wood or in the soil and have no definite central nest and others, such as the desert-inhabiting *Psammotermes,* construct extensive subterranean galleries. The Coptotermitinae construct nests of carton in wood or in the soil, although several of the Australian species (Gay and Calaby, 1970) construct mounds, the only termites not belonging to the Termitidae known to do so. The Termitidae exhibit a great variety of nesting habits, even within the various sub-families, ranging from small, diffuse systems of galleries with no distinct *endoecie* or *periecie* to immense structures often of great architectural complexity.

A. MATERIALS USED FOR CONSTRUCTION

The materials used by termites for constructing their nests and associated structures depend partly on their feeding habits and partly on the availability of material in their habitat. Although soil, excreta, plant remains and saliva are known to be used for construction (Emerson, 1938; Grassé, 1950; Harris, 1956; Maldague, 1959) there are few detailed observations of nest-building behaviour. The selection of materials by particular species, and the nature of the materials utilized has generally been deduced from the general appearance of the structures concerned. Noirot (1970) pointed out that laboratory experiments do not necessarily reflect the natural choice of building materials as *Cubitermes fungifaber* has been observed to incorporate much less excrement into its structure in culture than in natural conditions.

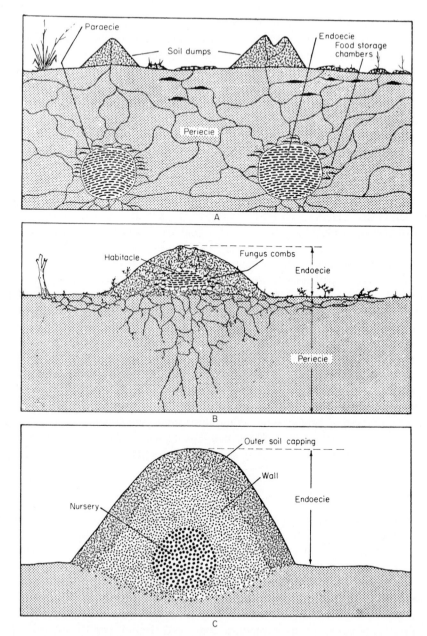

Fig. 4. Diagrammatic representation of different types of concentrated nest systems. A: *Hodotermes mossambicus*. (Reproduced with permission from Coaton, 1958.) B: *Macrotermes subhyalinus*. (Reproduced with permission from Grassé and Noirot, 1959a.) C: *Nasutitermes exitiosus*.

1. *Soil particles*

Soil particles are frequently used for nest construction and can be classified according to their size range as follows: gravel >2.00 mm, coarse sand 2.0-0.2 mm, fine sand 0.2-0.02 mm, silt 0.02-0.002 mm, clay <.002 mm. They are often the dominant constituents and only in the nest-systems of those species which have no contact with the soil, or in certain regions of the nests of other species, are they lacking or are a minor component.

In many species of termites there appears to be no precise selection of size particles. This was shown by our analyses (Lee and Wood, in press; and p. 102) of the mounds and other workings of a wide range of Australian termites. Most of the species we studied exhibited some preference in selecting a greater proportion of the finer particle size fractions, with the result that their mounds had a greater proportion (up to 20% more) of clay than any of the soil horizons. Such species included *Coptotermes acinaciformis, C. lacteus, Amitermes laurensis, A. meridionalis* and *Nasutitermes triodiae*. Concentration of clay particles in the mounds appeared to depend more upon the composition of the soil than the species of termite, as on a soil with a high content of clay in both A (53%) and B (71%) horizons *N. triodiae* selected a greater proportion of the coarse sand fraction for constructing its mounds. Concentration of clay in mounds of various species of *Cubitermes* in Africa has been noted by Kemp (1955), Maldague (1959) and Stoops (1964). Thus within wide limits species are able to construct mounds from available materials; this is well illustrated by our analyses (Lee and Wood, in press) of two mounds of *Amitermes meridionalis* about 100 m apart, one containing 13% of clay and 42% of fine sand and the other 27% of clay and 27-29% of fine sand. Our analyses showed that where several species occurred at the same site there were often, but by no means always, differences in the proportions of size fractions in the mounds of different species. For instance, both *Coptotermes lacteus* and *Nasutitermes exitiosus* on a podzolic soil near Braidwood, N.S.W., made use largely of subsoil to construct the soil capping which encased their mounds. The clay content of the subsoil and capping of the mounds of *C. lacteus* and *N. exitiosus* was 40%, 47% and 30% respectively, indicating preferential selection of clay by *C. lacteus*. On a solodic soil near Mareeba, North Queensland, *Nasutitermes triodiae* and *Drepanotermes rubiceps* largely utilized subsoil for construction of their mounds (clay content 25-26%) whereas *Amitermes laurensis* and *Tumulitermes pastinator* largely utilized topsoil (clay content of mounds 17-19%). Inter-specific differences are not always consistent as on a second solodic soil near Mareeba both *A. laurensis* and *N. triodiae* largely made use of subsoil for

mound-building and in fact the clay content of mounds of *A. laurensis* (24-34%) was slightly higher than in mounds of *N. Triodiae* (23-25%).

Certain species of termites construct their nests of soil from well-defined soil horizons or of precisely selected size fractions. The Macrotermitinae in Africa (Boyer, 1948; Grassé, 1950; Harris, 1956; Hesse, 1955; Nye, 1955; Stoops, 1964) construct their mounds from subsoil which contains a high proportion of clay. However, with the exception of the central portion of the nest, which contains a slightly higher proportion of clay than the subsoil, the proportions of the different size fractions in the mound are very similar to those in the subsoil. However, in some circumstances, there may be marked selection. Nests of *Macrotermes natalensis* on the sands of Kalahari contain 8.4% clay in the habitacle and 13% in the royal chamber, whereas the clay content of the sands was 1.8-5.4% to a depth of 84 m (Bouillon, 1970). In Australia *Coptotermes acinaciformis* and *Coptotermes brunneus* burrow deeply into the subsoil (Greaves, 1962a) and *C. lacteus* constructs special chambers in the subsoil for the purpose of obtaining clay (Ratcliffe and Greaves, 1940). Certain regions of the nest-system of a few species are constructed of precisely selected soil particles. The most notable example of this is exhibited by certain species of *Apicotermes* whose subterranean nests consist of 81-83% of fine sand mixed with organic matter (Stumper, 1923). A regional difference in the selection of materials is exemplified by *Coptotermes acinaciformis* in southern Australia where it nests within trees and hollows out the interior of trunks and large branches. The hollowed out core is packed with "mud-gut" which in south-western Australia contains a high proportion of soil but in south-eastern Australia consists largely of faecal material (Greaves, 1962a).

Soil particles used for construction may be carried by the termites in two ways. All termites carry particles in their mandibles and although this results in the re-distribution of the constituents there is little, if any, change in their composition. To some extent the size of particles carried must be limited by the maximum size that a worker can carry. Our analyses (Lee and Wood, in press) showed that *Drepanotermes rubriceps, Nasutitermes longipennis, N. magnus,* and *N. triodiae* incorporated a small proportion (1-3%) of gravel in their mounds. The workers of these species are comparatively large (5-6 mm long), whereas the workers of other species sampled are smaller (generally less than 5 mm long) and did not incorporate any gravel into above-ground portions of their mounds or other structures. Soil particles, particularly the finer size fractions, are also ingested and are subsequently regurgitated or excreted. Regurgitation appears to be practised by most species whereas passage of soil through the gut appears to be limited to the "humus-feeders", such as *Cubitermes* (Noirot, 1970). Micromorphological examination of the mounds and other structures of a wide range of Australian termites, none of which were humus feeders, indicated little more than incidental passage of soil particles through the termites' gut (Lee and Wood, unpublished data).

2. Plant material

Plant material is not often used until it has been digested (Adamson, 1943), although Noirot (1970) indicated that *Globitermes sulphureus* and *Cephalotermes rectangularis* incorporated some undigested wood into their nests, and we have noted (p. 36) that *Coptotermes acinaciformis* and *C. lacteus* incorporate masticated wood into their carton structures. Similar behaviour in several species of *Nasutitermes* was noticed by Emerson (1938) and in *Mastotermes darwiniensis* by Hill (1921). On the other hand the incorporation of grass into predominantly earthen mounds by several Australian grass-eating termites, e.g. *Drepanotermes* spp., is almost certainly incidental.

3. Saliva

Saliva has often been mentioned as a cementing material, although Noirot (1970) thought that it was generally of minor significance, as there were few direct observations of it being used. However, the use of saliva has been observed by Oshima (1919) in *Coptotermes formosanus*, Hill (1921) in *Mastotermes darwiniensis*, Emerson (1938) in *Anacanthotermes ochraceus*, *Speculitermes*, *silvestrii*, and *Microcerotermes arboreus*, J. A. L. Watson (personal communication) in *Drepanotermes* spp., and by ourselves in *Nasutitermes triodiae*. Although the observations are few, the wide range of species involved indicates that the use of saliva may be more frequent than Noirot (1970) suggested. Saliva may be more widely used by those species such as *Drepanotermes rubriceps*, which do not use their excreta as cementing material. The only group of termites known to make use of large quantities of saliva are the Macrotermitinae (Grassé, 1939; Noirot, 1970) which plaster their workings with rolls of regurgitated material containing soil and a considerable amount of saliva.

4. Excrement

Excrement is widely used in construction both as a cementing material and as a major structural component. According to Noirot (1970) the only group of termites that does not appear to use excrement for building is the Macrotermitinae. If this is true it is difficult to imagine where they put their excreta. The fungus combs of these termites appear to be constructed from excrement, at least in some species (Sands, 1960a), although Grassé and Noirot (1961) believed that they were constructed from masticated plant material, and lignin : cellulose ratios (p. 143) indicate that relatively undigested plant material is used. These conflicting opinions have been reviewed by Sands (1969). Nye's (1955) analyses of mounds of *Macrotermes bellicosus* showed that the interior of the mounds was constructed largely with soil particles that were of similar dimensions to soil particles in the gut of the termites, indicating that excreta might be used to some extent for construction purposes.

The excrement of humus-feeding termites contains a large proportion of soil and its general appearance is very much like soil. Mounds of humus-feeders, such as *Cubitermes* (Stoops, 1964), appear to contain a large proportion of such excreted material. Excreta of species which do not habitually ingest soil is usually darker than, and can be readily distinguished from, soil particles in the mounds. Wood-feeding species in particular produce large amounts of excrement which may be the dominant constituent of the nest or certain regions of the nest. This material, which is generally called carton (p. 139), is almost the only constituent of the nursery chambers of mounds of *Coptotermes acinaciformis, C. lacteus, Nasutitermes exitiosus* and certain workings of *Mastotermes darwiniensis*, and we found that samples of these materials contained 87-95% organic matter (Lee and Wood, in press). Excreta is often added to soil to produce composite soil/carton structures (Lee and Wood, in press), as in the wall material of *Nasutitermes exitiosus* (41-68% organic matter), mounds of *Microcerotermes nervosus* (25-31% organic matter), and the workings of *Tumulitermes comatus* and *Amitermes* sp. (31% and 21% organic matter respectively) in standing trees. Grass-feeding species produce less excrement than wood-feeding species as they can utilize a greater proportion of their food. In our survey of a range of Australian termites (Lee and Wood, in press) we found distinct, carton-like structures in the mounds of grass-feeding termites only in species (*Nasutitermes magnus, N. triodiae, Tumulitermes pastinator*) with populous colonies. The nursery chambers in mounds of these species were constructed of soil and excreta and had an organic matter content of 21-37%.

Excrement is also used to line the walls of galleries, to line the walls of chambers in regions of the nest constructed largely of soil and to fill in disused galleries. The quantities involved are small and we (Lee and Wood, in press) found the organic matter content of such structures to range from 2.5% (*Drepanotermes rubriceps*) to 11.0% (*Amitermes meridionalis* and *Tumulitermes hastilis*) in grass-feeding species and from 9.4% (*Nasutitermes exitiosus*) to 23% (*Schedorhinotermes intermedius actuosus*) in wood-feeding species.

Excrement is usually of fluid or pasty consistency but some of the primitive wood-feeding species, such as *Kalotermes* and *Neotermes* (Hegh, 1922) and *Mastotermes darwiniensis* and *Porotermes adamsoni* (p. 35), produce distinct pellets.

B. Methods of Construction

The nest-system is not a static structure and is enlarged as the colony grows. Species that do not have a concentrated nest-system enlarge their nests largely by excavation rather than by construction, and the formation of new galleries is often associated with feeding, as in the wood-feeding Kalotermitidae and Termopsinae. Some species with concentrated nest-systems have all or part of their nests below ground. Microscopic examination and physical and chemical analyses (Lee and Wood, in press) of the subterranean portions of nests of *Drepanotermes rubriceps* and *Tumulitermes hastilis* showed that the galleries were formed by excavation and re-packing of soil. In the case of the totally subterranean nests of *D. rubriceps* it appears that some coarse sand-sized particles (0.2-2.0 mm diameter) may be removed and spread over the surface of the nest, which lies flush with the soil surface (p. 102). *Hodotermes mossambicus*, which constructs entirely subterranean nests, dumps excavated soil on the surface in distinct heaps up to 20 cm high (Anon., 1960). In south-western Australia *Drepanotermes perniger* constructs subterranean nests and Watson and Perry (in prep.) have observed small soil dumps (approximately 15 cm diameter) made by this species. In the case of species, such as *T. hastilis* and *D. rubriceps*, which may have composite subterranean and epigeal nests, excavated soil is probably incorporated into the mound structure.

The growth of concentrated nests particularly those with a distinct architecture, involves a great deal of construction and Noirot (1970) distinguished two methods by which nests are constructed. Some species, such as *Cubitermes fungifaber*, extend their nests by adding new structures to already existing ones without any modification of the latter. Others, such as *Macrotermes bellicosus* in Africa and *Nasutitermes exitiosus* in Australia, in extending their nests modify and reorganize pre-existing structures, with the result that the nests grow from the inside outwards as material is moved towards the preiphery.

The behavioural basis of building is a response to a low level excitatory or "alarm" stimulus (Stuart 1967, 1969). The stimulus, which may be air movement, odour, light, temperature etc., upsets the normal state of the colony's environment. In *Zootermopsis* and *Reticulitermes*, the termites respond by depositing faecal cement and communicating "alarm" to other termites. This is followed by building which gradually eliminates the causal stimulus. The new structure may give rise to a secondary stimulus which may provide further stimuli and so on, this being the basis of Grassé's (1959a) "stigmergie" hypothesis of the mechanism of building behaviour. Thus, the immediate function of building is a homeostatic one of actively removing the stimuli which initiated the behaviour, but this does not explain how a complicated nest is constructed. However, it does provide a basis for explaining intra-specific variations in the architecture, size and shape of nests.

The mechanical process of construction has been observed directly by several workers (Smeathman, 1781; Beaumont, 1889, 1890; Drummond, 1888; Hill, 1921; Emerson, 1938; Grassé, 1937, 1939; Harris, 1956; Stuart, 1967; and others). The methods adopted by a wide variety of termites are basically similar and will be considered below in relation to the micromorphological structure of nests.

C. MICROMORPHOLOGY OF NESTS AND ASSOCIATED STRUCTURES

Microscopical examination of thin sections of soil permits the identification of various constituents and observation of the arrangement of particles, thereby contributing to an understanding of soil processes and soil formation (Kubiena, 1938, 1948, 1955). Similarly, microscopic examination of thin sections of structures built by termites permits identification of their constituents and their arrangement. The only work of this nature is that of Stoops (1964) who examined thin sections of material from mounds of *Macrotermes bellicosus, Cubitermes sankurensis* and *Cubitermes* sp. in Africa, and our observations of material from mounds and other structures of 15 species of Australian Termites.

1. *Fabrics dominated by transported and re-packed soil particles*

(a) *Without admixture of excreta.* Grassé (1937, 1939), Harris (1956) and Nye (1955) have observed the building behaviour of various African Macrotermitinae. The workers of these species carry a grain of sand in their mandibles and particles of subsoil (largely clay, but probably including particles of fine sand) in the crop and, on reaching the site of construction, place the sand grain in position using the fine material from the crop, which has been moistened with saliva, as a mortar around it. Emerson (1938) observed similar behaviour in *Anacanthotermes ochraceus*. New construction in *Macrotermes bellicosus* consists of a rather loose arrangement of these parcels of soil carried by individual workers, and results in the "pellet structure" observed in thin sections (Stoops, 1964). We have observed similar behaviour in *Coptotermes lacteus, Nasutitermes exitiosus* and *N. triodiae* during construction of the outer walls of their mounds, and the new construction has an open spongy appearance with many tunnels and pores (Fig. 5). At a later stage this open structure is filled in with transported soil particles and the fabric (in *C. lacteus*) of the completed capping has a dense, structureless appearance (Fig. 6). The completed outer casing of *Macrotermes bellicosus* has a similar appearance (Stoops, 1964). We found that structureless, re-packed soil dominated the fabric of the gallery walls in mounds of *Drepanotermes rubriceps* (Fig. 7), *Amitermes meridionalis, A. vitiosus, Tumulitermes hastilis* and also the outer soil capping of mounds of

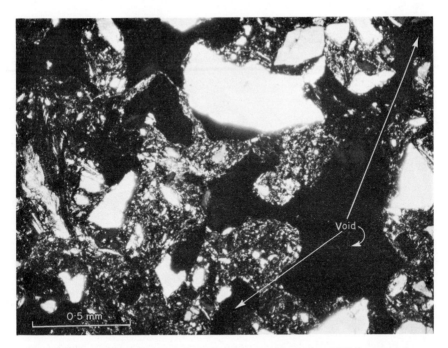

Fig. 5. Thin section of new construction in outer soil capping of *Coptotermes lacteus* mound, showing porous structure of loosely packed soil particles. (Crossed Nicols.)

Nasutitermes exitiosus, Coptotermes lacteus and *C. acinaciformis.* Zones of re-packed soil occurred among other types of fabric in the mounds of *Nasutitermes triodiae* and *N. magnus*, to a lesser extent in *Amitermes laurensis, Tumulitermes pastinator* and *Microcerotermes nervosus* and also in the workings of *Amitermes* sp. under the bark of a standing tree. Re-packed, structureless soil was not observed at all in the workings of *Mastotermes darwiniensis* and *Porotermes adamsoni.*

To some extent the intensity of re-packing will affect the hardness of the mounds. For instance the mounds of *Drepanotermes* are intensely hard, and the fabric contains much fewer pore spaces than the much softer mounds of *Tumulitermes hastilis.* Similarly, the soil capping of mounds of *Coptotermes lacteus* and *C. acinaciformis* is tightly packed and is harder than that of *Nasutitermes exitiosus.* Emerson (1938) reported that *Speculitermes silvestrii*, which constructs its mounds of re-packed soil particles without the addition of excreta, has mounds which are intensely hard.

(b) *With addition of excreta.* Emerson (1938) observed building behaviour in laboratory colonies of *Microcerotermes arboreus.* The workers placed a piece of soil, moistened with saliva, in place and then turned and excreted a drop of

Fig. 6. Thin section of outer soil capping of *Coptotermes lacteus* mound, showing closely packed soil particles of completed structure. (Crossed Nicols.)

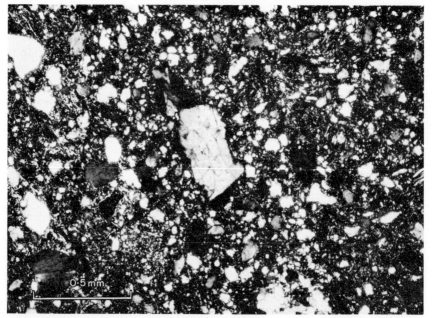

Fig. 7. Thin section of gallery wall in mound of *Drepanotermes rubriceps*, showing closely packed mainly mineral particles with virtually no spaces. (Crossed Nicols.)

thick, dark fluid on the newly-inserted piece of soil. A lenticular fabric that we have observed in thin sections of structures built by many species of termites would appear to result from this method of construction. This type of fabric appears in section as a mass of tightly fitting elongate to lenticular parcels of transported soil 0.5-2.00 mm long by 0.05-0.5 mm thick, each bounded by a thin coating (approximately 0.02 mm thick) of dark amorphous excreta. The outer wall of mounds of *Amitermes laurensis* (Fig. 8), *Microcerotermes nervosus* (Fig. 9) and *Tumulitermes pastinator* consists largely of this type of fabric. Similar lenticular fabric occurs sporadically among re-packed soil in the outer wall of mounds of *Nasutitermes triodiae*, and a similar but vaguer pattern (thinner and less continuous organic laminae) can be observed in parts of the outer wall of mounds of *Nasutitermes magnus* and *Amitermes meridionalis*, the outer soil capping of mounds of *Coptotermes acinaciformis* and *Nasutitermes exitiosus*, and the workings of *Amitermes* sp.

A similar pattern, with some variations, is apparent in sections of filled-in galleries of all the species noted above and also in filled-in galleries of *Amitermes vitiosus*, *Tumulitermes hastilis* and *Drepanotermes rubriceps*. The pattern varies from being very similar to the one described above (lenticular parcels of soil coated with thin laminae of excreta) to layers of soil separated by layers of excreta of equal or greater thickness. The full range of variation can be found within a single species and it appears that galleries are filled in by less methodical

Fig. 8. Thin section of outer wall of mound of *Amitermes laurensis*, showing lenses of mainly mineral particles with thin coatings of excreted organic matter.

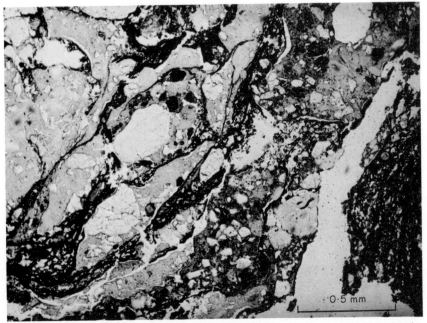

Fig. 9. Thin section of outer wall of mound of *Microcerotermes nervosus*, showing lenticular structure resembling that in *Amitermes laurensis* mounds. (Fig. 8.)

methods than are used to construct the walls of the galleries (Figs 10, 11). Lenticular fabric has not been observed in the workings of *Mastotermes darwiniensis*, *Porotermes adamsoni*, and *Coptotermes lacteus*.

More haphazard incorporation of excreta can be observed in the gallery walls of mounds of *Amitermes vitiosus* and *Tumulitermes hastilis* in particular, and to a lesser extent in the workings of other species, where small, discrete patches of amorphous excreta occur in a fabric dominated by re-packed soil particles.

2. Fabrics dominated by excreta

(a) *Fabrics of soil-ingesting termites*. None of the Australian species we studied appears to ingest soil other than incidentally during the course of feeding on wood, grass, or other plant tissue. Habitual ingestion of soil is probably confined to the humus-feeding species (see p. 16). The fabric of mounds of the humus-feeding *Cubitermes sankurensis* consists of mineral grains, fine soil particles, and residues from digestion, intimately mixed together (Stoops, 1964). The excreta is laid down in parallel or concentric layers, giving a lamellar structure to the fabric. The upper size limit ($<100\,\mu$) of the majority of the mineral grains is probably determined by the inability of the termites to swallow

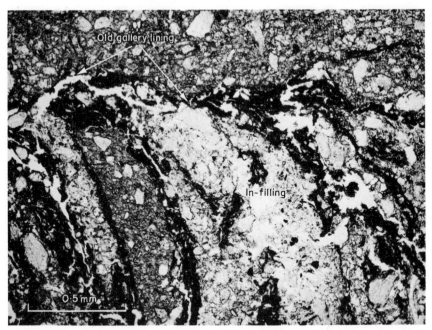

Fig. 10. Thin section of in-filled gallery in mound of *Drepanotermes rubriceps*, showing somewhat lenticular packing with much excreta, contrasting with close-packed mineral material of adjacent gallery wall. (Compare with Fig. 7.)

larger particles. Larger ($>500\,\mu$) sand particles in the fabric are probably transported in the mandibles and in section it is apparent that the laminar structure of the fabric goes around these large particles and does not include them.

(b) *Fabrics of predominantly undigested plant tissue or organic excreta.* Constructions in which undigested plant tissue or excreta, completely or almost completely free from soil, are used in large quantities are typified by the workings of *Mastotermes darwiniensis, Porotermes adamsoni,* the nursery and wall material of *Coptotermes lacteus* and *C. acinaciformis,* and the nursery and linings of galleries in the wall of *Nasutitermes exitiosus.* The microstructure of the fabric is pellet-like in *M. darwiniensis* and *P. adamsoni,* the material consisting largely of closely adpressed faecal pellets. Within the faecal pellets comminuted fragments of wood are visible. Our sections of *M. darwiniensis* workings (Fig. 12) are not as would be expected from Hill's (1921) description of the building behaviour of this species: ". . . building material is carried in the jaws in a condition susceptible of being moulded, and when laid in position is moistened further with saliva or fluid matter regurgitated from the stomach. The tip of the body is then brought into contact with the plastic mess, and the final

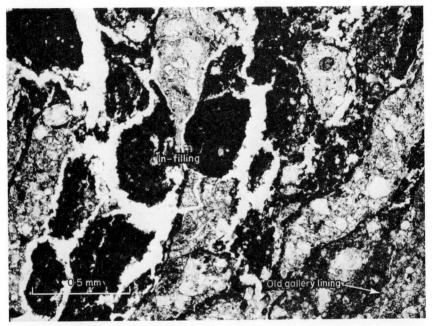

Fig. 11. Thin section of in-filled gallery in mound of *Amitermes laurensis,* showing some lenticular structure but more excreta than used in construction of gallery walls. (Compare with Fig. 8.)

moulding effected concurrently with the excretion of a copious flow of muddy fluid from the intestinal paunch". The discrepancy probably results from the use by this species, like many others, of different proportions of various constituents in different regions of its workings.

The microstructure of the fabric of carton wall material of *C. acinaciformis* mounds is lenticular; individual lenses consist mainly of fragments of comminuted wood with unmodified cellular structure, and the whole lens is surrounded by a thin layer of dark reddish-brown organic matter, apparently of faecal origin. (Fig. 13). The lenses are too large (up to *ca.* 2 mm long and 0.5 mm wide) to be faecal pellets, and are probably moulded from masticated wood, pressed into position, and coated with excreta, in the same way as soil is moulded and packed by some other termites, e.g. *A. laurensis* (Fig. 8) and *M. nervosus* (Fig. 9). In contrast, the microfabric of wall and nursery material of the closely related *C. lacteus* (Fig. 14) has a structure of thin parallel or concentric laminae, apparently laid down in a fluid state, and probably consisting of excreta; close examination of the material, however, shows that it includes many very finely comminuted but recognizable wood fragments, which have apparently passed through the alimentary system without being digested. A few

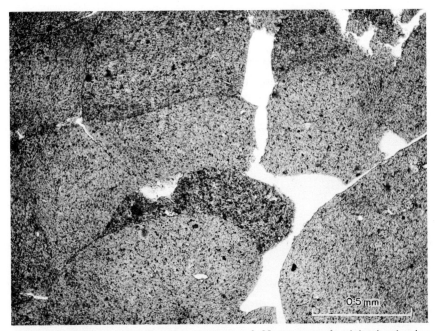

Fig. 12. Thin section of carton structure of *Mastotermes darwiniensis*, showing irregularly packed faecal pellets.

Fig. 13. Thin section of carton from mound of *Coptotermes acinaciformis*, showing lenticular structure and inclusion of coarsely comminuted wood.

mineral grains are included, the larger ones probably being transported in the mandibles, the smaller ones probably being ingested incidentally.

The use of undigested food material as a principal material for construction has not previously been conclusively demonstrated. Sands (1969, p. 511) states that there is no termite known that habitually uses its undigested food as a building material, and discusses the fungus combs of Macrotermitinae, which

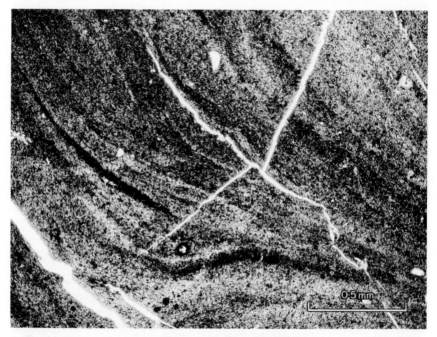

Fig. 14. Thin section of carton from mound of *Coptotermes lacteus,* showing parallel laminae of fluid excreta and absence of coarsely comminuted wood.

have been said to be constructed of masticated wood, but which he states are made of faecal material (see p. 39). The nature of the materials used for fungus comb construction could be determined by examination of thin sections, but this has not been done.

The fabric of nursery material and of the thick linings of gallery walls of *N. exitiosus* (Fig. 15) has a laminar form similar in appearance to that described above for the nursery of *C. lacteus,* but close examination of thin sections shows no recognizable wood fragments, and it appears to be all digested and of faecal origin. Emerson (1938) described similar structures made by *Crepititermes verruculosus,* composed of thick, dark, muddy excreta, laid down in a fluid state without being worked into position in any way.

Large quantities of excreta are also used in the nurseries of *Nasutitermes triodiae, Nasutitermes magnus,* and *Tumulitermes pastinator,* and the linings of galleries in walls of *Microcerotermes nervosus,* but the micro-structure of the fabric differs from the ones described above in having a distinctly fibrous appearance and also in having a constant, small proportion of mineral grains

Fig. 15. Thin section of gallery wall in mound of *Nasutitermes exitiosus*, showing internal region consisting of repacked mineral soil and external coating formed from thin layers of excreted organic matter.

included in the matrix (Fig. 16). The larger mineral grains must have been transported in the mandibles but the smaller grains could either have been ingested incidentally or carried in the mouth and "stirred" into the excreta. The fact that the fibrous fabric appears to flow around the larger grains but to enclose the smaller grains suggests that the first alternative is more likely than the second. The last three of the four species noted above are grass-feeders and it is likely that they ingest fine mineral particles (i.e. "dust") on the surface of grasses. Emerson (1938) observed building behaviour of *Nasutitermes guayanae* in which excretion was followed by the termite turning and working a piece of building material into place (in the excreta) with its mandibles. None of the structures we examined had a fabric consistent with this method of building.

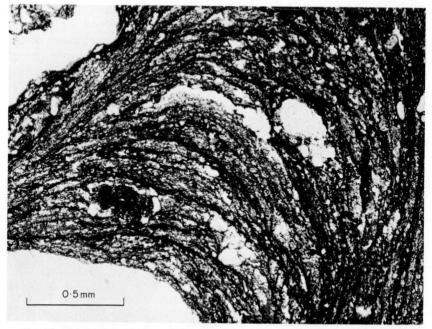

Fig. 16. Thin section of gallery lining in mound of *Microcerotermes nervosus,* showing fibrous structure, predominantly organic matter but including a small proportion of mineral grains.

With few exceptions excreta is used to line the walls of galleries. These linings are relatively thick, as already noted, in the wall material of *M. nervosus,* nursery and wall material of *N. exitiosus,* and the nurseries of *N. triodiae, N. magnus* and *T. pastinator.* In the outer walls of mounds of *N. triodiae, N. magnus, A. laurensis, A. meridionalis, A. vitiosus, T. pastinator* and *T. hastilis,* and the outer soil capping of mounds of *N. exitiosus* and *C. acinaciformis* the linings are thin. In the galleries from the outer soil capping of *C. lacteus* and the galleries of *Drepanotermes rubriceps* the linings are often extremely thin, difficult to detect in section and probably contain little excreta. Thin, organic strands running through regions consisting predominantly of re-packed soil, as in the hard basal core of mounds of *N. exitiosus, A. laurensis,* and *A. meridionalis,* indicate the outline of the walls of old galleries.

II. Nests and Mounds

A. SHAPE

Detailed descriptions of the structure of nests and mounds are beyond the scope of this book and can be found in the relevant literature (see Hegh, 1922;

Emerson, 1938; Hill, 1942; Grassé, 1949). The greatest structural complexity is evident in concentrated nests. The simplest forms of these are chambers sub-divided by thin walls, and the nest may consist of several such chambers ("calies", Grassé and Noirot, 1948) connected by subterranean galleries as in some of the Hodotermitinae. Generally, concentrated nests are single-unit structures and may be subterranean, epigeal (i.e. mounds), arboreal, or in wood. Noirot (1970) distinguished between two general types: those with a homogeneous structure consisting of chambers which are almost all alike and which lack important differences between the peripheral and internal regions, and those with a heterogeneous structure. The different regions of the latter often serve different functions, and may be constructed of different materials or different proportions of materials as indicated earlier in this chapter. The most complex structures are built by certain members of the Termitidae, among the most intricate being the subterranean nests of *Apicotermes* (Termitinae). These nests, described by Desneux (1948, 1952), are subterranean, sub-spheroidal in shape, and divided internally into a number of horizontal, parallel storeys, separated by thin lamellae. Communication between the different floors is either by direct or spiral ramps. The walls of the nest are perforated by a series of holes or slits for the purpose of ventilation and these holes may communicate with peripheral circular galleries within the wall. The architecture is very constant within species and specific diagnosis is sometimes more readily accomplished by examination of nests than of the termites themselves. Nests such as these, besides providing extraordinary examples of the ability of termites to modify their environment, are a record of the behaviour of the species and as such are useful material for students of the evolution of behaviour (Schmidt, 1955, 1958). Studies of termite nests have been interpreted in terms of phylogenetic relationships within the Isoptera in general (Emerson, 1938). At the generic level, as in *Apicotermes,* there is some justification for proposing phylogenetic relationships on the basis of nest structure although, as pointed out by Noirot (1970), homologies are difficult to prove since convergence is frequent. However, within the Isoptera in general, there appears to be little relationship between phylogeny and the architectural complexity of nest construction (Grassé, 1949). Certainly primitive families have simple nests (a notable exception being *Mastotermes darwiniensis*), but among the Termitidae there is every level of building behaviour from diffuse subterranean galleries to arboreal nests, even within a single genus (e.g. *Nasutitermes, Amitermes*). In addition, building behaviour is often influenced by the environment and this is particularly obvious in the case of mound-building termites.

Harris (1956) considered that termite mounds represented an equilibrium of three forces—behaviour, material and climate. He suggested that a species which is restricted in its distribution to a particular ecological niche or to zones where environmental factors, such as soil and climate, are relatively uniform, will build mounds of a uniform shape. On the other hand, a species occurring in a wider range of habitats will build mounds of variable appearance. The "magnetic ant-hills" built by *Amitermes meridionalis* in northern Australia are an outstanding example of uniform mound-building. These mounds are restricted to a small area south of Darwin where they are found only on grey soil flats subject to seasonal (summer) flooding (Hill, 1942; Ratcliffe *et al.,* 1952). Their adaptive significance is discussed later (p. 57) and it is interesting to note that in seasonally flooded areas on Cape York Peninsula *Amitermes laurensis,* which normally builds more or less regular conical mounds with rounded tops, builds mounds of the meridional form (Gay and Calaby, 1970). Convergent evolution of nest-building behaviour among unrelated species occurring in a similar habitat is well-illustrated by the rain-shedding devices (see p. 66) constructed by various species of Amitermitinae, Termitinae, and Nasutitermitinae in rain forest (Emerson, 1938).

Variability in mound-building behaviour is exhibited by *Macrotermes bellicosus* in Africa (Harris, 1956; Grassé and Noirot, 1961) and Hesse (1955) showed that variability in shape of mounds of *M. subhyalinus* is related to the sand : clay ratio of the soil used for construction (see p. 101). In addition, rainfall erodes away turrets and pinnacles and in areas subject to heavy rain there is a tendency for mounds to be domed. On the other hand, in South Africa mounds of *Trinervitermes trinervoides,* which are normally domed, are conical or turreted in wet regions (Fuller, 1915). Soil type appears to influence the shape of mounds of *Amitermes vitiosus* in northern Australia (see p. 74) but there are some species in which the variability in form of the mound does not appear to be related to obvious features of the environment. Our own observations and those of Hill (1942) and Ratcliffe *et al.* (1952) give some indication of the variation in form of mounds of *Nasutitermes triodiae* in northern Australia (Fig. 17). Mounds of the "Kimberley" type (Fig. 17A) attain a maximum height of about 4 m and a basal diameter of 3 m, near Derby in northern West Australia; other mounds are irregular cone- or dome-shaped structures (Fig. 17B). Modifications of this type of mound (Figs 17C, 17D) occur widely in northern West Australia, Northern Territory, Queensland and on a few islands in Torres Strait; a further modification, a smoothly contoured, domed structure (Fig. 17E) occurs around Mt. Isa (these mounds were attributed to *Drepanotermes rubriceps* by Hill, 1942). Irregularly turreted mounds, up to 2.5 m high, surrounded by many smaller ones (Fig. 17F) occur in the Northern Territory between Dunmara (16° 30′ south) and just north of Mataranka (14° 45′ south). However, there is a rapid change just south of Pine Creek (13° 55′) northwards to Darwin to mounds of the "fluted" or "columnar" type (Fig. 17G), which commonly exceed 4.5 m in height and reach up to heights approaching 9 m. We could not detect any relationship between the variations and soil type or vegetation, and although there is a pattern in the variation in

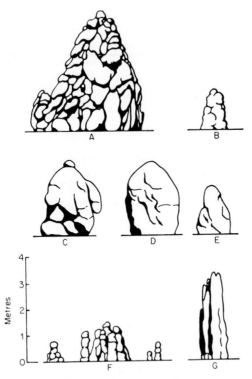

Fig. 17. Outline drawings of some common forms of mounds constructed by *Nasutitermes triodiae* in northern Australia. (Modified from Ratcliffe *et al.*, 1952.) See text for explanation of mound types.

form from western to eastern regions it is difficult to see how this could be consistently related to variations in climate.

B. Size

Termite mounds range in size from small domed or conical structures only a few centimetres in height and diameter to the colossal mounds built by some species of African Macrotermitinae which reach 9 m or more in height and 20-30 m in diameter at the base. The maximum height of termite mounds appears to be approximately 9 m. Harris (1955) illustrated a mound of *Macrotermes* sp. in Ethiopia of approximately this height, and mounds of *Nasutitermes triodiae* in Australia are known to exceed a height of 8 m. The weight of mounds and area of ground covered by them in various localities is shown in Table 3. In terms of space occupied and amount of soil deposited on the surface, the species of Macrotermitinae studied by Meyer (1960) in the

TABLE 3

Weight of Material in, and Area Occupied by, Termite Mounds in Various Habitats

Species	Percentage of total surface area	Dry weight (kg/ha)	Habitat	Author and reference
? *Anacanthotermes* *ahngerianus*	6.5[a]	–	Steppe, Central Asia	Ghilarov, 1962
? *Anacanthotermes* *ahngerianus*	10.0[b]	285 000	Steppe, Central Asia	Kozlova, 1951
Macrotermitinae (various species)	30.0[c]	2 400 000	Savanna, Congo	Meyer, 1960
Macrotermes *bellicosus*	0.3[d]	24 500	Savanna, Nigeria	Nye, 1955
Macrotermes *bellicosus*	3.7[e]	306 000	Savanna, Nigeria	Nye, 1955
⎰ *Tumulitermes* *hastilis*	0.2[f]	5000 ⎱	Savanna woodland, Australia	Williams, 1968
⎱ *Nasutitermes* *triodiae*	<0.1	7500 ⎰		
⎧ *Tumulitermes* *hastilis*	0.6[f]	30 000 ⎫		
⎪ *Amitermes* *vitiosus*	0.1	10 000 ⎪	Savanna woodland, Australia	Lee and Wood, unpublished
⎨ *Drepanotermes* *rubriceps*	0.9	21 000 ⎬		
⎩ *Nasutitermes* *triodiae*	<0.1	1500 ⎭		
⎧ *Tumulitermes* *hastilis*	0.1[f]	1000 ⎫		
⎪ *Amitermes* *vitiosus*	<0.1	425 ⎪	Savanna woodland, Australia	Lee and Wood, unpublished
⎨ *Nasutitermes* *triodiae*	<0.1	3500 ⎬		
⎩ *Coptotermes* *acinaciformis*	<0.1	1500[a] 650[b] ⎭		
Nasutitermes *triodiae*	0.1[g]	23 100	Tree savanna, Australia	Lee and Wood, unpublished
⎰ *Amitermes* *laurensis*	0.5[g]	45 000 ⎱	Savanna woodland (cleared), Australia	Lee and Wood, unpublished
⎱ *Nasutitermes* *triodiae*	<0.1	3300 ⎰		
Nasutitermes *magnus*	0.7[g]	36 000	Pasture, Australia	Lee and Wood, unpublished
Nasutitermes *exitiosus*	<0.1[g]	1200* 300†	Dry sclerophyll forest, Australia	Lee and Wood, unpublished
Cubitermes *fungifaber*	0.4[a]	17 600	Rain forest, Congo	Maldague, 1964
Trinervitermes *trinervoides*	2.5[a]	–	Savanna, South Africa	Murray, 1938

Congo are the most significant. The weight of soil in these mounds (2 400 000 kg/ha) is equivalent to a layer of soil 20 cm deep over the whole surface, and the fact that these mounds occupy 30% of the surface has a significant effect on the landscape, vegetation, and local agricultural practice. More often, lesser amounts of soil are involved as in the areas we have studied in Australia. However, mounds are not static objects but are continually being eroded by rainfall. Occupied mounds are repaired and enlarged by the termites while abandoned mounds are gradually eroded away. From the pedological point of view the significance of these mounds is the rate at which they are eroded and replaced, and the nature of their constituents. This aspect is considered in some detail in Chapter 7. Some mounds, such as those of *Coptotermes acinaciformis* and *Nasutitermes exitiosus* (Table 3), contain appreciable quantities of carton material, that is excretory products with a high content of partly digested organic matter, and the relative rates of production and decomposition of this material, as well as the quantities and chemical changes involved, are significant factors in the organic cycle (Lee and Wood, 1968). This aspect is discussed in more detail in Chapter 6.

III. Galleries and Runways

All termites construct a system of galleries or covered runways which they use in searching for requisites such as food, moisture and soil particles. Some species, notably members of the Kalotermitidae, Termopsinae, Stolotermitinae and Porotermitinae, excavate their nests and galleries solely within their food supply (wood) and rarely have any contact with the soil. Other species with similar habits are *Ahamitermes* and *Incolitermes* (Amitermitinae) which are obligate inquilines in the nests of *Coptotermes* in Australia (Gay and Calaby, 1970) and excavate galleries within, and feed on, the carton of their hosts' nest. Other termites construct galleries in the soil or make covered runways or sheetings on the soil surface, low-growing plants, fallen logs, or on the outside of standing trees.

Subterranean galleries appear to be constructed in two ways, not necessarily mutually exclusive. Greaves (1962a) described how *Coptotermes acinaciformis* and *C. brunneus* formed their subterranean galleries by compressing soil away from a central starting point to form a compact layer around the gallery. However, there is obviously some excavation of soil as the logs and tree stumps utilized by these and other species are often filled with copious quantities of soil

---

* Soil. † Carton.
[a] Numbers of mounds given in Table 5, Chapter 4.
[b] 570 mounds/ha.
[c] 4-7 mounds/ha.
[d] 5 mounds/ha.
[e] 62 mounds/ha.
[f] Numbers of mounds given in Table 9, Chapter 4.
[g] Numbers of mounds given in Table 12, Chapter 4.

brought up by the termites. Excavation has already been noted (p. 29) as a method of constructing subterranean nests. Subterranean galleries are often lined with excreta which may have a characteristic appearance peculiar to the species. Investigations in south-eastern Australia by Ratcliffe and Greaves (1940) showed that subterranean galleries of *Nasutitermes exitiosus* were lined with uniformly blackish-brown excreta whereas the linings of *Coptotermes* (*C. lacteus* and *C. frenchi*) galleries were "freckled", consisting of a mosaic of dark and light brown faecal material. Ebeling and Pence (1957) observed *Reticulitermes hesperus* making galleries in moist sand. The termites pressed sand particles sideways, primarily with the head and mandibles but occasionally with the whole body. The smaller sand particles were taken into the buccal cavity, mixed with a "gluey substance" (presumably saliva) and pushed out and spread along the walls of the gallery by means of the hypopharynx.

The construction of covered runways was vividly described by Drummond (1888) and appears to follow a similar pattern to nest-building. Depending on the species, runways are constructed of excreta or of soil particles cemented together with excreta or salivary secretions. The construction of covered runways follows odour trails laid by secretions of pheromones from the sternal gland (Stuart, 1969). Andrews (1911) demonstrated that odour trails were connected with foraging in *Nasutitermes*, and in *N. corniger*, Stuart (1969) observed that where the trail is distinct, soldiers line the edges with their heads pointing outwards. If the food source is too small these trails are only temporary, but if the food source is large (such as a log) workers deposit pieces of chewed wood and excrement along the edges of the trail. Eventually two walls, on which the soldiers mount guard, are formed and these bend towards each other and are eventually joined to form a covered runway. Runways often extend for considerable distances and rarely follow the shortest distance to the source of food. Emerson (1938) described how a covered runway built by *Nasutitermes guayanae* led from a nest 9.1 m up a palm tree, down some vine stems to the ground and to a small, dead tree. In all, the distance was 49.4 m, although the dead tree was only 10.7 m in a straight line from the palm tree. Some termites forage above ground without the protection of covered runways or sheetings. In general, these species appear to feed on materials which, in contrast to concentrated sources of food (logs, tree stumps etc.), do not occur in sufficiently large quantities at any one place to promote the building of semi-permanent covered runways. Among such species are the various grass-harvesting termites and the lichen-feeding *Hospitalitermes*.

Extensive covered sheetings are constructed by certain species. In contrast to covered runways, which protect the termites moving between the nest and the source of food, sheetings cover the source of food itself. Many scavenging termites feed under such protective sheetings. In Australia *Amitermes neogermanus*, which is a scavenger and a grass-feeder, often builds extensive sheetings (Ratcliffe *et al.*, 1952) and several dung-feeding species envelop dung pads with sheets of soil (Ferrar and Watson, 1970). Certain wood-feeding species, such as *Schedorhinotermes intermedius actuosus* in Australia (Fig. 18), feed beneath sheetings of soil. In the case of *Schedorhinotermes*, which can gain

Fig. 18. Thin soil sheeting built by *Schedorhinotermes intermedius actuosus* on fallen *Eucalyptus* trunk near Mareeba, Queensland.

protection within its food-supply, the purpose of the extensive sheeting is obscure.

There is no information on the quantities of soil transported above ground for the purpose of packing the eaten-out portions of fallen branches, logs, standing trees and tree stumps (Fig. 19) and for constructing covered runways and sheetings. In some instances considerable quantities of soil are involved and possibly are of similar magnitude to the quantities transported by mound-building species (Table 3, p. 44). These habits are widespread, being found within the Rhinotermitidae and all sub-families of the Termitidae and among mound-builders and non-mound-builders alike.

A. ARBOREAL-NESTING SPECIES

Termites that construct nests on the outside of tree trunks or branches communicate with the ground by covered runways built on the outside of the tree (Ratcliffe *et al.,* 1952; Noirot, 1970). These runways, or in some instances sheetings, may be continued on the soil surface; alternatively the termites may construct subterranean galleries.

Termites nesting within trees communicate with the soil either by covered runways or by galleries excavated within the tree, these galleries emerging from the tree below ground level as in *Coptotermes acinaciformis* in southern Australia. The gallery-systems of two colonies of this species in eastern Australia were studied in detail by Greaves (1962a). One colony had six main galleries leaving the tree below ground level. In section the galleries were uniformly 3 mm in height and their width varied from 6 mm to 63 mm, the width being proportional to the amount of traffic along them. The galleries branched and extended to and entered living trees and logs lying on the ground. The galleries were generally 15-28 cm below the surface but occasionally went deeper (over 70 cm) to avoid gravel or to locate pockets of moist clay. The galleries extended outwards for up to 30 m from the nest and the gallery system covered an area approximately of 0.16 ha. The other colony was older, had ten main galleries leaving the tree below ground level and these branched to a greater extent although covering a similar area to the first colony. Galleries from the first colony were traced to nine trees (two species) whereas the second colony attacked 15 trees (five species). A few tree-nesting species, notably the "black termites" (*Hospitalitermes* spp.) of Malaysia and Indonesia (Kalshoven, 1958), and *Grallatotermes grallator* of New Guinea (F. J. Gay, personal communication), do not build covered runways but leave their nests and forage on the surface in open columns. Their pigment probably serves to protect them from ultra-violet light and either their distastefulness or the secretions of the nasute soldiers protects them from predators. Kalshoven (1958) traced several foraging columns, two of which had trails exceeding 60 m in length.

Fig. 19. "Mudgut" pipe-like filling in centre of standing dead tree, occupied and apparently constructed by *Tumulitermes comatus,* near Mt. Molloy, Queensland.

B. MOUND-BUILDING SPECIES

The great majority of mound-building species construct subterranean galleries. In some species, such as the grass-feeding *Trinervitermes* in West Africa (Sands, 1961) and *Drepanotermes rubriceps* and *Nasutitermes triodiae* in Australia (Hill, 1942 and our observations) the galleries extend only a short distance from the mound and the termites emerge from these (occasionally they may emerge directly from the mound) and forage openly on the surface, usually at night or during the day in dull weather. In *Drepanotermes rubriceps* and *D. perniger* galleries extend for up to 20-25 m from the mound or nest and the termites forage for up to 0.5 m from each foraging exit (J. A. L. Watson, personal communication). In South Africa Fuller (1915) located 20 main galleries leaving the nest of *Trinervitermes trinervoides* and found that the gallery-systems of adjacent mounds were interconnected. Other species construct an elaborate system of subterranean galleries radiating out over a large area to sources of food. Ratcliffe and Greaves (1940) studied the gallery system of the wood-feeding *Coptotermes lacteus* and *Nasutitermes exitiosus* in south-eastern Australia, and Greaves (1962a) studied the gallery-system of *Coptotermes brunneus* and *C. acinaciformis* in western Australia. Two mounds of *C. lacteus* had 9 and 36 main galleries radiating from the nests and in five mounds of *N. exitiosus* the number varied from 18 to 36. The gallery-system of *C. lacteus* (Fig. 20) was similar in many respects to that of tree-inhabiting colonies of *C. acinaciformis* described above, in that the galleries usually ran 8-23 cm below the surface, occasionally going deeper (up to 60 cm) to avoid gravel or to locate moist clay, and extended a similar distance (approximately 30 m) from the colony. Avoiding gravel may be a general phenomenon as Ebeling and Pence (1957) observed that *Reticulitermes hesperus* could not progress through loosely-packed crushed cinders of particle sizes ranging from 1 mm to 1.5 mm. They also noted that the termites did not readily burrow from a sand of one range of particle sizes to a sand of larger particles. The gallery-system of *Nasutitermes exitiosus* studied by Ratcliffe and Greaves (1940) was traced for a distance of 30 m from the colony but differed from that of *C. lacteus* in having many cross-connections between galleries and no deep shafts into the clay subsoil although, as in *C. lacteus*, gravel was avoided by penetrating deeper into the soil.

C. SUBTERRANEAN-NESTING SPECIES

Little is known about the gallery systems of species with subterranean nests. Many of these species do not have a concentrated nest-system but live in small colonies under stones, at the base of tussocks of grass and similar cryptic habitats. Some of these species such as *Amitermes neogermanus* in Australia (Ratcliffe *et al.*, 1952) may construct covered runways or sheetings. Many other species appear to be entirely subterranean.

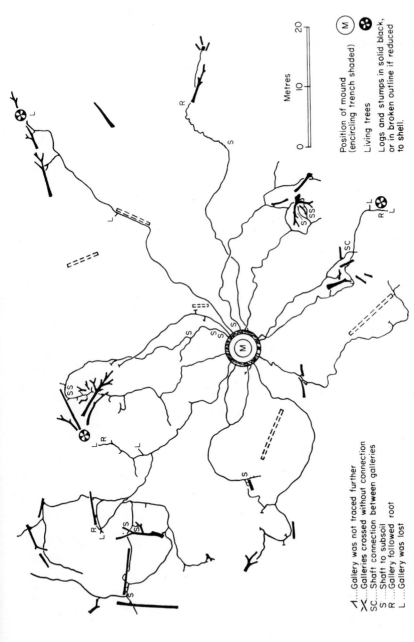

Λ....Gallery was not traced further
X....Galleries crossed without connection
SC....Shaft connection between galleries
S ....Shaft to subsoil
R ....Gallery followed root
L ....Gallery was lost

Metres

0   10   20

⊙ (M) Position of mound
      (encircling trench shaded)

❀ Living trees

● Logs and stumps in solid black,
  or in broken outline if reduced
  to shell.

Fig. 20. The subterranean gallery system of a colony of *Coptotermes lacteus*, near Braidwood, N.S.W. (Reproduced with permission from Ratcliffe and Greaves, 1940.)

Some species have concentrated nest-systems, such as certain members of the Hodotermitinae, Rhinotermitidae and Termitidae. Some of these species appear to be entirely subterranean while others forage on the surface. The latter may forage in the open, for example the Hodotermitinae in Africa (Coaton, 1958), which construct a network of interconnecting subterranean galleries some of which lead to the surface, and certain species of *Drepanotermes* (Amitermitinae) in Australia (Watson and Perry, in prep.). Other surface-foragers construct covered runways or sheetings, such as those of *Schedorhinotermes intermedius actuosus* referred to earlier (p. 47).

From the foregoing account it will be apparent that the gallery-systems of different termites are similar in many respects although differing in details. Apart from special purpose galleries penetrating deep into the subsoil (up to depths of 70 m; Yakushev, 1968) either to avoid drought, to obtain clay for building purposes or for moisture, the majority of galleries are either on or near the surface where there are the greatest concentrations of food. Galleries and runways often extend for considerable distances from the central nest, often exceeding 30 m, and Kalshoven (1958) observed *Hospitalitermes* foraging more than 60 m from the nest. A considerable amount of time must be spent foraging at such distances as Skaife (1955) found that at a temperature of 25°C workers of *Amitermes hastatus* took 2 h to travel 23 m and back to their nests. No attempts have ever been made to make quantitative estimates of all termite galleries in a given area or to estimate the proportion of space in the soil occupied by galleries. The extent and ramifications of the galleries of single species, discussed earlier, indicate that in areas where there are many species of termites exploiting a wide range of food resources (humus, plant litter, grass and herbs, dead and living wood) their galleries and runways are likely to be as important, although less conspicuous, a feature of the ecosystem as are, in certain areas, the mounds of mound-building species.

CHAPTER 3

Termites as Soil Animals

I. The Soil as an Environment for Termites

Soil consists of a heterogeneous mixture of mineral and organic particles and aggregates, ranging in size from colloidal particles to huge boulders, and separated by air- and water-filled spaces. It offers many advantages as an environment for animals. Chief among these are a high degree of protection from predators, protection from light, buffering of ambient temperature and moisture variations, and access to large quantities of living and dead plant material as a food supply. On the other hand, soils may have properties that impose limits on soil-inhabiting animals. Chief among these are the small dimensions and irregular shape of the majority of natural interstices, intermittent flooding or desiccation of surface layers, where most of the organic matter is located, abrasiveness of coarse textured mineral particles, and adverse ionic conditions (especially low pH and high salinity).

Soil animals inhabit the interstitial spaces; they include at one extreme minute aquatic forms such as protozoa and nematodes, that live in water-filled spaces throughout their lives, and a gradation through a series of forms whose requirements for free water are less and less stringent, to animals such as some spiders, with highly developed physiological mechanisms for water conservation, that can live in air-filled interstitial spaces or burrows in soils of arid regions. Disregarding the wholly aquatic forms, soil animals may be divided into those that are unable to burrow and are therefore confined to naturally occurring interstices, and those that burrow and can reshape the soil to their own requirements.

Termites have developed the capacity to burrow and to mould structures from soil and organic matter to a level unknown in any other group of soil animals. Termite nests, mounds, and gallery systems are sealed off from the external environment except when they are deliberately opened by the termites to allow air to circulate or to permit the exit of foraging parties or flight of alates. Noirot (1970) considered that active regulation by termites of the environment in their nests and mounds has been often postulated, but rarely demonstrated. In contrast, Bouillon (1970) considered that termites do not merely occupy a niche, but model it within the dimensions of their tolerances and preferences. The composition of the atmosphere within nests and mounds, their temperature and moisture content, are related to those of the external environment, but there is abundant evidence that many termites exercise some control over them. Control results from the cumulative effects of various adaptations of behaviour and methods of construction, and varies in its effectiveness.

II. The Environment in Mounds, Nests, and Subterranean Galleries

A. OXYGEN AND CARBON DIOXIDE CONCENTRATIONS

Few measurements have been made of oxygen and carbon dioxide concentrations in termite nests. Day (1938) found that in four mounds of the Australian *Nasutitermes exitiosus* carbon dioxide concentration ranged from 1.00% to 1.89%. Concentration of oxygen varied from 19.10% in the mound with highest carbon dioxide concentration to 19.91% in that with lowest carbon dioxide concentration. Total carbon dioxide and oxygen was fairly constant, varying only between 20.91% and 21.04%.

Termites are capable of surviving high carbon dioxide and low oxygen tensions. Day (1938) subjected *Nasutitermes exitiosus* to air containing up to 18.87% carbon dioxide; the termites were anaesthetized at this level but recovered when fresh air was admitted. Cook (1932) showed that for *Zootermopsis nevadensis* oxygen consumption did not fall materially with decreasing oxygen tension until a concentration of approximately 2% was reached. Below this level *Z. nevadensis* continued to deplete the oxygen tension in closed containers, though at a reduced rate. In the absence of oxygen the termites were immobilized but some anaerobic respiration (probably attributable to micro-organisms in the gut) continued for up to two days, and if oxygen tension were increased during this treatment the animals recovered and showed no indication of oxygen debt. The termites survived and respired normally in an atmosphere containing 20% oxygen and 20% carbon dioxide. Higher concentrations of carbon dioxide induced anaesthesia but the animals recovered when returned to air after exposure to 40% carbon dioxide. *Z. nevadensis* is a "dry wood" termite and would not normally be exposed to very high carbon dioxide concentrations, as may a soil-inhabiting termite when soil becomes waterlogged. Cook concluded that ability to withstand high carbon dioxide concentrations is probably a characteristic of all termites; this is a common characteristic of most insects, but it may have special significance to soil-inhabiting species.

Limited control over the gaseous environment in mounds and nests may be exercised by some termites. Lüscher (1955) found the volume of air in a mound of *Macrotermes bellicosus* to be about 500 litres. He estimated that there were about two million termites in the colony, and that their oxygen requirement would be about 240 litres per day (i.e. 1200 litres of air). He described two patterns of air circulation and exchange with outside air, one in mounds from the Ivory Coast and the other from Uganda; in both cases the air circulation was driven by convection currents, induced by heating of the air in the fungus combs, but the geometry of the air spaces in the mounds differed, and he considered that the two types of mound might reflect behavioural differences between two morphologically indistinguishable geographical races of *M. bellicosus*. Ruelle (1964) made casts of the space inside mounds of *M. bellicosus* and showed that the arrangement of interconnecting spaces above and below the central nest and their connections with openings to the exterior favour massive air flow through the mound. Loos (1964), using small anemometers located in the air spaces within *M. bellicosus* mounds, demonstrated convection currents and also showed that air currents within mounds are related to, but are much less than, outside wind speeds and directions.

Carbon dioxide concentration is related to the intensity of metabolic activity of termites within mounds, and this in turn depends on temperature. Ruelle (1964) recorded diurnal fluctuations in the nest chambers of *M. bellicosus*. Concentration rose to a maximum of about 3% in the middle of the day and fell during the night to a minimum of 0.6% in the dry season and 1.0-1.5% in the wet season. Fluctuations in carbon dioxide concentration closely paralleled diurnal temperature fluctuations recorded in the wall of termite mounds and in adjacent soil at 20 cm depth. Skaife (1955) found that in mounds of the South African *Amitermes hastatus* carbon dioxide concentration was usually about 4-5%, but reached 15% in mid-summer when colonies were very active. Hébrant (1970) placed whole nests, which included colonies of *Cubitermes exiguus*, in respirometers and measured oxygen consumption for three days at 30°C. Of 25 colonies tested, 23 displayed circadian rhythms of oxygen consumption, with two peaks (at 8 a.m. and 8 p.m.) and two troughs (at 2 a.m. and 2 p.m.). Average oxygen consumption at the extremes of the cycle, in ml/h (corrected to 0°C and 760 mmHg) was: 8.3 at 2 a.m., 13.7 at 8 a.m., 5.4 at 2 p.m., 13.6 at 8 p.m. Hébrant correlated the variations with circadian rhythms in foraging and resting behaviour of the termites, but was not able to determine whether the rhythmic variations in oxygen consumption derived from endogenous or exogenous stimuli. On hot days some termites (e.g. *Nasutitermes triodiae* in northern Australia) make temporary openings at the top of their mounds to promote ventilation. Ruelle (1964) covered a mound of *M. bellicosus* with a sealed plastic dome. In less than 48 h the termites built a large porous addition to the top of the mound, apparently in an attempt to promote air flow. One day after the dome was fitted, carbon dioxide concentration in the air inside the mound was 4.5%. When the dome was removed carbon dioxide concentration fell very rapidly to about 0.5%. Although the termites then sealed the porous top of the mound it was a week before maximum diurnal carbon dioxide concentration (usually attained between 3 p.m. and 4 p.m.) reached 1.0%.

B. TEMPERATURE

The temperature inside termite nests varies diurnally and from day to day. Holdaway and Gay (1948) measured temperatures in mounds of *Nasutitermes exitiosus*. They found that the temperature in the central nursery chamber was always higher than soil or air temperatures, but varied less than temperatures in other parts of the mound. Occupied mounds were always warmer (by 8.6-10.3° C) than unoccupied mounds, apparently due to metabolic heat. The presence of alates resulted in an increase of 5.6-7.2° C above the temperature of similar mounds without alates. Ruelle (1964) found that temperatures in the central nest of the large mounds of *Macrotermes bellicosus* were 4-5° C higher in occupied than in unoccupied mounds. The mean daily temperature in the nest was approximately 30° C and did not vary more than 0.5° C throughout the year, but diurnal fluctuations paralleled ambient temperature variations and sometimes exceeded 3° C. Mean daily temperature during August to October in mounds of *Trinervitermes trinervoides,* in Natal, was 20.2° C and the difference between mean daily maximum and minimum was 4.4° C (Cowles, 1930). Greaves (1964), in Australia, measured temperatures in nests of *Coptotermes acinaciformis* and *C. frenchi* built inside the trunks of trees. He found that in *C. acinaciformis* temperatures in the nursery varied from 33° to 38° C, i.e. 13-20° C above that at the centre of portions of the same tree trunk without termites. Nursery temperatures in nests of *C. frenchi* varied from 27° to 36° C, with little diurnal variation, and were highest in November when alates were present in large numbers.

Some degree of temperature control in mounds and nests, or at least in part of these structures, is exercised by many termites. Various methods are used, and they may be summarized as follows.

1. *Site selection*

In very hot climates the mounds of some termites are commonly built in the shade of trees or woody shrubs. The small conical mounds of *Tumulitermes tumuli* in central Australia are almost invariably built close to the trunks of small woody shrubs. Large mounds of *Nasutitermes longipennis,* seen by the authors near Daly Waters (Northern Territory), were similarly situated. Sands (1965a), in northern Nigeria, studied the distribution of mounds of four species of

Trinervitermes; 75% of mounds of *T. oeconomus* and *T. occidentalis* were located in the shade of trees, while 90% of mounds of *T. geminatus* were located in full sun (see p. 78). All the above species are grass-feeders, so the selection of sites near trees is not due to food preferences. In the Sahara desert, species of *Anacanthotermes, Psammotermes,* and *Amitermes* build subterranean nests with chambers deep in the soil, apparently to minimize the effects of diurnal temperature fluctuations (Grassé, 1949).

In cooler climates some species show a preference for sites exposed to the sun. In dry sclerophyll forest on the hills east of Adelaide *Nasutitermes exitiosus* mounds are numerous on slopes with a northerly aspect and low-growing vegetation and are rare or absent on adjacent shaded southerly slopes with tall trees (Wood and Lee, in press); this species shows a similar preference for slopes with a northerly aspect in the Canberra district (J. A. L. Watson, personal communication). Aggregations of *Heterotermes ferox, Amitermes neogermanus, A. xylophagus,* and *Microcerotermes* sp. are commonly found under stones in the same area (Table 14, p. 90); all species show a strong preference for sites under stones exposed to the sun, as compared with stones in shaded areas.

2. Architecture of mounds

Several species of *Amitermes* in northern regions of Australia build tall mounds, elongated in a roughly north-south direction. The best known of these is *Amitermes meridionalis* which invariably builds such elongated mounds; *A. laurensis* and *A. vitiosus* sometimes build mounds of similar form, but not always with a north-south orientation. Various hypotheses have been proposed to explain this behaviour in *A. meridionalis,* but the most plausible explanation (Hill, 1942) is that the shape minimizes heat gain in the middle of the day. Whether this is or is not the principal reason for the mounds having such a form, it must greatly affect diurnal variations in mound temperature in the hot climate of northern Australia. Variation in the proportion of mound-nest construction above or below ground level also appears to be related to climatic variation in some wide ranging species. *Nasutitermes exitiosus,* in South Australia where winters are mild, builds nests that are almost wholly above ground level, while near Canberra, where winters are more severe, about half of the nest is below ground level and mounds are correspondingly smaller. Variation of mound form has been noted by Noirot (1959) over the range of the widely distributed *Macrotermes bellicosus,* which is found from Tchad to Uganda, and builds its mounds not only in the humid savannas where it is most common, but also in the steppes of Tchad and Nigeria, in the swampy savannas of Gabon, and even occasionally in forest. The nest is entirely above ground in the swamps of Gabon, while in some of the dry savanna areas of Oubangui the nest is largely subterranean. Harris (1961) also reported subterranean nests of *M. natalensis* on the high plateaux of South Africa, where winters are cold. The differences may be due to differences in environment or they may sometimes reflect, over such vast areas, differentiation of geographic races with differing mound architecture, as was suggested by Grassé and Noirot (1961) to explain differences between nests within species of *Macrotermes* in Africa. Several kinds of mounds are known in the widespread northern Australian species *Nasutitermes triodiae* (see p. 42).

3. Ventilation

Temporary modifications of mound structure to promote air flow are discussed above (p. 55) in connection with oxygen and carbon dioxide concentrations. Dissipation of excess heat appears to be accomplished in the same way by many termites, and may be more important to a mound population than reduction in carbon dioxide concentration, since many, if not all, species can tolerate high concentrations of carbon dioxide.

4. Insulation

The mounds and nests of termites, though their primary function is to provide a protected living and food storage space for the animals, themselves insulate the central regions of the nest from variations in ambient temperature. Many species construct insulating layers around the periphery of their mounds. We have observed that *Amitermes vitiosus, Drepanotermes rubriceps, Nasutitermes triodiae, Tumulitermes hastilis*, and *T. pastinator*, among Australian termites, fill the outer galleries of their mounds with loosely packed fragments of grass, which would provide insulation as well as food storage (Fig. 1, p. 9). Especially in *N. triodiae*, and to some extent in *Drepanotermes* spp., the outer grass-filled galleries are larger and have thinner dividing walls than those of the inner portion of the mound. In *Nasutitermes magnus* harvested grass is often concentrated in a zone of galleries surrounding the central nursery chamber. We do not presume that insulation is necessarily the primary purpose of such placement of stored grass, but whatever the primary purpose some insulation of the inner mound galleries must result.

Some species construct their mounds with the inner nest separated by an air space from the outer soil wall. *Coptotermes acinaciformis* builds mounds, usually leaning against tree trunks but sometimes free-standing, in northern Australia. The mounds have a space up to about 8 cm wide between the thick outer soil wall and the carton interior (Fig. 21). Tenuous connections of carton material join the inner nest to the soil wall. A similar separation of outer wall and inner nest is noted in the earth mounds of *Macrotermes bellicosus* near Ibadan (Nigeria) by Nye (1955). The subterranean nests of *Apicotermes* spp. and

Fig. 21. Section of outer region of mound of *Coptotermes acinaciformis,* showing air space between soil outer capping and carton interior.

of some fungus-growing termites have a sharply defined outer casing and are almost entirely separated from the surrounding soil (Noirot, 1959), or may have a surrounding space filled by the termites with loose sand.

5. Metabolic heat

Crowding together of large numbers of termites in the central portion of the nest during cold weather is a commonly used device for maintaining high nest temperatures. Holdaway and Gay (1948), in a study of mound populations of *Nasutitermes exitiosus,* attributed the constantly high temperature of the nursery to metabolic heat. They showed that numbers of termites in mounds were low when ambient temperatures were high, and vice versa. The metabolic rate of individual termites is higher when ambient temperatures are high than when they are low, and smaller numbers of termites can maintain an elevated nursery temperature when ambient temperature is high than when it is low. Thus the mound temperature, particularly in the nursery, is probably buffered by movement of individuals between peripheral galleries and the mound.

Lüscher (1951a) has suggested that a primary function of fungus gardens in mounds of *Macrotermes bellicosus* is to maintain constant temperatures for the raising of young by production of metabolic heat. He found that an almost constant temperature of about 30°C was maintained throughout the day in fungus gardens. Bachelier (1963) also reported constant temperatures of 28-30°C in fungus gardens of macrotermitids. Cheema *et al.* (1960) measured temperatures in the fungus gardens of the Indian macrotermitid *Odontotermes obesus*. They found that during winter fungus garden temperatures varied from 18° to 25°C, while corresponding ground surface temperatures were 10-30°C; in summer fungus garden temperatures were 28-32°C and corresponding ground-surface temperatures 30-40°C. Fungus garden temperatures did not follow diurnal fluctuations of ambient temperature and there was little difference between temperatures of fungus gardens in mounds exposed to the sun compared with others built in shaded situations. Noirot (1970) considered any thermo-regulatory function of fungus gardens to be incidental to their principal function, which he regarded as the digestion of lignin-cellulose complexes and probably as a source of vitamins and nitrogen (p. 127).

6. Mass movements of mound populations

Grassé and Noirot (1948) reported that at the end of the dry season in the hot savannas of Northern Guinea and Upper Volta the mounds of *Cubitermes* are almost devoid of inhabitants, which take refuge in underground galleries at the base of the mound, or deeper in the soil. This may be more to escape desiccation than a direct response to high temperatures, but the two are related. Hill (1942) reported that large mounds of *Drepanotermes rubriceps* in the Mt. Isa district of Queensland are similarly deserted in the dry season. We have found that these mounds are built by *Nasutitermes triodiae*, not *D. rubriceps*, though it may be that the mounds reported by Hill had been secondarily occupied by *D. rubriceps*. Noirot (1970) and Bouillon (1970) listed several examples of vertical migration of mound populations correlated with diurnal temperature fluctuations.

C. MOISTURE

Termite species differ in their moisture requirements, some being able to live in dry wood above ground in deserts while many are restricted to wetter regions, or to subterranean nest and gallery systems (Collins, 1969).

Bouillon (1970) discussed various sources of water used by African termites. These included water produced metabolically, free water in the soil and from the water table, even when it is very deep, water from rain, and condensation within nests or other termite structures. Resorption of water from faeces before they are voided is practised only by termites living in dry wood (Bouillon, 1970).

Some species, (e.g. *Bifiditermes durbanensis*) which feed on dead wood, build their nests in living trees immediately adjacent to living tissue, apparently to take advantage of the moisture available in the living tissue (Kemp, 1955).

Moore (1969) commented that in general termites are very susceptible to desiccation, for their cuticle is exceptionally soft and its water-retaining properties are poor. Collins (1969) compared the survival time of a variety of North American species when subjected experimentally to drying at 34-35°C and 0-4% relative humidity, without food or water. In Hodotermitidae, Rhinotermitidae, and Termitidae survival times extended only for minutes or hours, while the more desiccation-tolerant species of Kalotermitidae survived for days or weeks, and for some death from starvation would precede desiccation. Among the Kalotermitidae discussed by Collins three species could not live in very humid atmospheres, but most species preferred relative humidities of 90-97%.

The maintenance of high humidity in nests, mounds and galleries is an essential requirement for the survival of most species of termites, especially for those that live in arid and semi-arid regions. Mechanisms that contribute to humidity control are considered under the following headings:

1. Active transport of water.
2. Use of absorbent materials for construction of nests.
3. Metabolic water.
4. Protection from excess water.

1. Active transport of water

Termites that live in arid or seasonally arid regions frequently have vertical galleries descending to the water table and transport water to the nest to maintain suitable humidity. Water is carried in the crop and regurgitated.

Hill (1921) recorded a covered way, built by *Mastotermes darwiniensis,* which began from a horizontal gallery in soil at the surface of the underlying rock at a depth of about 1 m and descended vertically down the side of a well to a depth of about 3.3 m, at which level the sides of the well were moist. Ratcliffe and Greaves (1940) traced the extensive network of galleries (see p. 50) radiating to food sources (logs and living trees) from a mound of *Coptotermes lacteus* in New South Wales. At various points close to the mound and close to food sources, shafts went down 30-60 cm into the moist subsoil; some of them led to large irregular cavities, apparently sources of clay for mound construction, but most were apparently to obtain water.

Grassé and Noirot (1948) described the habits of several species that live in the Sahara. At the oasis of Tit, *Psammotermes* brings water from a depth of several metres to humidify its shallow subterranean nests; there is no continuity between the moist nest and the underlying water table. *Macrotermes subhyalinus,* during the dry season at Fort Lamy, maintains high humidity in the inhabited parts of its nest, especially in the vicinity of the royal chamber, while the remainder of the mound is allowed to dry out. Near Bongor (Tchad), *Odontotermes magdalenae* was observed rebuilding its mounds at the end of the dry season with moistened soil, and maintaining a trail of moistened soil for the columns of workers involved in rebuilding. Bodot (1967a) found deep shafts penetrating to the water table below mounds of *Macrotermes bellicosus.* Bodot calculated that, with an average volume of 2 m³, about 200 litres of water was required to achieve the observed water content of 15-30%. She was unable to measure rate of water loss, so could not calculate the rate of replacement of water by the termites.

Ghilarov (1962) found galleries of *Anacanthotermes ahngerianus* descending from the nests about 1.5 m below the ground surface to moist soil at 10-15 m, and considered that these allowed moist air to ascend to the nest. Yakushev (1968) quoted observations of West in Africa of termite galleries going to the water table at a depth of 70 m.

2. Absorbent material in nests

By introducing absorbent materials into their living space many termites are able to store water. The absorbent materials are of three main kinds, i.e. clay, "carton", and "fungus gardens".

(a) *Clay.* The clay content of mounds is discussed later (p. 101). Clay is used as a structural and cementing material, but sometimes its distribution in mounds indicates that it is important for water conservation. Boyer (1948) found that in *Macrotermes subhyalinus* the central portion of the nest, including the queen's chamber, contained up to 70% clay, transported from deep soil layers, and this portion was maintained during dry seasons at 25-32% moisture content with water transported from below by the workers; outer regions of the mound were predominantly sand, cemented with clay, and were not kept moist. Gay and Calaby (1970) noted that in mounds of the Western Australian species *Coptotermes brunneus* the clay superstructure of the mound is usually moist and plastic, and may even include small pools of free water. They considered the water to be probably of metabolic origin and regarded the presence of the wet clay as a reservoir of suitable material for mound construction and repair during dry periods.

(b) *Carton.* Carton consists largely of the excreta of termites, usually incorporating some mineral particles and often undigested fragments of wood, grass or leaves of trees. It is formed into a labyrinth of laminar or alveolar structure and makes up the galleries of the central portion or sometimes the whole of mounds and nests of many species of termites. In many other species similar material is used to line earthen galleries within the mound or to line galleries that provide access to food supplies.

Fyfe and Gay (1938) studied moisture relationships in mounds of *Nasutitermes exitiosus,* near Canberra, Australia. Mounds of this species have an outer covering, about 1-4 cm thick, of soil which is transported from the subsoil by the termites, contains 12-35% clay, and is cemented by the addition of faeces and probably saliva into a compact layer. Internal to the soil layer is a thick layer, alveolar in structure, consisting of thick-walled cells of carton and soil, with the proportion of organic matter increasing from 20-45% in outer regions to about 75% in the inner portion; in the centre at the base of the mound is the nursery, in which the young are raised, with thin-walled cells composed of carton and consisting largely of organic matter. Fyfe and Gay found that relative humidity throughout the mound was usually above 95% and probably never less than 92%; the saturation deficit in mounds probably never exceeds 2 mmHg, while that of the external atmosphere in the sampling area may frequently exceed 20 mmHg. Measurements of mound temperature showed that, in summer, nursery temperatures commonly rise to about $36°C$; temperatures in the outer alveolar regions within the soil wall are generally lower than in the nursery, and the difference may occasionally exceed $8°C$. Fyfe and Gay measured the absorptive capacity of mound material from the various layers at $26°C$ and $36°C$ and at a range of relative humidities from 100% to 10%. Material from the nursery absorbed about twice as much water per unit dry weight as that from the outer alveolar region, at all temperatures and relative humidities (Table 4). If the mound material were uniformly absorptive, a difference of $10°C$ between nursery and outer layers, combined with the high humidities recorded, would lead to distillation of water from inner to outer layers and consequent accelerated loss by evaporation. Fyfe and Gay concluded that this tendency would be countered by water movement in the opposite direction due to the higher absorptive capacity of the inner material. For a short time on hot days the outer layers reach temperatures similar to the nursery; subsequent relatively rapid cooling could lead to temporary dew formation in outer galleries, but not in the nursery and adjacent regions of the mound where the termites are concentrated. Water loss from mounds to the outside air is further inhibited by the relatively impervious outer soil covering. The contribution of carton to water conservation has not been studied in detail for any other species of termite, but it may reasonably be inferred that processes operating in mounds of *N. exitiosus* are paralleled in similar mounds built by many other species.

Bouillon (1964a, 1970) investigated relationships between the moisture content of surrounding soil and the structure of the walls of peripheral galleries of *Cubitermes exiguus.* In moist sand the faecal lining of galleries was incomplete and the galleries were narrow. In dry sand the faecal lining was complete, and the galleries broad and sheet-like. Since faecal material used for gallery linings is

TABLE 4

Average Moisture Content of the Different Regions of Mounds of *Nasutitermes exitiosus* at Various Relative Humidities and Temperatures. (Reproduced with permission from Fyfe and Gay, 1938.)

Relative humidity %	Temp. °C	Moisture content %			
		Nursery	Alveolar wall region		Outer soil layer
			Inner portion	Outer portion	
100	26	36.75	32.69	16.72	10.52
	36	33.77	31.10	15.60	9.36
95	26	32.14	30.18	14.71	8.56
	36	29.59	28.68	14.05	8.30
90	26	27.32	26.90	13.09	7.96
	36	25.65	25.45	12.06	7.55
80	26	20.88	20.96	10.44	6.23
	36	18.68	18.44	9.44	5.64
70	26	16.75	16.76	8.39	4.84
	36	15.15	15.06	7.69	4.44
50	26	12.84	12.94	6.37	3.73
	36	11.50	11.47	5.77	3.48
30	26	9.40	9.42	4.82	2.72
	36	8.59	8.46	4.30	2.46
10	26	4.16	4.18	2.20	1.36
	36	3.90	3.85	2.07	1.22

similar to carton, it probably served a similar moisture-holding and -conserving function.

(c) *Fungus gardens.* The cultivation of fungus gardens is confined to species of the subfamily Macrotermitinae, a predominantly African group, also represented in Madagascar and Indo-Malaya. Fungi are grown on complex convoluted structures, referred to as "fungus combs", with a large surface area (see p. 143). The fungus combs are situated in the central nest or in ancillary chambers excavated specially for them, and on their surfaces grow various species of fungi, frequently but not always in monoculture. It has been supposed that fungus combs are constructed and fungi are deliberately grown to provide the principal food resource of the colony, but Grassé (1949) has pointed out that although the fungi are eaten, and may be a source of vitamins or similar dietary requirements, the amount of fungus present is entirely inadequate to provide the principal food supply. Furthermore, Grassé and Noirot (1948) found structures indistinguishable from fungus combs, but without fungi, in above ground nests of *Sphaerotermes.*

Cheema *et al.* (1960) measured relative humidity in the air around fungus gardens of *Odontotermes obesus* and found that it varied only between 85% and 95%. It differed little from relative humidity of the soil air immediately adjacent to the fungus gardens but differed markedly from that of soil air at a distance from the gardens.

Hesse (1957) considered that fungus gardens function primarily to control humidity by taking up excess moisture or by releasing water to a drying atmosphere within mounds. They present a very large absorptive surface to the air and might serve the same function in controlling humidity as was attributed by Fyfe and Gay (1938) to carton (see p. 63), with the additional advantage that the metabolic heat of the fungi would contribute to temperature control.

3. Metabolic water

Decomposition of cellulose, which is the principal food resource of termites, results in release of water. Fyfe and Gay (1938) considered that most of the water required to maintain the observed high humidity in mounds of *Nasutitermes exitiosus* could be produced from carbohydrate metabolism. No reliable measurements have been made of production of metabolic water by termites in the field, but extrapolation from the results of laboratory feeding trials conducted with *N. exitiosus* by the authors indicates that metabolic water may be important in replacing losses by evaporation. The trials were conducted with artificial colonies in glass jars in a humid chamber (75% relative humidity), maintained at $26°C$. Weights of wood (*Eucalyptus obliqua* l'Herit) eaten, carbohydrate content of the wood and excreta, showed that 1 000 000 termites, a reasonable average for a colony of this species, would consume 21.93 g of carbohydrate per day, which yields 12.19 g of water. Measurement of a large number of *N. exitiosus* mounds near Adelaide showed that the average volume of the galleried portion of mounds is about 260 litres, of which about one-quarter (65 litres) is air space. At 100% relative humidity 65 litres of air contain 1.58 g of water at $26°C$ and 2.71 g of water at $36°C$. In the absence of measurements of water loss from mounds in field conditions no accurate assessment of the water balance of mounds can be attempted, but it is apparent that in the tightly sealed mounds of *N. exitiosus* addition of 12.19 g of water per day from carbohydrate metabolism must contribute significantly to the maintenance of high humidity.

Hesse (1955) found that the moisture content of inhabited mounds of three East African species of *Macrotermes* was higher than that of adjacent uninhabited mounds, and inferred that metabolic water was largely responsible for the difference. He did not consider active transport of water, which is well known in *Macrotermes* spp., but the very large populations that sometimes inhabit *Macrotermes* mounds must contribute much metabolic water to the mounds.

It seems likely that the fungi in fungus gardens of Macrotermitinae supply metabolic water to the environment in the mound, but no information on their significance is available.

4. *Protection from excess water*

For species that inhabit regions of heavy rainfall, especially rain forests, maintenance of high humidity presents no problems, but protection from flooding and excessive erosion may be important. Many rain forest termites build arboreal nests, often with covered runways descending to the soil. Grassé (1949) and Emerson (1938, 1956) described such nests which have special structural features, apparently for shedding water. *Amitermes excellens,* in the forests of Guyana and *Cubitermes subarquatus,* in Congolese forests, build nests consisting of a series of superposed "half hats" spaced down tree trunks; the nests of *Amitermes evuncifer* are similarly spaced and consist of a series of overlapping sheet-like flanges projecting outward and downward from tree trunks, and with their edges prolonged into finger-like projections from which water is shed; *Procubitermes niapuensis* and *Constrictotermes cavifrons* build a herring-bone pattern of covered ways on tree trunks above their nests, apparently to divert water running down the trunk away from the nest. Noirot (1959) pointed out that, at least in the genus *Procubitermes,* other species that live in the same environment do not build such "rain-shedding" structures, and questioned the idea that protection of the nest from rain damage is their true function. Emerson (1956) similarly considered the "hats" of the mushroom shaped nests of *Cubitermes* as primarily a rain-shedding device; his observation that some species construct nests with "hats" in the wetter parts and without "hats" in the drier parts of their range adds weight to his conclusion on the function of the "hats".

In northern Australia, and in much of tropical Africa, southern Asia and South America, widespread seasonal flooding temporarily prohibits access to the soil for termites in low-lying areas. During the wet season grass-feeding termites such as *Amitermes meridionalis* in northern Australia, retreat into their mounds and apparently live on grass collected and stored during the dry season.

D. Termite Nests as an Environment for Other Animals

The physical protection and equable environmental conditions provided by termites in their nests, mounds, and other structures attract many animals, mostly insects, to spend part or all of their lives in association with termites. These animals are known collectively as termitophiles. Their activities are largely irrelevant to the aims of this book, and the reader is referred to the work of Hegh (1922), Kistner (1969) and Harris (1961) for an account of the animals involved in such associations. Many species of termites are obligate or facultative inquilines in the nests of other termites. Hill (1922a, 1935) and Ratcliffe *et al.* (1952) report such associations in Australian termites, while Bouillon (1964a), Harris (1961), Kemp (1955) and Sands (1965a) report similar associations in African termites.

Reptiles, birds, and mammals also frequent termite mounds, both as permanent living places and as nest sites. Goodland (1965) found armadillo, foxes, lizards and rattlesnakes living in termite mounds in Guyana; Cowles (1930) made a detailed study of the use of mounds of *Trinervitermes trinervoides* as incubation sites for the eggs of the monitor *Varanus niloticus* L. in Natal; Mitchell (1965) found a gecko, *Gehyra pilbara* Mitchell, living in mounds and feeding on the termites (probably *Nasutitermes triodiae*) in north-western Australia, together with a small python (*Liasis perthensis* Stull) which preys on the gecko; Murray (1938) found birds frequenting termite mounds in South Africa, and it is known that several species of Australian parrots excavate, and nest in, holes in mounds. Araujo (1970) has summarized information on a variety of similar associations of animals with termite mounds in South America; he applied the term "termitariophiles" to such animals, to distinguish them from the true termitophiles.

CHAPTER 4

Termite Populations

The significance of termites in soils is related to their numbers and the effects they have in transporting and transforming the mineral and organic components of soils and plants. The numbers of termites, or more precisely the numbers of termite mounds, have always impressed travellers in the tropics, where mounds are often sufficiently numerous to be a dominant feature of the landscape. Their extreme abundance may impinge directly on man's activities, for instance providing cover for hunters in Africa (Drummond, 1888) or endangering air-strips in northern Australia (Ratcliffe et al., 1952). However, in contrast to the wealth of quantitative information on the populations of other soil animals, such as earthworms, mites and collembola, in a wide variety of habitats, the little available information on termites is largely qualitative. Quantitative data are incomplete, there being no estimate of the total termite population for any single habitat. This lack of quantitative information is partly due to inadequate investigations and partly due to the difficulties involved in sampling termite populations (see Appendix).

I. Distribution and Abundance of Termites

A. TERMITE MOUNDS

Termite mounds are relatively easy to count and there are a number of estimates of their abundance, some of which are shown in Table 5 (see also Tables 8, 9 and 10). The densities of the large mounds of Macrotermitinae in Africa and of *Nasutitermes triodiae* (Nasutitermitinae) in northern Australia, which support colonies of several million individuals, are usually less than 10/ha, while densities of the smaller mounds, which support colonies of several thousand individuals, may approach 1000/ha. Mounds are more numerous in tropical and subtropical regions than in temperate regions, although Kozlova (1951) recorded densities of 570/ha for mounds of a species, which was

TABLE 5

Abundance of Some Termite Mounds

Species	Numbers/ha	Habitat and locality	Author and reference
Hodotermitidae			
?*Anacanthotermes ahngerianus*	162	Steppe, Central Asia	Ghilarov, 1962
Rhinotermitidae			
Coptotermes lacteus	1-2	Sclerophyll forest, S. Australia	Wood and Lee (in press)
Termitidae			
Macrotermitinae			
Odontotermes sp.	5-7	Savanna, Kenya	Glover *et al.*, 1964
Macrotermes bellicosus	2-3	Savanna, Congo	Bouillon and Kidieri, 1964
Macrotermes spp.	3-4	Savanna, E. Africa	Hesse, 1955
Nasutitermitinae			
Nasutitermes exitiosus	4-9	Sclerophyll forest, S. Australia	Wood and Lee (in press)
N. triodiae	3-7	Tree savanna, N. Australia	Wood and Lee (in press)
N. magnus	61	Pasture, E. Australia	Wood and Lee (in press)
Trinervitermes trinervoides	534	Savanna, S. Africa	Murray, 1938
Amitermitinae			
Amitermes laurensis	28-210	Savanna woodland, N. Australia	Wood and Lee (in press)
Drepanotermes spp.	up to 350	Semi-arid woodland, Australia	Watson and Gay, 1970
Termitinae			
Cubitermes fungifaber	875	Tropical rain forest, Congo	Maldague, 1964
C. exiguus	} 0-652	Steppe savanna,	Bouillon and Mathot, 1964
C. sankurensis	} 8-550	Congo	

probably *Anacanthotermes ahngerianus*, in Central Asia. High densities of the large mounds are reached only in savanna or sparsely timbered scrub or tree savanna, while smaller mounds can be extremely abundant in both savanna and dense forest.

There are few estimates of the abundance of mounds of all species in selected habitats, but our own observations in northern Australia (Wood and Lee, in press) and those of Sands (1965a) in West Africa indicate that numbers may approach or even exceed 1000/ha (see Tables 8 and 9).

B. SUBTERRANEAN TERMITES

The subterranean termite fauna is made up of species which build distinct subterranean nests, species which are entirely subterranean but whose nests are rudimentary, and also species which build nests above the ground and have foraging galleries in the soil.

The abundance of subterranean nests is difficult to estimate. Hartwig (1966), making use of trenches dug for civil engineering purposes, estimated the density of nests of *Odontotermes latericius* in veld near Bloemfontein, South Africa at about 1/ha. Nel (1968) made use of the mutual hostility shown by workers from different colonies and estimated the mean area of the territory of *Hodotermes mossambicus* to be 92 m², and as the whole of the area investigated appeared to be divided up into termite territories, their density was calculated at 110/ha.

Estimates of the total subterranean termite fauna for a variety of habitats in Africa, West Indies and Panama are shown in Table 6 and for some arid and

TABLE 6

Abundance of Subterranean Termites in Various Habitats
(Sampling details are given in the Appendix)

Habitat	Numbers/ m²	Percentage of total macro- arthropods	Author and reference
Brachystegia "shadowy forest", Congo	500	not known	Maldague (1964)
Various habitats, Congo	1800	75	Harris (1963)
Various grasslands, E. Africa	1395	6	Salt (1952)
Dry savanna, Trinidad	27	0.6	Strickland (1944)
Rain forest, Trinidad	4450	43	Strickland (1944)
Various forests, Trinidad	2790	34	Strickland (1945)
Rain forest, Panama	12	0.5	Williams (1941)

semi-arid habitats in Australia in Table 7. As mentioned in the Appendix, most of the estimates are not particularly accurate but are included here as they are the only ones available. They show, nevertheless, that the subterranean termite fauna is appreciable and in some instances constitutes half or more of the soil macro-arthropod fauna. In *Brachystegia* forest in the Congo (Maldague, 1964) subterranean termites constituted over half the total termite population.

TABLE 7

Abundance of Subterranean Termites in Some Arid and Semi-arid Habitats in Australia (Lee and Wood, unpublished data) (5 to 6 cores 20 cm^2 area at each site)

Habitat	Number of sites	Frequency of occurrence (%)	Density (nos./m^2)	Percentage of total macro-arthropods
Southern Australia				
Desert grassland and steppe	17	11.8	12	3
Semi-arid woodland	32	18.8	69	11
Shrub steppe	18	22.2	290	25
Semi-arid mallee	13	16.5	131	6
Savanna woodland	8	18.8	50	3
Northern Australia				
Native grassland	2	50.0	2000	45

II. Factors Affecting Distribution and Abundance

A. TERMITE MOUNDS

Generally, factors such as climate, vegetation, and soil interact in their effects on the distribution and abundance of termites, so that it is often not possible to say which factor is the most important on the basis of observational evidence alone. For instance, *Amitermes meridionalis* which constructs the famous "magnetic ant-hills" in northern Australia, is confined to a small area south of Darwin. Its mounds are abundant on grey soils around the margins of poorly-drained, treeless flats, which are waterlogged in the wet season (summer); they are less abundant on grey, poorly-drained soils in the adjacent sparsely timbered country and are not found at all on the surrounding, slightly more elevated red earths (Hill, 1942) which are well-drained and support woodland or forest. It is not obvious whether seasonal inundation, soil type, or vegation are the principal factors determining its distribution. Murray (1938) showed that near Frankenwald, South Africa, the abundance of termite mounds increased as secondary plant succession advanced (Fig. 22) from two-year-old fallow to undisturbed veld, and she attributed this to an increase in the binding of soil particles which rendered the soil texture more suitable for termites. However, the situation is almost certainly more complex than this, with factors associated with increasing complexity of the vegetation, such as shade, and variety and

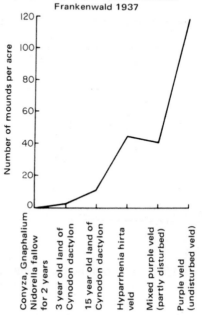

The abundance of termite mounds increases as plant succession advances. The slight fall in the number of termite mounds in "mixed purple veld" might be due to this area's riverine situation.

Frankenwald 1937

Fig. 22. Abundance of termite mounds in relation to succession of plant communities near Frankenwald, South Africa. (Reproduced with permission from Murray, 1938.)

quantity of food, probably playing an important role. The interaction of various factors is demonstrated by Bodot's (1964, 1967a) study of the distribution of termites in various types of savanna in the Ivory Coast of West Africa (Table 8). Coarse-textured sandy soils (silt and clay : sand = 13 : 1) in area I had a low water-holding capacity and supported a vigorous growth of tussock grasses, such as *Loudetia,* which are long lived and which provided an abundance of dry grass for harvesting termites (*Trinervitermes* spp.), roots for *Amitermes evuncifer,* and humus for the humivorous *Cubitermes severus.* On the other hand, in areas II and III, where the surface of the soil had a higher water-holding capacity due to its greater content of clay, as a result of excess water in the wet season, there was only a sparse cover of grasses and therefore, less food for the termites and fewer termite mounds. In area I, mounds of *Trinervitermes* spp. and *Macrotermes bellicosus* were localized in valleys or at the base of slopes where the ratio of silt and clay : sand tended to be greater than 13 : 1, due to the accumulation of water-borne fine material, whereas in areas II and III, where the ratio was greater than 28 : 1, *Trinervitermes* spp. and *Amitermes evuncifer* were localized along drainage lines. However, in spite of the complexity of the

TABLE 8

Abundance of Mounds and Frequency of Occurrence of Subterranean Termites in Different Types of Savanna in the Ivory Coast, W. Africa (Adapted from Bodot, 1964, 1967a)

Density of mounds in numbers/ha; frequency of subterranean species as % occurrence in 12 samples

	Area I	Area II	Area III
Dominant grass	Loudetia	Anadelphia	Schizachyrium
Ratio clay + silt : sand	13.5	29.8	28.3
%C in surface soil	0.66	0.39	0.15

	Total	Abandoned	Total	Abandoned	Total	Abandoned
Mound-building termites						
Cubitermes severus	131	85				
Amitermes evuncifer	17	2	4	1	6	1.5
Trinervitermes trinervius	9	1	3	1	4	0.5
Trinervitermes occidentalis	31	12	6	1	7	1
Macrotermes bellicosus	68	66	2	2	3	2.5

Subterranean species	Frequency	Frequency	Frequency
Anoplotermes spp. (3 spp.)	58	33	50
Allognathotermes hypogeus	84		
Hoplognathotermes subterraneus	58		
Euchilotermes tensus	33		
Basidentitermes potens	58		
Pericapritermes urgens	25		
Mimeutermes sorex	25		
Ophiotermes sp.	20		
Allodontotermes giffardi	+	+	
Ancistrotermes cavithorax ⎱ Ancistrotermes crucifer ⎰	50		
Microtermes subhyalinus	50	16	25
Macrotermes subhyalinus	42		

environment one can sometimes see the effects of isolated factors on the distribution and abundance of termites, and some examples are discussed below.

1. Soils

The most significant feature of soils for mound-building termites is the proportion of sand, silt, and clay and the distribution of these constituents throughout the profile. A certain amount of clay, or other colloidal material such as saliva or faecal matter, is required to cement particles together, which accounts for the general absence of mounds on pure sands. For instance, in south-western Australia, the only *Eucalyptus* community from which *Coptotermes acinaciformis* is absent is "mallee" growing on deep sand (Calaby and Gay, 1956). A group of soils known as cracking clays (Ug soils, Northcote, 1965; black earths and some red, brown and grey clays, Stace *et al.*, 1968) are widely distributed in Australia. These soils have a high clay content throughout the profile, are self-mulching, are subjected to seasonal inundation, and crack deeply in the dry season. It is likely that the disturbance caused by seasonal cracking prevents termites from building stable structures such as mounds and galleries, as Ratcliffe *et al.* (1952) observed that mounds did not occur on these soils, even though they were abundant on adjacent soils (desert loams). Our own observations confirm this, with the single exception of a small area of cracking clays near Dunmara in northern Australia, where there were a number of mounds of *Nasutitermes longipennis*. These mounds, which were up to 1 m high and constructed largely of soil, were invariably built against the base of living *Eucalyptus* trees. This species of termite is predominantly a grass- and litter-feeder and the trees may have provided shade (see p. 56), but also the soil around the base of the trees may have had a slightly different texture than the surrounding cracking clays.

The distribution of *Amitermes vitiosus* in northern Australia illustrates the importance of soil texture. On shallow soils with a uniform sandy or sandy-loam profile it is either absent or builds small, conical mounds up to 0.5 m high (Fig. 23). With an increasing proportion of clay, as in soils of the earth type, its mounds are often extremely abundant (several hundred per hectare) and also larger, up to 1.5 m high (Fig. 24). Even larger mounds, although not in such great numbers, are found in situations where silt or clay tends to accumulate, such as on outwash fans and levees alongside watercourses and in shallow depressions (Fig. 25) or on the lower slopes of hills, although heavy-textured soils are avoided. The mounds are rarely found on well-developed duplex soils, that is soils which have a predominantly sandy A horizon sharply separated from a predominantly clayey B horizon. It is possible that in these soils *A. vitiosus* is unable to obtain the clay required for mound-building. In contrast, *Amitermes laurensis*, which is widely distributed in eastern Queensland, is particularly abundant on the solodic (duplex) soils around Townsville and the Atherton Tableland, but is rare on adjacent soils of the earth type (Wood and Lee, in press).

A relationship between the abundance of large mounds of Macrotermitinae in the Congo and the clay content of the soil was noticed by Sys (1955) and Meyer (1960). Sys showed that on soils with 60%, 50%, 40% and 30-35% of clay, there were 4.9, 4.0, 3.7 and 2.7 mounds/ha occupying 7.8%, 6.4%, 5.9% and 4.3% of the surface respectively.

The depth of soil appears to have some significance for species which build

Fig. 23. Small conical mounds of *Amitermes vitiosus* on shallow earthy sands near Tennant Creek, N.T., Australia.

Fig. 24. Aggregation of mounds of *Amitermes vitiosus* on a red earth near Tennant Creek, N.T., Australia.

Fig. 25. Large mounds of *Amitermes vitiosus* on grey earths in a broad depression near Newcastle Waters, N.T., Australia.

very large mounds. In northern Australia *Nasutitermes triodiae* builds large mounds up to 5 m or more high and often exceeding 2 m in diameter. These mounds are found on a wide variety of soils but never on shallow soils. In undulating country, shallow soils often predominate on hillsides below rocky outcrops and *N. triodiae* mounds are found only in valleys or on flats where there is a sufficient depth of soil to enable large mounds to be constructed.

A comparison of three sites in northern Australia (Table 9) illustrates the influence of soils on the distribution and abundance of termite mounds, although other factors are involved. The three areas lie within 240 km of each other and are subject to very similar climates. All the species, apart from *C. acinaciformis*, are grass-feeders. In each area the vegetation is savanna woodland (Wood and Williams, 1960) with a dense cover of tall tropical grasses dominated by various species of *Sorghum, Heteropogon* and *Chrysopogon*. At Larrimah, where the density of mounds exceeded 1000/ha, the soil was a red earth and our observations have indicated that, in northern Australia, the various types of "earth" support the greatest numbers of termite mounds. At Pine Creek, in undulating country, soils on slopes were shallow, gravelly loams which supported only small mounds of *A. vitiosus* and *T. hastilis* at a density of about 240/ha. The scarcity of soil could possibly limit the abundance of mounds and almost certainly was the reason for the absence of the large mounds of *N. triodiae* which were confined to the deep colluvial loamy "earths" in valleys between the slopes. At Brock's Creek, on loamy duplex soils (solodic soils), there were no *A. vitiosus* (see above), somewhat higher densities of *T. hastilis* (*T. pastinator* was the less abundant species of the two), and a few *N. triodiae*, the latter being

TABLE 9

Abundance of Termite Mounds (Numbers/ha) in Three Areas of Savanna Woodland in Northern Territory, Australia

Species	Larrimah Wood and Lee (in press)		Pine Creek Lee and Wood (unpublished)		Brocks Creek Williams (1968)	
	Total	Abandoned	Total	Abandoned	Total	Abandoned
Tumulitermes hastilis	486	177	180		500	326
Tumulitermes pastinator	–	–	–			
Nasutitermes triodiae	< 1	not known	< 1	not	1	not known
Amitermes vitiosus	268	72	60	known	–	
Drepanotermes spp.*	354	94	–		–	
Coptotermes acinaciformis	–		5		–	

* Mainly *Drepanotermes rubriceps* but including at least one undescribed species of *Drepanotermes*.

more abundant on the deeper earths on lower slopes and in valleys (Williams, 1968 and personal communication). However, the absence of *Drepanotermes rubriceps* from the Pine Creek and Brock's Creek sampling sites cannot be satisfactorily explained by differences between soils, as this species is probably the most widely distributed mound-building termite in Australia and occurs on a great variety of soils, including the ones dominant in these two areas. *Coptotermes acinaciformis* is a wood-eating species and its absence from the Larrimah and Brock's Creek areas is more likely to be due to factors associated with vegetation (see below) than with soils.

2. Vegetation

As plant tissue is either directly or indirectly the source of food for termites, vegetation must be an important factor in determining their distribution and abundance. This is illustrated by the distribution of the genus *Coptotermes* in Australia (Calaby and Gay, 1956, 1959). Mound-building is unknown in this genus outside Australia, whereas four of the six species in Australia regularly construct mounds, and all but one species are dependent on *Eucalyptus* spp. for food. The whole of Australia, with the exception of the cold, wet south-east and the rain-forest areas, is climatically suitable for *C. acinaciformis*. However, in the dry inland of Australia, where the dominant trees are various species of *Acacia*, it is found only in *Eucalyptus* logs and trees along watercourses. In southern Australia, its nests are generally made within the trunks of trees whereas in northern Australia it builds large, domed mounds and Calaby and Gay (1959) suggested that the *Eucalyptus* spp. of the northern woodlands were not large enough to support the populous colonies of this species, which contain over a million individuals.

The structure of the vegetation is also of importance, particularly through its effect on the amount and distribution of shade. Sands (1965a) studied the distribution and abundance of several species of *Trinervitermes* in northern Nigeria (Table 10), in habitats ranging from more or less closed woodland to grassland (cleared woodland). He attributed the different densities of *Trinervitermes* in his areas I, II and III to differences in the form of the vegetation. *T. geminatus* built nests in unshaded areas, 90% of all the nests found being in "fully exposed" sites. In the closed woodland it was confined to the few open spaces and was much less abundant than in partly cleared (area II) and cleared (area III) habitats. On the other hand, 75% of the mounds of *T. oeconomus* and *T. occidentalis* were found in shaded sites, and these species were most numerous in area I and least numerous in area III. Shade may be particularly important in hot, dry areas. Kemp (1955) found that in the dry thickets of inland Tanzania, termite mounds only occurred in shaded sites. *Tumulitermes tumuli* is abundant in the arid regions of central and western

TABLE 10

Abundance of Mounds and Frequency of Occurrence of Subterranean Termites in Northern Nigeria (Adapted from Sands, 1965a)

Density of mounds in numbers/ha; frequency of subterranean species as mean number of occurences in 50 pits 1.68 m² in area by 0.91 m deep

Species	Area I Closed woodland (climax vegetation)		Area II Partly cleared woodland (scrub)		Area III Totally cleared (grassland)	
	Total	Abandoned	Total	Abandoned	Total	Abandoned
Mound-building termites						
Trinervitermes geminatus	63	5	440	207	753	248
Trinervitermes trinervius	1.7*		0.5		1.2	
Trinervitermes togoensis	0.2*		2.5		1.0	
Trinervitermes oeconomus	2.5*		0.7		0.7	
Trinervitermes occidentalis	0.5*		0.5			
Macrotermes bellicosus	25	10	10	10	2.5	2.5
Macrotermes subhyalinus			2.5	2.5		
Odontotermes sudanensis	15	10	2.5	2.5		
Cubitermes sp.	2.5	2.5			2.5	2.5
Procubitermes sp.	2.5	2.5				

Subterranean species	Frequency	Frequency	Frequency
Anoplotermes spp.	0.52	0.81	2.80
Amitermes evuncifer	0.02		0.04
Eremotermes nanus		0.02	
Microcerotermes spp.		0.08	
Allognathotermes sp.	0.12		
Promirotermes spp.	0.04		
Pericapritermes sp.		0.02	
Pseudacanthotermes militaris	3.28	0.24	0.24
Pseudacanthotermes spiniger	0.12		
Allodontotermes sp.	0.22	0.04	
Odontotermes spp.	0.02	0.26	1.12
Ancistrotermes spp.	0.62	0.56	0.40
Microtermes spp.	2.54	5.02	4.84

* Data for occupied mounds only.

Australia. According to Calaby and Gay (1959) its distribution more or less coincides with that of the mulga (*Acacia* spp.) scrub. It is a grass- and litter-feeding species and may not, therefore, depend on the mulga trees for food. Its mounds, which are conical structures 0.2-0.6 m high, are most often found at the base of the trees (Fig. 26) and it is likely that shade is the important

Fig. 26. Mound of *Tumulitermes tumuli* at base of a mulga (*Acacia* sp.) tree, near Coober Pedy, central Australia.

factor. On the other hand, an excess of shade can lead to the exclusion of termites. In southern Australia, *Nasutitermes exitiosus* is an abundant and widely distributed mound-building, wood-eating species in *Eucalyptus* woodland and forest. In areas where the native vegetation has been felled and replaced with exotic *Pinus* plantations, the colonies decline and gradually die out (Ratcliffe *et al.*, 1952), even though there is abundant food in the form of logs and stumps of *Eucalyptus* trees. The mounds are not affected until the pine trees have formed an almost closed canopy and it is likely that the shutting out of sunlight is at least partly responsible for the death of the colonies (see also p. 7). This suggestion would be supported by the fact that in sclerophyll *Eucalyptus* forests its mounds are rarely found in steep, well-shaded gullies with a dense shrub stratum (Wood and Lee, in press).

3. Climate

Climate affects the distribution and abundance of termites on a geographical scale and its effect is difficult to dissociate from geographical distribution of the species of termites themselves (see p. 19) and differences in soil and vegetation. Grassé (1950) noted that fungus-feeding termites were rare or absent from dry areas in West Africa, their preferred habitats being humid savanna and forest. Kemp (1955) found a similar distribution in East Africa where the humid woodland near the coast supported many more species and a greater proportion of mound-builders (Table 11) than the dry inland areas. In Africa, species of *Cubitermes* are abundant in regions of heavy to moderate rainfall, rare in regions of light or more seasonal rainfall, and absent from regions with an annual rainfall of less than 25 cm (Williams, 1966). As species of this genus are humus-feeders, they are probably more directly dependent upon soil moisture than are species which feed on wood, grass, or leaf-litter. Although the Australian termite fauna has approximately the same number of species north and south of the Tropic, there are more species of Termitidae north of the Tropic and more species of the primitive families south of the Tropic (Calaby and Gay, 1959). However, there are many more mound-building species north of the Tropic, as is demonstrated by the fact that six of the seven mound-building species of *Amitermes* are tropical, and the northern species of *Nasutitermes* largely build mounds, whereas the southern species are largely subterranean. This tendency towards mound-building in the northern, tropical regions has already been noted in the case of *Coptotermes acinaciformis*, and it is possible that in the tropics termites can control their environment more readily in mounds than in subterranean galleries (see Chapter 3).

The effect of a relatively rapid change in climate over a short distance can be seen in the depletion of the fauna with increasing altitude. This was illustrated by Kemp's (1955) study of the Tanzanian fauna (Table 11) and can be seen in

TABLE 11

Number of Species of Termites Recorded from Different Types of Vegetation in North-eastern Tanzania (Adapted from Kemp, 1955)

	Coastal plains <3000 ft	Northern bushland	Mid-northern bushland	Eastern bushland	Riverine forest	Mountain rain forest	Mountain cedar forest	Cultivated >4000 ft
Kalotermitidae	5	4	3	0	1	2	1	0
Hodotermitidae	0	0	1	1	0	0	0	0
Rhinotermitidae	2	1	0	0	1	0	0	0
Termitidae	53	31	22	16	6	8	3	2
Total	60	36	26	17	8	10	4	2
Nesting habits:								
Dead trees and logs	10	8	7	2	2	3	1	0
Subterranean	14	11	10	4	1	0	0	0
Mounds	32	17	9	11	4	6	3	2
Arboreal nests	4	0	0	0	1	1	0	0

the Snowy Mountains of south-eastern Australia, where *Coptotermes lacteus,* a common mound-building species in woodland and sclerophyll forest on the eastern plateaux, rarely occurs above 1200 m and the even more abundant *Nasutitermes exitiosus* rarely occurs above 900 m.

4. Other animals

There is little information on the effects of other animals, including other species of termites, on the abundance and distribution of termites. One can conveniently consider other animals in the termites' environment in three categories, (i) predators and parasites, (ii) "competitors", and (iii) termitophiles. Discussion of termitophiles, which include snakes, lizards, and birds, as well as many arthropods (see p. 66), is outside the scope of this book and interested readers are referred to the review of Kistner (1969).

(a) *Parasites and Predators.* Snyder (1956, 1961, 1968) has given an extensive bibliography of work on the parasites and predators of termites. Although a wide range of parasites, including fungi, protozoa, nematodes, mites, and insects, have been recorded from termites, little is known of their incidence in termite populations and their effects on different species of termites. There is more information on predators and the best known are those arthropods and vertebrates that prey on the swarms of winged termites (Nutting, 1969). These animals consume enormous quantities of termites, but such predation appears to be largely opportunistic and may account for as little as 1% of the predators' diet (Knight, 1939). However, Bont (1964) suggested that termites were vital to the survival of many of the migratory insectivorous birds of Europe which spend the northern winter in Africa. There are a number of specially adapted predators (see Hegh, 1922) that probably have a more significant effect on termite populations. Among vertebrates are the scaly ant-eater (*Manis crassicaudata* Geof. St Hilaire) in India (Mathur, 1962), ant-eaters (*Myrmecophaga* spp.) in South America (Araujo, 1970), the armadillo in Texas (Kalmbach, 1943), the numbat (*Myrmecobius f. fasciatus* Waterhouse) (Calaby, 1960) and echidna (*Tachyglossus aculeatus* (Shaw)) in Australia. Termites appear to be the principal item of diet of the numbat and they formed about 30% of the stomach contents of armadillos (Araujo, 1970). Although there is no precise information on the effect of these predators on termite populations, they would appear to have some significance as some termites have developed mechanisms, such as the distasteful sticky fluid secreted by soldiers of the Nasutitermitinae and the long slender mandibles of certain genera such as *Amitermes* and *Orthognathotermes*, to repel vertebrate predators (Stuart, 1969). Ants are generally regarded as being the most important predators of termites (Wheeler, 1936), and there is some evidence that they may occasionally have a profound effect on termite populations. Wheeler (1936) discussed, in general terms, the relationships between ants and termites and recognized four categories of predatory ant-termite relationships.

(i) Cleptobiotic ants: these ants attack other ants, particularly injured individuals, which have been raiding termite colonies and wrest their prey from them.

(ii) Termitolestic ants: these are small ants which live in the walls or partitions of termite nests and prey on the host colony.

(iii) Certain inquiline ants: these ants occupy portions of inhabited or abandoned mounds and are extremely aggressive towards the host termites. Sands (1965a) found four genera of ants, one (*Megaponera* sp.) of which was known to eat termites, inhabiting mounds of *Trinervitermes* spp. in northern Nigeria. When such mounds were opened, there was immediate and indiscriminate conflict between the ants and termites. There was a general tendency for more abandoned mounds than occupied mounds to be colonized by ants, and in one area where mounds were not particularly abundant, the termites tended to occupy their mounds more fully and permanently, thus excluding mound-sharing species such as ants and other termites. The implications are that these ants can only occupy abandoned mounds or mounds in which the colonies are of low vigour and, in the latter case, they may hasten the decease of the colony. Hill (1922b) gave a lucid description of a similar situation in northern Australia involving the "meat ant", *Iridomyrmex purpureus* F. Smith, and two mound-building termites, *Amitermes laurensis* and *Drepanotermes rubriceps*. Around Townsville, he estimated that this ant occupied up to 80% of all termitaria. Our own observations around Townsville (Wood and Lee, in press) indicate that *Iridomyrmex* occurs more frequently in abandoned mounds of the grass- and litter-feeding *A. laurensis* than in occupied mounds. In addition one of the sites we studied included a heavily overgrazed area where 50% of *A. laurensis* mounds were abandoned, and an adjacent lightly grazed area where 22% of the mounds were abandoned. The proportion of abandoned mounds occupied by *Iridomyrmex* was similar in the two areas (82% and 72% respectively), but the proportion of occupied mounds colonized by ants (70% and 46% respectively) was much greater in the over-grazed area, possibly due to the "low vigour" of the termite colonies, induced by shortage of food.

(iv) Termitharpactic ants: these ants habitually raid colonies of termites and include some, such as some Ponerinae, which feed exclusively on termites and others, such as some Dorylinae, Myrmicinae, and Ponerinae, for which termites constitute a large proportion of the food. In northern Nigeria, Sands (1965a) observed that whenever *Dorylus* spp. were found in termite mounds, they appeared to be exterminating the inhabitants. Termites such as *Anoplotermes* and *Trinervitermes* were observed to vacate their mounds *en masse* when invaded and to return when these ants had disappeared. Bodot (1961, 1967a) observed that *Dorylus (Typhlopone) dentifrons* Wasmann frequently launched massive attacks on mounds of *Macrotermes bellicosus* in the Ivory Coast. A few of these attacks were repulsed, but most of the attacked colonies were exterminated. *M. bellicosus* was attacked in preference to other species of termites and Bodot (1967a) attributed the large proportion of abandoned mounds (see Table 4) and the recent regression of this species to attacks by the ants. Another instance of a specialized predatory relationship is that of the ponerine ant *Termitopone commutala* (Roger) which specializes in raiding various species of *Syntermes* (Emerson, 1945).

(b) *"Competitors"*. If one accepts Milne's (1961) definition of competition, included in the category "competitors" are those animals which utilize the same resources, such as space or food, as termites with the result that the intensity of competition increases as the ratio of population to resource increases. Due to their specialized feeding and nesting habits, the most important competitors of termites, with some exceptions which will be noted later, are other termites of the same or different species. There is, however, little information on the significance of competition among termite populations although, among mound-building species at least, over-dispersion of mounds indicates that competition may be a general phenomenon. The relationship between density of mounds per unit area (m), the mean distance between pairs of nearest-neighbouring mounds $(\bar{r})$ and the dispersion coefficient (a) may be expressed as: $m = a/\bar{r}^2$ (Clark and Evans, 1954; Waloff and Blackith, 1962; Wood and Lee, in press). The value of the dispersion coefficient ranges from a theoretical minimum of zero when the mounds are aggregated into a single mass to a maximum of 1.158 when the mounds are situated at the corners of a network of regular hexagons. A completely random distribution of mounds gives a value of 0.25. Thus values of less than 0.25 indicate aggregation and values greater than 0.25 indicate over-dispersion. The tendency for mounds to aggregate in favourable localities is opposed by increasing competition between colonies as the distance between mounds decreases and the foraging area per colony is reduced. Thus, the intensity of competition between colonies is reflected in the value of the dispersion coefficient and the tendency for mounds to be spaced hexagonally. A study of mound-building termites in Australia (Wood and Lee, in press) showed that in 11 out of 13 populations values of a exceeded 0.25, indicating that mounds were over-dispersed (Table 12). There were two populations in which mounds appeared to be randomly distributed or slightly aggregated and in one of these, *Nasutitermes exitiosus* (site 9a in Table 12), it was shown that this was due to heterogeneity of the habitat resulting in the exclusion of mounds from certain areas, and that within the aggregations (9b and 9c in Table 12) mounds were over-dispersed. The most obvious resources for which mound-building termites might compete are food, space, and suitable sites for nesting and mound-building. We suggested (Wood and Lee, in press) that in a population of *Amitermes vitiosus* in northern Australia (site 2 in Table 12) competition for suitable nesting sites may have been partly responsible for marked over-dispersion of mounds. Although Sands (1965a) suggested that competition for food was unlikely to be a limiting factor for the termite populations he studied in northern Nigeria, there is no information regarding the requirements of termites for food; in addition, competition for food itself is complicated by competition for suitably sized foraging territories in which to locate food. Large colonies appear to maintain larger territories than small colonies as we (Wood and Lee, in press) found a positive correlation ($r = 0.88$) between the size of nearest-neighbouring mounds of *Nasutitermes exitiosus* and the distance between them.

Where the habitat is exploited by man, competition for food may be of more obvious significance. For instance, we showed (Wood and Lee, in press) that mounds of the grass- and litter-feeding *Amitermes laurensis* were more over-dispersed in areas subject to heavy grazing by cattle than in adjacent, lightly grazed areas. In South Africa (Coaton, 1954; Anon., 1960), harvester termites (Hodotermitinae) reach "saturated" population levels in over-grazed areas of veld and destroy practically all the grass. In these areas, there is competition for food among the termites themselves and between the termites and grazing animals.

In populations of more than one species, the tendency for mounds of one

TABLE 12

Densities of Termite Mounds and Values of the "Dispersion Coefficient" in Various
Habitats in Australia (After Wood and Lee, in press)

Site	Species	Vegetation*	No. of mounds per hectare		Mean of nearest-neighbour distances (metres)	Dispersion coefficient (a)
			Occupied	Total		
1	Amitermes vitiosus	Low woodland	no data	330	3.93	0.51
2	Amitermes vitiosus	Savanna woodland	no data	123	7.45	0.68
3	Tumulitermes hastilis Amitermes vitiosus Drepanotermes spp.	Savanna woodland	755	1108	3.38†	0.86†
4a	Nasutitermes triodiae	Tree savanna	1.7	3.4	25.60	0.22
4b	Nasutitermes triodiae		no data	6.6	22.75	0.34
5a	Amitermes laurensis	Savanna woodland	217	268	4.42	0.52
5b	Amitermes laurensis	(cleared)	129	154	4.94	0.38
6a	Amitermes laurensis	Savanna woodland	105	210	5.14	0.55
6b	Amitermes laurensis	(cleared)	111	142	5.76	0.47
7	Amitermes laurensis	Savanna woodland	21	28	12.42	0.43
8	Nasutitermes magnus	Pasture	38	60	6.42	0.30
9a	Nasutitermes exitiosus	Dry sclerophyll forest	2.9	3.7	24.55	0.22
9b	Nasutitermes exitiosus		6.6	8.6	18.90	0.31
9c	Nasutitermes exitiosus		9.2	9.2	22.18	0.45
10	Coptotermes lacteus Nasutitermes exitiosus	Dry sclerophyll forest	1.9	2.4	51.20	0.63

* Vegetation formations as defined by Wood and Williams (1960).
† Calculated on basis of occupied mounds only.

species to be over-dispersed must be influenced by the reaction of that species to
the other species. If the species are hostile or avoid each other, over-dispersion
will be produced by inter-specific competition as well as intra-specific
competition. In a mixed population of *Tumulitermes hastilis, Amitermes
vitiosus, Drepanotermes rubriceps* and *Drepanotermes* sp., all of which are grass-,
or grass- and litter-feeders, in northern Australia (site 3 in Table 12) mounds
were highly over-dispersed and we showed (Wood and Lee, in press) that *A.
vitiosus* occupied a greater mean area per colony than the other two species, and

competed with them for space. On the other hand, there appeared to be little competition for space between *T. hastilis* and *Drepanotermes* spp. We also suggested that the marked over-dispersion of the wood-eating *Coptotermes lacteus* and *Nasutitermes exitiosus* (site 10 in Table 12) was largely due to inter-specific competition. Competition between species of quite different feeding habits is indicated by Mathot's unpublished observations (Bouillon, 1970) near Kinshasa in the Congo, where the area in the immediate vicinity of a mound of *Macrotermes bellicosus* was not occupied by mounds of *Cubitermes sankurensis*, which were very abundant elsewhere.

Bouillon (1970) discussed some aspects of competition among termites, such as adaptations and niche specificity, which are concerned with natural selection and are of obvious significance on an evolutionary time scale. From the ecological point of view the processes of competition are of greater significance and our use of the term "competition" includes "interference", which involves attempts to oust established individuals, "exploitation", which involves utilization of a common resource (Park, 1954), and avoidance. There is little information on the relative significance of these processes in termite populations, although all seem to be operative. Nel (1968) demonstrated that aggressive behaviour among colonies of *Hodotermes mossambicus* leads to the maintenance of well-defined territories. On the other hand, this species and a co-existing species, *Trinervitermes trinervoides,* fought only if they were forcibly mixed and their normal reaction was to avoid each other. A similar situation may exist among the wood-eating *Coptotermes* in southern Australia (Calaby and Gay, 1959), as where the species are sympatric (*C. lacteus* with *C. acinaciformis* and *C. acinaciformis* with *C. frenchi*) they never occur in the same log. On the other hand, Noirot (1959) often found three or four species inhabiting the same log and frequently observed fighting between species, although they generally lived in mutually exclusive galleries. Greaves (1962a) observed that in the case of *Coptotermes acinaciformis,* termites from one colony are able to take over the galleries and workings of another colony, and Noirot (1961) quoted the case, confirmed in greater detail by Bodot (1967a), of *Amitermes evuncifer* which entered mounds of *Cubitermes* and *Trinervitermes* in the Ivory Coast, eventually displacing the original inhabitants. Species may be displaced without their mounds being taken over, as in northern Australia where we found (Wood and Lee, in press) a much higher proportion (60.5%) of abandoned mounds of *Amitermes laurensis* around occupied mounds of *Nasutitermes triodiae* than in areas (16.8% abandoned) widely separated from mounds of *N. triodiae.* Competition between grass-feeding termites and grazing animals would seem to operate largely through "exploitation", although the effects of trampling (Williams, 1959) and buffeting of mounds (Hill, 1942) are also factors to be considered. Thus, knowledge of the significance of competition among termite populations is largely fragmentary, and its role in the regulation of populations and relative abundance of different species is a virtually unexplored field of research.

B. SUBTERRANEAN TERMITES

One might expect species living a subterranean existence and only appearing above ground for foraging and mating flights to be less affected by certain factors, such as structure of vegetation, that are of importance to mound-building species. This could be illustrated by Sands' (1965a) work in northern Nigeria (Table 10, p. 79). The distribution and abundance of the various species of mound-building *Trinervitermes* was primarily determined by the availability of shaded or exposed situations. On the other hand, although the frequency of occurrence of the entirely subterranean species of Macrotermitinae (*Pseudacanthotermes, Allodontotermes, Ancistrotermes* and *Microtermes*) differed in the three areas, the total occurrences of all these species were very similar, which suggests that the availability of nesting sites for subterranean Macrotermitinae was similar in each area. However, *Pseudacanthotermes militaris* was more abundant in area I than in areas II and III, and its nest chambers occurred at a mean depth of 40 cm in area I compared with about 53 cm in areas II and III. Sands (1965a) suggested that some effect arising from the less shaded surface of the two latter areas, such as higher soil temperatures, was responsible for the differences in depth of nesting sites, and through restricting the availability of nesting sites, was responsible for the lower populations. *Microtermes* spp. appeared to be more adaptable in this respect and were more abundant in areas II and III, being able to take advantage of nesting sites unsuitable for *P. militaris*. However, in general, areas favourable for mound-building termites can also be expected to be favourable for subterranean species, as is illustrated by the abundance and frequency, respectively, of these groups in savanna in the Ivory Coast (Table 8, p. 73). The effects of isolated factors, discussed below, are even more difficult to demonstrate than for the mound-building species.

1. Soils

As with the mound-building species, the proportions of sand, silt and clay are important in determining the stability of subterranean galleries, although in the construction of galleries the soil is used more or less *in situ*, there being less mixing of soil from different horizons than with the mound-building species. Subterranean gallery systems of *Coptotermes acinaciformis* are better developed in well-structured soils than in more compact soils with a high content of clay; in loose sandy soils galleries are not constructed at all, the underground movement of the termites being confined to the roots of trees (Greaves and Florence,

(1966). Harris (1963) observed high frequencies (Table 13) and densities (Table 6, p. 70) of subterranean termites in seven out of eight habitats examined in the Congo, the exception being savanna on a deep, sandy soil where there was a complete absence of subterranean termites.

TABLE 13

Occurrence of Subterranean Termites in Different Habitats in the Garamba National Park, Congo (After Harris, 1963)

Core samples 15 cm deep, 75 cm² in area

Habitat	Number of cores	Frequency of occurrence (%)	Number of species
Gallery forest	15	60	9
Dry woodland	3	100	5
Wooded savanna	20	75	7
Wooded savanna on slope	10	100	5
Wooded savanna on plateau	8	60	3
Grassy savanna	8	85	7
Grassy savanna with rock outcrops	6	83	2
Grassy savanna on sandy soil	11	0	0

Factors associated with soil type have been implicated in the distribution of *Mastotermes darwiniensis* in northern Australia, where it is widely distributed but is absent from the deep red, basaltic soils (krasnozems) carrying rain forest, or which once carried rain forest (Ratcliffe *et al.,* 1952), and also from bauxite soils (pisolitic red and yellow earths) on Cape York Peninsula (Calaby and Gay, 1959). In the Sahara, *Anacanthotermes ochraceus* is restricted to areas where there is a proportion of clay or alluvium in the soil, and in sandy regions is replaced by the sand termite, *Psammotermes hybostoma* (Harris, 1970).

2. *Vegetation*

The effects of shading on the distribution and abundance of certain subterranean Macrotermitinae (Sands, 1965a) has already been noted, and its effects are also demonstrated by our own work in dry sclerophyll forest in southern Australia (Table 14). Here the shrub layer consists of various species of *Leptospermum, Acacia* and *Hakea* which vary from being very dense to widely spaced, thus giving varying amounts of shade to the soil surface. Various species of subterranean termites occur under stones on the ground, but they occur far more frequently under stones in open situations than under stones shaded either by shrubs or grass tussocks. The nature and degree of cover may also affect the

TABLE 14

The Effect of Shade on the Occurrence of Subterranean Termites under Stones in Dry Sclerophyll Forest in South Australia (Lee and Wood, unpublished data)

Species	Stones in shade	Stones not shaded
Heterotermes ferox	1	6
Heterotermes sp.	2	8
Amitermes neogermanus	3	17
Amitermes xylophagus	0	2
Amitermes sp.	4	10
Microcerotermes sp.	0	2
Total	10	45

establishment of colonies, as Anon. (1960) and Hartwig (1955) maintained that, where grass-cover in the South African veld had been reduced by over-grazing or drought, there were a greater number of favourable nesting sites for the winged reproductives of the harvester termites (Hodotermitinae).

3. Climate

The greater abundance of mound-building termites in tropical than in temperate areas has already been mentioned, and a comparison of the frequency of occurrence of termites in soil cores taken in tropical and temperate regions illustrates a similar pattern for the subterranean species. The only information for temperate regions is our data from arid and semi-arid habitats in southern Australia (Table 7, p. 71), where the frequency of occurrence varied from about 10% in the arid habitats to about 20% in semi-arid habitats and a negligible frequency in sub-humid habitats (not shown in Table 7). In contrast, Harris (1963) obtained frequencies greater than 50% and up to 100% in the Congo (Table 13, p. 89), and similarly high frequencies are indicated in northern Australia (Table 7).

Subterranean species appear to be relatively more abundant than mound-building species in hot, dry areas. For instance, Kemp's (1955) study of termites in Tanzania (Table 11, p. 82), showed that the ratio of mound-building species to subterranean species was 2.3 in the humid coastal plains, 1.5 in "northern bushland" with an annual rainfall of less than 760 mm and 0.9 in the even drier "mid-northern bushland". In a small area of semi-arid mallee in southern Australia (annual rainfall of 250 mm), in the course of a day's collecting, we found nine species of termites, none of which were mound-builders. In the Sahara desert, two of the dominant termites, *Psammotermes hybostoma* and *Anacanthotermes ochraceus*, construct entirely subterranean nests (Bernard, 1954)

III. Numbers, Biomass and Metabolic Activity of Termite Populations

We have already indicated that there are no reliable estimates of the total numbers of termites for any habitat. Maldague (1964) made a single estimate of the population of subterranean ($500/m^2$) and mound-building ($337.6/m^2$) termites in *Brachystegia* forest in the Congo, and estimated the total population at $1000/m^2$ with a biomass of 11 g/m^2. In dry sclerophyll *Eucalyptus* forest in South Australia, we (Lee and Wood, 1968) have estimated the population of *Nasutitermes exitiosus*, the only mound-building species in the habitat, at $600/m^2$ and the biomass at 3.0 g/m^2. In this habitat there are at least eight other species of termites (Table 24, p. 133) and although their numbers have not been estimated, the total biomass of termites probably does not exceed 6 g/m^2. Termite populations are greatest in the tropics, the highest population recorded being $4450/m^2$ in Trinidad rain forest (Strickland, 1944; see Tables 6 and 7), although this included only the subterranean population. By combining estimates of the sizes of colonies of various mound-building species (Table 17, p. 97) with estimates of the abundance of mounds (Tables 5, 9, 10 and 11), the populations of various habitats in northern Nigeria (Sands, 1965a) and the Ivory Coast (Bodot, 1967a) can be estimated at $1000\text{-}10\,000/m^2$ with a probable biomass of 5-50 g/m^2.

Maldague (1964) estimated that in *Brachystegia* forest in the Congo, the termite biomass of 11 g/m^2 consumed 8 ml $O_2/m^2/h$ which corresponded to 329 $kcal/m^2/year$. This is the only published estimate of the metabolic activity of the entire termite population of a habitat, but it appears to be based on erroneous assumptions (see p. 134). The oxygen consumption was calculated from Zeuthen's (1953) generalized relationship between body weight and consumption of oxygen, which for a mean weight of an individual of *Cubitermes fungifaber* of just over 10 mg gave a figure of 800 μl $O_2/g/h$ at 15°C. However, Hébrant (1964, 1967) made direct measurements on the smaller *Cubitermes exiguus* and obtained figures of about 165 μl $O_2/g/h$ for workers (3.44 mg) and 245 μl $O_2/g/h$ for stage V nymphs at 30°C; at 15°C the corresponding consumption of oxygen would be about 100 $\mu l/g/h$ and 150 $\mu l/g/h$ respectively, indicating that Maldague's (1964) figures are about ten times too high.

Bouillon (1970) estimated the biomass and oxygen consumption of a population of *Cubitermes exiguus* using Hébrant's (1964, 1967) estimates of numbers, biomass and oxygen consumption of colonies (Table 15), and Bouillon and Mathot's (1964) estimates of the abundance of colonies. There were 650 occupied mounds per hectare. The population of an average colony weighed

TABLE 15

Numbers, Biomass (mg) and Oxygen Consumption ($\mu l/h$) of Colonies of *Cubitermes exiguus* (Adapted from Bouillon, 1970)

Type	Individuals[a]		Society before swarming			Society after swarming		
	Weight[b] (mg)	Consumption of O_2	Numbers	Biomass	Consumption of O_2	Numbers	Biomass	Consumption of O_2
Royal pair	57.50	32.50	1	57.50	32.50	1	57.50	32.50
Imagoes	7.25	3.65	594	4306.50	2168.10	0.2	1.45	0.73
Stage V nymphs	7.30	1.77	242	1766.60	428.34	1	7.30	1.77
Stage IV nymphs	6.30	1.60	28	176.40	44.80	8	50.40	12.80
Stage III nymphs	2.50	0.66	5	12.50	3.30	0.5	1.25	0.33
Stage II nymphs	1.50	0.42	22	3.00	0.84	0.7	1.05	0.29
Stage I nymphs	0.60	0.17	0	0	0	0.8	0.48	0.14
Eggs	0.05	0.016	1942	97.10	31.07	2253	112.65	36.05
Stage I larvae	0.35	0.15	927	324.45	139.05	1068	373.80	160.20
Stage II larvae	0.90	0.29	920	828.00	266.80	792	712.80	229.68
Young workers }			162 }			113 }		
Workers	3.44	0.55	5838	20 722.56	3313.20	5099	18 001.52	2878.15
White soldiers }			24 }			21 }		
Young soldiers }	3.72	0.80	5 }	290.16	62.40	2.6 }	188.23	40.48
Soldiers			73 }			48 }		

[a]The royal pair are considered together.
[b]The intestinal contents of earth are not included.

28.59 g and consumed 6.49 ml O_2/h before swarming, and after swarming weighed 19.51 g and consumed 3.39 ml O_2/h. On the basis that the combustion of 1 litre of O_2 produces 4.7 kcal the biomass, oxygen consumption, and population metabolism of the population before swarming is 1.86 g/m², 3.70 l O_2/m²/year, and 17.4 kcal/m²/year respectively. The corresponding figures after swarming are 1.27 g/m², 1.93 l O_2/m²/year and 9.0 kcal/m²/year. In addition to *C. exiguus* this habitat supported *Cubitermes sankurensis* (8 mounds/ha), *Apicotermes gurgulifex, Macrotermes bellicosus, Pseudacanthotermes militaris, Odontotermes snyderi* and *Microcerotermes parvus*. It is likely that the total termite metabolism in tropical habitats with high populations of termites, approaches or exceeds 100 kcal/m²/year.

TABLE 16

Biomass and Metabolic Activity of soil and Litter Invertebrates in Oak Woodland (After Macfadyen, 1963 and based on data of Drift, 1951)

	Biomass (g/m²)	Metabolic activity kcal/m²/year
Large herbivores (mollusca, arthropods)	9.2	57.3
Large decomposers (earthworms, arthropods)	66.0	128.5
Small decomposers and herbivores (mites, Collembola, Enchytraeidae, nematodes)	3.8	175.7
Predators (arthropods)	0.9	22.2
Total	79.9	383.7

It is useful to compare this with Macfadyen's (1963) estimates of the population metabolism of soil invertebrates in oak woodland in Holland (Table 16) based on the population studies of Drift (1951). The metabolic activity of "large herbivores" and "large decomposers" was estimated to be 57 kcal/m²/ year and 129 kcal/m²/year respectively. Thus it is likely that, where termites are abundant, their population metabolism will be of the same order of magnitude as the "large herbivore" and "large decomposer" groups of invertebrates in temperate woodland habitats.

IV. Growth, Size and Phenology of Populations

A. FOUNDATION OF COLONIES

Colonies are founded either by a single pair of winged sexual forms or by a group, consisting of all castes, separating from an established colony. Grassé

(1949) and Nutting (1969) gave details of flight and pairing behaviour which appear to be similar in many species. Flight, or swarming, is usually synchronized, not only within the one colony, but also between different colonies of the same species. It is commonly associated with seasonal weather patterns, such as well-defined periods of rainfall, but there is often no such relationship among primitive dry-wood termites belonging to the Kalotermitidae. Generally, primitive termites are the strongest fliers, while some of the Termitidae are capable of only a brief period of fluttering (Ratcliffe *et al.,* 1952). Selection of a nest site usually follows pairing (for details see Nutting, 1969) which occurs when a female successfully attracts a male, but may precede it, in which case either sex chooses a nest site and attempts to attract members of the opposite sex by extending the abdomen (Weesner, 1960). The foundation of colonies by groups of individuals from an established colony can be achieved in two ways. Fragmentation of colonies followed by migration of swarms containing all castes ("sociotomie") has been observed in *Constrictotermes cavifrons* and others in South America (Emerson, 1938), and *Anoplotermes* and *Trinervitermes* (Grassé and Noirot, 1951) in Africa. A less positive method is practised in some Rhinotermitidae, such as *Reticulitermes* (Grassé, 1949), where the colony appears to have little cohesion and spreads out forming new colonies as soon as contact with the main nest is lost. Ratcliffe *et al.* (1952) suggested that new colonies of *Mastotermes darwiniensis* could be formed in this way.

B. GROWTH AND AGE OF COLONIES

There is a general correlation between evolutionary complexity and fecundity. According to Grassé (1949) the relatively primitive Kalotermitidae and Termopsinae lay 200-300 eggs per year, Rhinotermitidae lay some thousands of eggs per year, and Termitidae lay up to several million per year (*Cubitermes exiguus* lays 185 per day; *Macrotermes bellicosus* lays 40 000 eggs per day; Bouillon, 1970). In tropical regions, these rates may be maintained throughout the year, whereas in sub-tropical regions, egg-laying is interrupted during the cold season (Bodenheimer, 1937). These are maximum figures for mature colonies, whereas the early growth of colonies is relatively slow. Primitive termites (Kalotermitidae) excavate nests in wood which serves also as food, and as it is relatively not very nutritious, colonies grow very slowly at first (Brian, 1965), *Cryptotermes havilandi* laying four eggs and *Kalotermes flavicollis* laying six or seven (Luscher, 1951b). The latter species lays eggs over a period of 30-35 days, rests for 10-40 days and then lays again (Grassé and Noirot, 1958b). The eggs hatch after 50-60 days and there may be 55 individuals after 12 months. *Neotermes tectonae* has only 30-70 individuals after 1-2 years (Kalshoven, 1959). Higher termites form a chamber in the soil, and the body reserves of the queen, the fat body and wing muscles, are utilized for production of eggs and nutrition of the first brood, with the result that the growth of the colony is more rapid than in the primitive termites. In the laboratory, *Tenuirostritermes tenuirostris* laid five eggs per day three days after pairing and there were 60 eggs after 30 days (Light and Weesner, 1955); the eggs hatched after 35 days, and 60 days after pairing the first workers were foraging for food. A similar rate was observed in the fungus-growing species *Ancistrotermes guineensis* (Sands, 1960a), and in five grass-feeding species of *Trinervitermes* (Sands, 1965d).

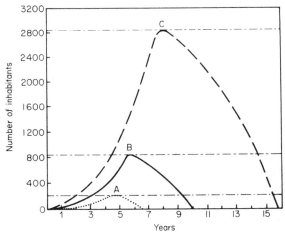

Fig. 27. Growth curves for small (A), medium (B), and large (C) colonies of *Neotermes tectonae*. (Reproduced with permission from Bodenheimer, 1937; data from Kalshoven, 1930.)

There is little information on the rate of growth and longevity of termite colonies. It is generally accepted that there is a high mortality in the early stages, as demonstrated by Kofoid (1934) who observed a first-year survival of 3.6% in *Kalotermes minor*. Bodenheimer (1937) fitted logistic curves to Kalshoven's (1930) data on the growth and senescence of colonies of *Neotermes tectonae* (Fig. 27). Small, slowly growing colonies (A in Fig. 27) reached their maximum size (240 individuals) at the age of 4½ years and died at the age of 6-7 years. Most colonies (B) reached their maximum size (844 individuals) after 5½ years and died after ten years, while larger, rapidly growing colonies (C) reached their maximum size (2844 individuals) after eight years and died after 15-16 years. However, the innate capacity for increase (see Andrewartha and Birch, 1954) of the small colonies (1.66 individuals/individual/year) was greater than that of the large colonies (0.57 individuals/individual/year). Colonies of some higher termites are known to live for much longer periods and those which produce supplementary kings and queens are potentially immortal, although

Bodenheimer (1937) was of the opinion that colonies had a definite longevity. Ratcliffe *et al* (1952) estimated that colonies of *Nasutitermes exitiosus* attained their full size after 20-25 years and that the average colony lived for at least 50 years. The same authors knew of a colony of *Nasutitermes graveolus* in northern Australia that was over 30 years old. Skaife (1955) estimated that colonies of *Amitermes hastatus* took 25-30 years to reach their full size and that the average life-span of a colony was 30 years, with a maximum of 50 years. Even longer life-spans have been estimated for some species. Hill (1942) reported on a large mound of *Nasutitermes triodiae* in northern Australia which had the top few feet removed in 1872 and was still occupied and in good repair in 1935, and Grassé (1949) noted that nests of some species of *Macrotermes* were occupied by the original reproductives, which were 80 years old. Some colonies are apparently very short lived, as Nye (1955) observed that mounds of *Macrotermes bellicosus* grow and decay to about half their maximum height in 5-10 years, and Williams (1968) noted that about half of the active mounds of *Tumulitermes hastilis* and *T. pastinator* near Brock's Creek in northern Australia had developed in a period of nine months. Noirot (1969) observed that colonies of *Cubitermes fungifaber* did not live for more than five years after egress of the nest from the soil. He recognized three stages in the growth and senescence of colonies: a juvenile period, during which only soldiers and workers are produced; an adult period, during which alates are regularly produced; a senile period, during which production of alates diminishes and finally ceases altogether. Bodot (1969) showed that for *Cubitermes severus* in the Ivory Coast juvenile colonies had an average size of 5600 individuals, adult colonies an average size of 30 000, and senile colonies an average size of 50 000. The percentage of larvae in these three types of colonies was 52%, 36%, and 14% respectively.

C. The Size of Colonies

Some estimates of the size of colonies of different species of termites are listed in Table 17. In general, the lower termites have rather small colonies numbering several hundred or a few thousand individuals, whereas the higher termites often support extremely populous colonies, the most notable of which are some of the Macrotermitinae in Africa, whose colonies support several million individuals. In areas of settlement, the primitive *Mastotermes darwiniensis* maintains large colonies, whereas under natural conditions they number only tens of thousands of individuals (Gay and Calaby, 1970). On the other hand, many of the Termitidae, particularly those building numerous small mounds, such as some species of *Trinervitermes* and *Cubitermes* in Africa, often have colonies numbering only tens of thousands or even less than 10 000; species such as *Amitermes vitiosus, A. laurensis, Tumulitermes hastilis,* and *Drepanotermes rubriceps* which, in parts of northern Australia, construct mounds in great abundance, probably fall into this category.

TABLE 17

Populations in Colonies of some species of Termites

Species	Numbers $(\times 10^3)$	Site of nest	Country	Authority and reference
Mastotermitidae				
Mastotermes darwiniensis	10->1000	Tree or subterranean	Australia	Hill (1921)
Kalotermitidae				
Kalotermes flavicollis	0.5-10			Bodenheimer (1937)
K. minor	2.6	Branch of tree	N. America	Kofoid (1934)
Neotermes tectonae	0.2-3	Branch of tree	Malaya	Kalshoven (1930)
Hodotermitidae				
Zootermopsis angusticollis	4	Rotting wood	N. America	Kofoid (1934)
Rhinotermitidae				
Reticulitermes hesperus	3-100	Subterranean	N. America	Kofoid (1934)
Coptotermes acinaciformis	1250	Living tree	Australia	Greaves (1967)
C. frenchi	750	Living tree	Australia	Greaves (1967)
C. lacteus	614-1108	Mound	Australia	Gay and Greaves (1940)
Termitidae				
Odontotermes redemanni	up to 3000	Mound	Ceylon	Bodenheimer (1937)
Macrotermes subhyalinus	2000	Mound	E. Africa	Harris (1955)
M. falciger	"Several" 1000	Mound	E. Africa	Bachelier (1963)
M. bellicosus	"Several" 1000	Mound	E. Africa	Bachelier (1963)
	2000	Mound	W. Africa	Luscher (1955)
Trinervitermes geminatus	19-52	Mound	W. Africa	Sands (1965b)
Nasutitermes rippertii	632	Arboreal	Jamaica	Andrews (1911)
N. surinamensis	3000	Mound	S. America	Emerson (1938)
N. exitiosus	747-1807	Mound	Australia	Holdaway *et al.* (1935)
Amitermes hastatus	11-40	Mound	S. Africa	Skaife (1955)
Cubitermes ugandensis	35	Mound	E. Africa	Harris (1955)
C. fungifaber	7-69	Mound	Congo, Africa	Maldague (1964)
C. exiguus	4-25	Mound	Congo, Africa	Bouillon and Mathot (1964)
Microcerotermes arboreus	5.8	Arboreal	S. America	Emerson (1938)

D. PHENOLOGY

Any attempt to assess the significance of termites must take into account seasonal variations in numbers and activity. However, little is known of their phenology (Noirot, 1969), apart from a few observations on seasonal movement, such as instances of deeper penetration into the soil during the dry season

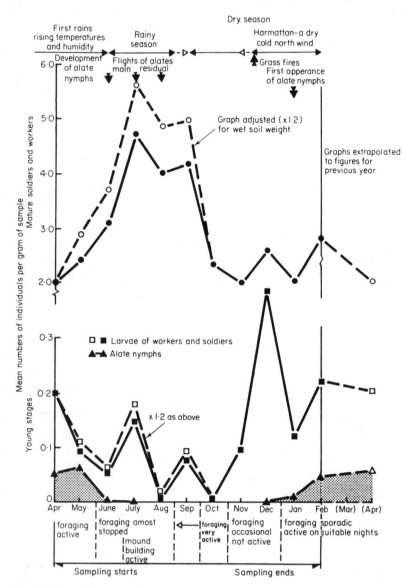

Fig. 28. Fluctuations in population density in mounds of *Trinervitermes geminatus*. The scale for the young stages is ten times that for the mature forms. (Reproduced with permission from Sands, 1965b.)

(Grassé and Noirot, 1948; Harris, 1961; Hill, 1942), and a wealth of information on swarming and flight activities (Nutting, 1969). Detailed investigations in West Africa by Sands (1965b) and Bodot (1967b) showed distinct patterns of building, foraging and flight activity which appeared to be related to seasonal weather patterns, although there were differences between species. In northern Nigeria, *Trinervitermes geminatus,* which stores chaffed grass in its mounds, commenced foraging in September and October after the flight of alates (Fig. 28), when the grass was at its highest nutritive content, and was curtailed by the onset of the wet season in May. The population in the mound increased between January and June until the flight of alates depleted the population once again. In contrast, Bodot (1967b) showed that in the Ivory Coast *Trinervitermes trinervius,* which does not store grass in its mounds, forages all the year round, although the intensity of foraging is related to the seasonal weather pattern, with maximum activity in September and October after the heavy rains and minimum activity in the dry season (December to May). *T. trinervius, Amitermes evuncifer* and *Cubitermes severus* apparently rely on moisture in the upper regions of the soil, and their maximum building activity coincided with the onset of heavy rains and the flight of alates, whereas *Macrotermes bellicosus* can build all the year round as it largely uses clay from the moist subsoil (Bodot, 1967a).

Bouillon (1970) has summarized the literature on the phenology of termites in the Ethiopian region. In general, it appears that the activities of egg-laying, swarming, building and foraging are broadly correlated with seasonal climatic events and in species with a wide distribution, the timing of these activities is related more to local climate than to the time of the year. Furthermore, sympatric species tend to time their activities, particularly swarming, at different times of the year, although there is often some degree of overlapping between the species.

CHAPTER 5

Effects on Physical and Chemical Characteristics of Soils

Construction of mounds, nests, or gallery systems, from soil or mixtures of soil and other materials, or within soil horizons, must affect the physical and chemical characteristics of both the soil used for construction and the soil of the surrounding areas from which the materials are derived. Soil particles are selected, transported, rearranged, cemented together, and mixed with organic matter. Organic debris or living plant tissue is collected, often over extensive foraging areas, transported to mounds, nests, or subterranean depots and subjected to intense degradation when it is digested by termites (Chapter 6). Some mounds and nests are inhabited and maintained for long periods (probably 50 years or more for mounds of *Nasutitermes exitiosus*), while others are more transient structures, lasting for periods of less than ten years (p. 96). Plant nutrients and organic matter that they contain are withheld from circulation in the plant-soil system until they finally decay.

Much work has been done on physical and chemical changes in soils due to termite activity, but it is difficult to relate the results of analyses reported by the various workers. The elements estimated vary from one investigation to another, methods of analysis differ or are not mentioned, and some comprehensive chemical studies lack identifications of the termites responsible for the mounds or other structures sampled. We have recently (Lee and Wood, in press) selected 17 species of Australian termites, sampled their mounds or other structures and soils from the same sites, and conducted a wide range of physical and chemical analyses on the samples. In preparing this portion of the present work, we have used our studies as a basis for comparison with results obtained by other workers.

I. Physical Effects

A. PARTICLE SIZE

Particle size analyses of soil from termite mounds and other structures, when compared with those of adjacent soil samples, show that some degree of selection of particular size fractions is general, but that few species consistently select material within a precise range of particle sizes. The maximum size of particles that can be transported and incorporated in structures is limited by the ability of the workers to carry them, and this is related to the size of the workers (see p. 26).

Particle size analyses of mounds of *Macrotermes* spp. in Africa (Hesse, 1955; Nye, 1955; Harris, 1956; Maldague, 1959; Stoops, 1964) show that their composition is close to that of subsoil, but there is some selection in favour of the finer size fractions (Nye, 1955; Stoops, 1964) in soils that are not rich in clay, or against the finer fractions in soils rich in clay (e.g. in a mound at Arusha, Tanzania, described by Hesse, 1955). Hesse (1955) also noted that changes in *Macrotermes* mound shape in eastern Africa were related to the ratio sand : clay in the mounds and the subsoil from which materials were obtained. Tall, thin mounds had sand : clay ratios of 1 : 1 to 3 : 1, while larger, dome-shaped mounds had ratios of 2 : 1 to 18 : 1.

Particle size analyses of mounds of African *Cubitermes* spp. by Kemp (1955) and Stoops (1964) show considerable enrichment in clay relative to the deep soil horizons from which materials for construction are derived. Kemp (1955) found 67.2% clay and 26.5% sand in mounds of *C. umbratus,* compared with 30.8% and 63.0% respectively for surrounding soil. Stoops (1964) analysed mounds of *C. sankurensis* and another *Cubitermes* sp.; he found that, relative to the soil, mounds had a very low proportion of particles of 100-500 μ size, but a higher proportion of <100 μ and >500 μ sized particles. *Cubitermes* spp. swallow fine soil particles, carry them in the crop and excrete them, while larger particles are carried in the mandibles. Stoops concluded that particles of 100-500 μ size are probably too large to be swallowed and too small to be conveniently carried. Harris (1956) described similar techniques for carrying soil by *Macrotermes bellicosus,* but apparently found no comparable discrepancies in the particle size fractions of their mounds. Watson's (1960) analyses of mounds of *Cubitermes* sp. from Rhodesia showed little difference between soil in mounds and in the deeper horizons of the surrounding soil.

Joachim and Kandiah (1940) found that mounds of *Odontotermes redemanni* in Ceylon always contained more clay and less coarse sand than the soils from which they were derived, and this was particularly so of mounds in sandy soils. In contrast, they found that mounds of *Odontotermes obscuriceps* did not differ significantly in physical composition from surrounding soils. Pathak and Lehri (1959) found a great increase in clay and silt relative to sand in mounds of *Odontotermes obscuriceps* built on very sandy soils.

The most remarkable structures built by termites, the subterranean nests of African *Apicotermes* spp., provide an example of precise and consistent selection of particle size fractions (see p. 26).

Our results (Lee and Wood, in press) of particle size analyses of structures built by *Schedorhinotermes intermedius actuosus, Coptotermes acinaciformis, C. lacteus, Amitermes laurensis, A. meridionalis, A. vitiosus, Drepanotermes rubriceps, Nasutitermes exitiosus, N. longipennis, N. magnus, N. triodiae, Tumulitermes hastilis* and *T. pastinator,* from a wide range of habitats in Australia, may be summarized as follows.

(i) The species sampled usually select the finer (clay and silt) in preference to the coarser (sand) soil particles for construction. Some examples are listed in Table 18. Species do not, however, appear to have precise requirements of particle sizes for their structures.

(ii) Most species obtain soil for their structures from deep soil horizons, but topsoil is sometimes used. A particular species does not always obtain soil from the same horizon, e.g., soil used in *Coptotermes acinaciformis* mounds at two sampling sites was predominantly from the subsoil (B horizon), at a third site, where the topsoil (A horizon) contained a high proportion of clay (53%), it was predominantly from the A horizon, and at a fourth site it was a mixture of A horizon and B horizon material.

(iii) Particle size analyses alone are not always adequate to determine the origin of soil used for construction. For example, nests of *Drepanotermes rubriceps* are excavated just beneath the ground surface, and may or may not extend into an above-ground mound. The subterranean portion of nests at two of our sampling sites, one in South Australia that had no above-ground mound and the other in Northern Territory that extended upward into a mound, had more clay and less sand than the surrounding A horizon, suggesting that at least some of the soil in them was derived from deeper clay-rich horizons. Identification of clay minerals, however, showed that the clay in the nests was the same as that in the A horizon, and differed from that in the B horizon. The termites must therefore have altered the ratio of clay to coarser materials by removing a proportion of the sand to the ground surface and building with the remainder. At the first site it was calculated that removal of 20% of the coarse sand and 10% of the fine sand from the A horizon would yield a soil with physical composition almost identical with that of the nest. Nests of *D. rubriceps* in that area have flat tops, more or less level with the ground surface, and often have a thin layer of loose sand on them. At the second site, similar reductions in the coarser fractions of the A horizon would provide a soil approximating in physical composition to the subterranean portion of the nest, but slight enrichment with clay from deeper horizons may also have occurred.

(iv) The moving of selected particle size fractions from deep horizons to surface mounds and other structures, where they are eventually eroded and spread over the surface, has considerable significance in pedogenesis. This subject is discussed on pp. 152-156.

TABLE 18

Comparison of Physical Composition of Soil Materials Used in Structures of Some Australian Termites with Soil from which the Materials are Derived. (Data from Lee and Wood, in press)

Coarse fraction = sand; fine fraction = silt + clay

Termite species	Type of structure	Origin of material (soil horizon)	Physical composition			
			Termite structure		Soil	
			Coarse fraction %	Fine fraction %	Coarse fraction %	Fine fraction %
Coptotermes acinaciformis	Capping of mound	B	62	36	77	24
Coptotermes acinaciformis	Capping of mound	B	50	45	47	52
Coptotermes acinaciformis	Capping of mound	A	23	75	26	77
Coptotermes lacteus	Outer layer of mound	B	42	54	52	49
Amitermes laurensis	Whole mound	A	53	42	68	30
Amitermes laurensis	Outer galleries of mound	B	58	38	67	31
Drepanotermes rubriceps	Above-ground galleries of mound	B	73	23	80	18
Drepanotermes rubriceps	Below-ground galleries of mound	A	75	25	84	13
Nasutitermes exitiosus	Capping of mound	B	57	39	52	49
Nasutitermes exitiosus	Capping of mound	B	38	62	35	64
Nasutitermes magnus	Outer galleries of mound	B	48	48	54	45
Nasutitermes magnus	Outer galleries of mound	A	73	25	73	26
Nasutitermes triodiae	Outer galleries of mound	B	59	37	65	32
Nasutitermes triodiae	Outer galleries of mound	B	65	31	67	31
Tumulitermes hastilis	Above-ground galleries of mound	B	60	36	55	48
Tumulitermes pastinator	Outer galleries of mound	A	49	46	68	30

B. Structure

Pathak and Lehri (1959) studied the degree of aggregation of soil from mounds of *Odontotermes obscuriceps* and compared it with that of samples of adjacent soil. They found that in the mound soil 67.7% of clay aggregates had particle sizes $>2\,\mu$, compared with 48.1% in undisturbed soil. 19.2% of silt sized particles were incorporated in aggregates in the mound soil, while 5.0% were aggregated in undisturbed soil. Aggregates from undisturbed soil were more easily dispersed in water than those from mound samples. Joachim and Pandittisekera (1948) similarly found increased aggregation in soil from termite mounds (termite species not named) in Ceylon. They distinguished "crude" crumbs, separated by sieving, from "true" crumbs, separated by a combination of sieving, washing, and separation of gravel, and found that "crude" crumbs comprised 61% and "true" crumbs 30% of mound samples, compared with 33% and 25% respectively for undisturbed soil. We have found (Lee and Wood, in press) that there is a correlation between the proportion of organic matter in mound samples and their susceptibility to dispersion for particle size analyses. Of 27 samples whose loss on ignition exceeded 20%, only two (with 21% and 23% loss on ignition respectively) were satisfactorily dispersed using the methods of Hutton (1955). Even after prolonged (24 h) treatment with hydrogen peroxide it was not possible to disperse the other 25 samples. The nature of the flocculating agents in the organic matter, which consists principally of termite excreta, is not known.

Probably more important than their contribution to aggregate formation is the ability of some termites to cement soil particles into massive structures that are extremely resistant to erosion. Boyer (1958) noted that *Macrotermes subhyalinus* brings much fine material to the surface and cements it into a concrete-like material on and around its mounds. Water cannot readily penetrate through this material to the underlying soil, so the normal processes of soil development are arrested. In extreme cases, Boyer claims that previously formed soil horizons may disappear. Cemented material from mounds of a variety of species has been used for roads, paths, tennis courts, earth floors in buildings, and even to make bricks for house construction (see p. 168). Several workers have noted cementing of the walls of subterranean galleries. *Anacanthotermes ahngerianus* is found in sandy soils in central Asia; Ghilarov (1962) has described galleries whose walls are strengthened and cemented with clay, extending down into the sands to depths of 10-15 m. Greaves (1962a) described subterranean gallery systems of *Coptotermes brunneus,* in compact red sandy soils in Western Australia, radiating up to about 45 m from the mound. The galleries can be dug out of the surrounding sandy soil as tubular structures with cemented sandy walls about 6-18 mm thick and a central horizontal slit-like opening. Greaves considers that cementing materials deposited on the gallery walls by the termites probably diffuse out into the surrounding sand when it is wet, thus producing the thick cemented wall. Adamson (1943) described cement-like soil linings on the walls of subterranean galleries of the common *Heterotermes tenuis* of Trinidad.

Excreta is commonly used as a cementing matrix for soil. We have examined thin sections of mound materials of a variety of Australian termites (see pp. 30–40) and in some species there are distinct laminae of excreta coating and bonding together discrete aggregates or grains of inorganic soil particles. In other species soil particles are sorted and packed so that there are virtually no spaces between them. No organic laminae can be seen between the particles, but they are cemented and highly resistant to fracture. It seems most likely that some colloidal organic material is used to bond the particles together.

C. Bulk Density

Very few measurements have been made of the bulk density of termite-modified soils. Ghilarov (1962) reported studies, made by Dimo, of termitaria (probably of *Anacanthotermes ahngerianus*, but Ghilarov does not mention the species involved) in virgin soils of the Golodnaya Steppe in Central Asia. Bulk density of samples from termitaria was 1.112 g/cm^3, compared with 1.226 g/cm^3 for samples of the surrounding grey desert soil. Maldague (1964) measured the bulk density of forest soils in the Congo, which had a termite population of about 1000/m^2 and that of nearby parasol-covered fallow lands. The forest soils had a bulk density of 1.00 g/cm^3, compared with 1.27 g/cm^3 in fallow lands; Maldague attributed the difference to the effect of the termites, but this does not seem an entirely reasonable deduction. Lower bulk density of termite-affected soil compared with unaffected soil must result from increased porosity, due to termite galleries, or to incorporation of organic matter in the soil, or both. Termites that repack soil particles so that pore spaces are minimal (e.g. *Drepanotermes rubriceps* and *Coptotermes acinaciformis* in Australia) must increase bulk density, but no measurements are available.

D. Water-holding Capacity

The little information available indicates that there is considerable variation in water-holding capacity. Pathak and Lehri (1959) found that mounds of *Odontotermes obscuriceps* in India had a water-holding capacity about five times that of adjacent soil, while Kemp (1955) reported a small increase in mounds of *Cubitermes umbratus* in Africa, and Pendleton (1941) measured increases ranging from nil to about 50% relative to adjacent soil in mounds of unidentified termites in Thailand. The mounds of *O. obscuriceps* contained 62.76% organic matter while those of *C. umbratus* contained 2-3%, and those analysed by

Pendleton contained 0.6-7.9% organic matter. Pathak and Lehri considered that increased water-holding capacity was related to organic matter content. The role of organic matter in absorbing large quantities of water is discussed elsewhere in this book (p. 62).

Ghilarov (1962) reported a fall in water-holding capacity of about 8% relative to surrounding soil in mounds (probably of *Anacanthotermes ahngerianus*) in Central Asia, and Goodland (1965) found a reduced capacity in samples from mounds (termite species not identified) in the Rupununi savanna lands of Guyana.

E. GALLERY SYSTEMS

Gallery systems associated with mounds, nests, and foraging territories of termite colonies are known to affect pore space, infiltration of water into the soil, aeration, and penetration of plant roots. The nature and extent of gallery systems are discussed in Chapter 2.

Ghilarov (1962) noted an increase in porosity from 54.3% in grey desert soils of the Golodnaya Steppe of Central Asia to 57.8% in termitaria (probably of *Anacanthotermes ahngerianus*). Termitaria occupied 6.5% of the ground surface at the site sampled. Maldague (1964) reported a porosity of 58% in Congo soils under forest with high termite populations (ca. $1000/m^2$), compared with 48% in adjacent parasol-covered fallow lands with few termites and attributed the difference to termites. Pendleton (1941) measured pore space of termite mounds (species of termite not identified) and adjacent soils at nine localities in Thailand, and found increases in the mounds ranging from <1% to about 17%. The principal effects of the increased pore space are on water infiltration and aeration. Ghilarov (1962) reported that capillary water capacity was markedly reduced (17%, compared with 32.6%). He also measured the time required for capillary rise of water, and found that this was 175 min for a 16-cm rise in samples from termitaria, compared with 100 min in undisturbed soil. Microscopic examination of the fabric of termite structures (pp. 30–40) shows that soil particles are repacked, often leaving little pore space apart from that in the relatively large galleries.

We know of no measurements of infiltration rates nor aeration of termite-modified soils. Adamson (1943) and Robinson (1958) consider that infiltration is promoted by gallery systems. Boyer (1958) points to an opposite effect of *Macrotermes subhyalinus*; the termites bring much fine material to the surface and cement it, forming a layer that is not easily penetrated by water; normal processes of soil development are arrested and in extreme cases, under mounds, underlying soil horizons may disappear. Robinson (1958) states that galleries of *Odontotermes badius* improve aeration in topsoil and subsoil of coffee fields in Kenya. Adamson (1943) distinguishes between occupied burrows, which have compact or cemented walls and probably have little, if any, effect on aeration, and abandoned burrows, where wall linings are not maintained, which may promote soil aeration.

Robinson (1958) studied the development of roots of coffee plants in infilled termite galleries in Kenya. At depths of 60-120 cm in subsoil he noted that old galleries were filled with dark soil, richer in nutrients and less compact than the surrounding soil. Where axial roots had grown into such tunnels there was a high degree of fine root proliferation. Watson (1960) recorded tube-like zones of grey soil at depths up to about 850 cm in West African soils; they contained up to 94% fine material (clay and silt), compared with 52% in adjacent soil, and he considered the filling material to have been washed down from overlying soil horizons into abandoned termite galleries. Roots were found to follow the grey soil zones, and Watson considered that the roots take advantage of the less compact soil that they contain to penetrate the weathering rock crust and obtain water. Ratcliffe et al. (1952) noted that in a semi-arid area of New South Wales termite galleries extend to considerable depths below the surface, sometimes penetrating masses of limestone; they found that plant roots frequently followed the course of deserted and soil-packed galleries.

II. Chemical Effects

Since termites commonly bring soil for above-ground structures from considerable depths, it is most important to identify the source of soil when comparing chemical properties of soil in termite structures with surrounding soil. Frequently this has not been done, and it is impossible to make meaningful comparisons between results for individual samples. The only comprehensive series of analyses done by consistent methods, and relating to a range of termite species, are those of Stoops (1964) for three species from the Congo, and those of Lee and Wood (in press) for 17 Australian species.

A. pH

Nearly all workers note an increase in pH relative to surrounding soil (Boyer, 1955, 1956b; Kemp, 1955; Nye, 1955; Robinson, 1958; Sys, 1955; Watson, 1962; Wild, 1952) for various African termites; Gokhale et al. (1958), Sen (1944) and Shrikhande and Pathak (1948), for some Indian termites. A few (Maldague, 1959; Pathak and Lehri, 1959) note a decrease. Stoops (1964) found that pH of mounds differed little from that of adjacent subsoil in the African species Macrotermes bellicosus, Cubitermes sankurensis and Cubitermes sp.

Increased pH, especially in mounds of *Macrotermes* spp., is often associated with accumulations of calcium carbonate (p. 113). Decreased pH may be associated with high organic matter content in mounds, as in mounds of *Odontotermes* sp. studied by Shrikhande and Pathak (1948).

For Australian species, we have found (Lee and Wood, in press) that the pH of soil in mounds and other structures is usually lower than the pH of the soil horizon from which building materials are derived, but the differences are small; in a few species the pH is higher, but again the differences are small. Relative raising or lowering of pH does not correlate with any other of a wide variety of chemical properties tested, nor with taxonomic groupings nor food preferences of the termites studied, and would seem to be of little significance.

B. Organic Matter, Organic Carbon, Total Nitrogen

Most termite mounds and other structures have organic matter contents higher than the soil from which they are constructed; this is not surprising, as termites use organic materials (salivary or faecal) to cement soil particles or aggregates (pp. 30–40). Grassé and Joly (1941), Hesse (1955), and Stoops (1964) have reported organic matter contents of the earth (subsoil) mounds of African *Macrotermes* spp.; their analyses show that some mound samples contain less organic matter than surrounding soils, but Stoops (1964) found an increase in organic matter from the outer mound casing to the innermost royal chamber, where the organic matter content was higher than in soil samples, and Grassé and Joly similarly found a high organic matter content in the material of the royal chamber. Organic matter contents in structures built by other African termites are reported by Stumper (1923) for *Apicotermes occultus,* Stoops (1964) for *Cubitermes sankurensis,* and *Cubitermes* sp., Kemp (1955) for *Cubitermes* sp., and Grassé and Joly (1941) for *Cubitermes* sp. and *Amitermes evuncifer.* Other analyses include those of mounds of *Odontotermes redemanni* and *Odontotermes obscuriceps* from Ceylon by Joachim and Kandiah (1940), mounds of *O. obscuriceps* from India by Pathak and Lehri (1959), galleries of an Indian *Odontotermes* sp. by Shrikhande and Pathak (1948), and mounds of *Nasutitermes exitiosus* from Australia by Holdaway (1933). In all cases there was an increase relative to soil, except in mounds of *Odontotermes redemanni,* where there was a slight decrease. We have similarly found a general increase, but occasionally a decrease, in our studies of the structures of Australian termites (Lee and Wood, in press). A distinction must be made between structures composed largely of soil, in which differences in organic matter content relative to soil are small, and may be positive or negative, and structures composed largely of carton or of a mixture of soil and carton-like materials, which contain a high proportion of organic matter relative to surrounding soils. The organic matter of carton consists principally of the excreted end-products of digestion of plant tissue, sometimes with a proportion of fragmented but relatively undigested plant tissue. It contains much polyphenolic material (up to 16.5%) similar to the alkali-soluble acid-insoluble humic materials of soils, lignin (up to 64.1%), little carbohydrate, and is sometimes highly resistant to microbial decomposition (Lee and Wood, 1968). Transformations of organic matter resulting from its digestion by termites are discussed in Chapter 6.

The organic carbon content of mounds and other structures parallels the organic matter content, i.e. it is generally higher and occasionally lower than that of adjacent soils. Similarly, nitrogen content roughly parallels organic matter content, but not necessarily in the same proportions as for carbon content. Plant tissue, humus, dung, and other foods of termites contain little nitrogen. Moore (1969) discussed the recycling of nitrogen in termite colonies through eating of dead and injured or surplus members of any caste, and in cases of extreme nitrogen deprivation by quite extensive cannibalism. It seems likely that the meagre supplies of nitrogen available from the primary food are supplemented in many termites by digestion of fungi growing on the food (see p. 6). Accumulation of nitrates in mounds of *Anacanthotermes ahngerianus* in Central Asia was noted by Kozlova (1951). Mounds contained $0.85\% \text{ NO}_3'$, compared with $0.022\% \text{ NO}_3'$ in surrounding soils. Kozlova estimated that the mounds (>500/ha) contained 208 kg/ha of NO_3' or 47 kg/ha of readily available nitrogen, and considered that the favourable conditions of temperature and moisture in mounds favoured mineralization of nitrogen contained in the organic matter in mounds. The mounds are used by farmers as fertilizer in the initial stages of agricultural development.

The ratio carbon : nitrogen has been recorded for the structures of a variety of termites. The mounds of Macrotermitinae are sometimes little different in C : N ratio from the subsoil of which they are built (Hesse, 1955; Maldague, 1959). However, Boyer (1955) found that the outer layer of *Macrotermes bellicosus* mounds had a C : N ratio of about 10–12, while for inner portions of the mound the ratio was about 6.5, and Boyer (1956b) found C : N ratios of 2.7 in the royal cell of *M. bellicosus* and *M. subhyalinus*, compared with 6–7 in outer mound layers and 10–12 in the soil of termite galleries surrounding the mound. Some other C : N ratios reported for termite structures are lower and some are higher than those of surrounding soils. Among African species the mound of *Nasutitermes latifrons* had a C : N ratio of 12.12, compared with 15.00 in the soil (Maldague, 1959), a mound of *Thoracotermes brevinotus* had a C : N ratio of 4.2 (Boyer, 1956b), while a mound of *Amitermes unidentatus* had a ratio of 18.7–18.82, compared with 8.26–10.31 for surrounding soil. In Ceylon, Joachim and Kandiah (1940) reported C : N ratios slightly lower than surrounding soils for mounds of *Odontotermes redemanni* and *O. obscuriceps*, while Shrikhande and Pathak (1948) recorded a lower C : N ratio (5.63) in material from galleries of *Odontotermes* sp. compared with adjacent soil (6.19),

TABLE 19

Organic Carbon, Total Nitrogen, and Carbon : Nitrogen Ratios of Mounds, etc., of Some Australian Termites and the Soil from which They are Constructed, with Notes on Principal Sources of Food. The Structures Listed are Composed Predominantly of Soil. Data from Lee and Wood (in press)

Termite species	Principal food	Type of structure	Mounds, etc. Organic C%	Total N%	Ratio C:N	Horizon*	Soil Organic C%	Total N%	Ratio C:N
Schedorhinotermes intermedius actuosus	Dead eucalypt wood	Thin sheath of soil on log	7.4	0.16	46.3	B	0.6	0.046	13.0
Coptotermes acinaciformis	Living and dead eucalypt wood	Capping of mound	2.7	0.08	33.8	B	0.2	0.014	14.3
		Capping of mound	2.4	0.10	24.0	B	0.4	0.036	11.1
Coptotermes lacteus	Dead eucalypt wood	Capping of mound	2.4	0.077	31.2	B	0.3	0.04	7.5
		Capping of mound	4.8	0.14	34.3	A_1	6.3	0.23	27.4
						B	1.9	0.057	33.3
Amitermes laurensis	Grass and organic debris	Whole mound	2.9	0.13	22.3	A	0.8	0.055	14.5
		Outer galleries of mound	2.1	0.19	11.1	B	0.3	0.028	10.7
Amitermes	Grass and organic	Outer galleries of mound	4.6	0.26	17.7	A_1	0.6	0.040	15.0

Species	Material	Structure				Horizon			
...vilosus	debris					B	0.5	0.020	15.0
Drepanotermes rubriceps	Grass	Mound	1.4	0.085	16.5	B	0.2	0.022	9.1
	Grass	Mound	1.6	0.076	21.1	B	0.4	0.044	9.1
		Below-ground nest	1.4	0.12	11.7	A	0.9	0.075	12.0
		Below-ground nest	0.8	0.081	9.9	A	0.4	0.055	7.3
Nasutitermes exitiosus	Dead eucalypt wood	Capping of mound	2.8	0.095	29.5	B	0.3	0.040	7.5
		Capping of mound	6.6	0.14	47.1	B	0.8	0.048	16.7
Nasutitermes longipennis	Grass and organic debris	Mound	3.5	0.19	18.4	A	0.9	0.071	12.7
						B	0.2	0.024	8.4
Nasutitermes magnus	Grass	Outer galleries of mound	1.5	0.081	18.5	B	0.5	0.039	12.8
		Outer galleries of mound	1.0	0.068	14.7	A	0.9	0.067	13.4
Nasutitermes triodiae	Grass	Outer galleries of mound	2.7	0.10	27.0	B	0.2	0.020	10.0
		Outer galleries of mound	4.4	0.15	29.3	B	0.4	0.044	9.1
Tumulitermes hastilis	Grass and organic debris	Mound	2.4	0.084	28.6	A	1.1	0.059	18.6
						B	0.3	0.020	15.0
Tumulitermes pastinator	Grass	Outer galleries of mound	3.7	0.17	21.8	A	0.8	0.055	14.5

* The soil horizons from which materials were derived were identified by comparison of physical and chemical analyses and clay minerals of samples from termite structures with those of samples from adjacent undisturbed soil. In doubtful cases, or where the termites apparently use material from more than one horizon, figures are given for A and B horizons.

and Pathak and Lehri (1959) recorded a higher ratio (7.1) compared with soil (5.0). Lower values of C : N ratios in termite structures recorded elsewhere contrast with our measurements (Lee and Wood, in press) on the structures of Australian termites. Of 46 samples consisting mainly of soil and taken from mounds, etc., of 13 species (examples are listed in Table 19), only two samples had C : N ratios lower than the soils from which they were derived, while of 26 samples (from 10 species) consisting of carton or containing a high proportion of carton all had C : N ratios much higher than surrounding soils (see Table 27, p. 141). Considering only those samples consisting principally of soil, if the C : N ratio of termite-modified samples is expressed as a ratio of the C : N ratio of adjacent unmodified soil samples a distinction may be made between termites that feed mainly on grass or on grass and organic debris and those that feed mainly on wood. For grass-feeding species the C : N ratio of modified samples is 0.8–2.0 (mean 1.4) times that of unmodified samples, while corresponding figures for wood-feeding species are 1.1–2.7 (mean 1.9) times those of unmodified samples. The difference is probably due to the generally higher C : N ratio of wood compared with grass, which is carried over into the faecal material used in making carton. We do not know why C : N ratios of samples from Australia should be generally higher than those from other countries.

C. Calcium, Magnesium, Potassium, and Phosphorous

1. Calcium

An increase in calcium content, relative to surrounding soils, is noted in nearly all chemical analyses of termite mounds. In extreme cases, especially in the mounds of African Macrotermitinae, concretions of calcium carbonate are occasionally found, usually in a band near the base of the mound and sometimes in quantities sufficient that the mounds may be used as a fertilizer in the initial agricultural development of the land (Milne, 1947). Boyer (1956c), Hesse (1955), and Wild (1952) reported calcium concentrations in African macrotermitid mounds; Burtt (1942), Milne (1947), Sys (1955) and Watson (1962) reported similar concentrations in African mounds, probably of macrotermitids, but the termites responsible were not identified. Goodland (1965) reported calcium concentrations in termitaria (of non-macrotermitids) averaging more than three times, and sometimes up to seven times those in soil in the Rupununi savanna lands of Guyana. In India Pathak and Lehri (1959) found more than five-fold concentrations in mounds of *Odontotermes obscuriceps*, while Sen (1944) found up to about two-fold concentrations in the soil of termite runways, and Gokhale *et al.* (1958) found slight concentrations in soil packed inside the stems of tea plants by *Microcerotermes* sp. Shrikhande and Pathak (1948) alone reported a small reduction in total calcium concentration in soil from galleries of *Odontotermes* sp. (at Kanpur, India). For Australian termites we have found (Lee and Wood, in press) that the calcium content of mounds and other structures is almost invariably higher (usually two to five times, but up to ten times) than that of the soil from which they are constructed. In general, calcium content increased with increasing organic matter content, but there is no precise correlation between the two. None of the termite structures we have sampled have calcium carbonate concentrations like those reported from some African termite mounds. Analyses of carton structures built by various Australian termites (Lee and Wood, in press) showed calcium levels much higher than in soils, and this calcium must be derived from ingested plant tissue. Since excreted material similar to carton is incorporated with soil in mounds, etc., composed predominantly of soil, the smaller concentrations of calcium noted in such structures are probably also excreted constituents of digested plant tissue.

Calcium carbonate concretions in termite mounds are probably not derived from concentration of calcium salts from excreta. The mounds of Macrotermitinae (especially *Macrotermes* spp.) from which concretions have been reported are very large, composed of soil originally brought up from deep soil horizons, frequently with their own peculiar vegetation, and are prominent features of the landscape (pp. 43, 194). Meyer (1960) considered that macro-termitid mounds in the central Congo Basin, which are not now inhabited by the species that built them, date from a drier period, going back to the beginning of the Quaternary. Pedological processes within them may be quite different from those in surrounding soils (Leenheer *et al.*, 1952). Hesse (1955) studied mounds of *Macrotermes falciger*, *M. subhyalinus* and *M. bellicosus* in Kenya. In the Magadi district all mounds, regardless of age and condition, contained finely divided calcium carbonate, but they contained no more than the surrounding soil, which was highly calcareous. In all other districts he found that mounds were calcareous only if they were built in special conditions. Inhabited mounds were calcareous only if built from calcareous soil. In old, uninhabited mounds there was a definite correlation between concentration of calcium carbonate and proximity to areas with impeded drainage. Of 24 calcareous mounds examined, 20 were on or near seasonally waterlogged ground and the remainder were associated with poorly drained soils. He attributed calcium carbonate accumulation in the mounds to periodic inundation of the lower portions with calcium-charged groundwater, and evaporation of water from the raised mound surface, possibly accentuated by transpiration of the plants growing on the mound surface, resulting in accumulation in the mound of salts from the groundwater. Long continuation of the process, in very old mounds, would lead to the formation of a layer of calcium carbonate concretions at the base of the mound, i.e. the process is pedological, not biological. Hesse found that the chemical constitution of nodules at the base of mounds closely resembled that of similar concretions in the adjacent subsoil. Very large quantities of calcium carbonate were found in some mounds by Hesse (Table 20).

TABLE 20

Volume and Weight of Some Calcareous Termite (*Macrotermes* spp.) Mounds from Kenya, with Their Approximate Calcium Carbonate Content (Data from Hesse, 1955)

Volume of mound above ground (m³)	Weight of mound above ground (kg)	Approximate calcium carbonate content (kg)
84.0	188 000	2440
57.0	103 000	1020
8.0	17 700	410
0.3	710	30

We have examined mounds of Australian termites at poorly drained sites, and have not found any great accumulation of calcium carbonate (Lee and Wood, in press). The time-scale of nodule formation by pedological processes would require mounds to persist for at least hundreds or even thousands of years; to our knowledge no Australian termite builds mounds that last so long.

2. Magnesium

Increased magnesium content relative to adjacent soil has been noted by Boyer (1956c) in mounds of *Macrotermes bellicosus*, Wild (1952) in mounds of *Macrotermes natalensis*, Pathak and Lehri (1959) in mounds of *Odontotermes obscuriceps*, Goodland (1965) in termitaria from the Rupununi region of Guyana, and by Shrikhande and Pathak (1948) in galleries built by *Odontotermes* sp. Lee and Wood (in press) also noted increased magnesium in mounds and other structures of various Australian termites. The increases are small and, like the general increases noted in calcium levels, must result from incorporation of organic matter with soil during construction.

3. Potassium

Potassium levels in mounds, galleries, etc., roughly parallel those of calcium and magnesium, and increases must also result from additions of organic matter. Increased potassium has been noted by Boyer (1956c), Wild (1952), Sen (1944), Goodland (1965), and Shrikhande and Pathak (1948); Pathak and Lehri (1959) found less potassium (0.254%) in mounds of *Odontotermes obscuriceps* than in surrounding soil (0.608%). We have found (Lee and Wood, in press) generally slightly more potassium than in adjacent soil samples in structures built by Australian termites, but in a few mound samples slightly less than in soils.

4. *Phosphorus*

There are some records of concentration of phosphorus in mounds. Increased phosphorus relative to surrounding soils was found by Kemp (1955) in mounds of *Cubitermes umbratus,* Pathak and Lehri (1959) in mounds of *Odontotermes obscuriceps* and by Sen (1944) and Shrikhande and Pathak (1948) in galleries and runways built by some Indian termites. Gokhale *et al.* (1958) found no significant difference in phosphorus in soil packed in galleries in the stems of tea bushes by *Microcerotermes* sp. compared with adjacent soils, and we (Lee and Wood, in press) found little difference in mounds and other structures of a variety of Australian termites, relative to the soil from which they were built. Hesse (1955) examined 56 mounds of *Macrotermes falciger, M. bellicosus,* and *M. subhyalinus,* and recognized two main types of phosphate distribution in mounds. Phosphate was either fairly uniformly distributed through the mounds, approximating to the concentration in nearby subsoil (from which mounds of *Macrotermes* spp. are constructed), or it increased down through the mound, reaching a maximum concentration at about ground level, and then decreased with increasing depth below the mound. The latter type of phosphate distribution was found only in large mounds near sites with impeded drainage, i.e. in conditions closely resembling those that favour accumulation of high concentrations and concretions of calcium carbonate (p. 113). Distribution of phosphorus in mounds, etc., of Australian termites (Lee and Wood, in press) resembles the first type of distribution recognized by Hesse.

Available phosphorus (i.e. citric acid soluble) has been estimated by a few authors. Griffith (1938) and Gokhale *et al.* (1958) found little difference from adjacent soils, while Shrikhande and Pathak (1948) found a slight decrease in termite structures relative to adjacent soil samples.

D. EXCHANGEABLE CATIONS

Changes in exchangeable cation content relative to surrounding soils have been noted in nearly all chemical analyses of termite structures and termite-modified soils. Some analyses are listed in Table 21. In most cases total exchange capacities are higher than in soil, but sometimes there is little difference, e.g. in galleries of *Odontotermes* sp. (Shrikhande and Pathak, 1948), and occasionally there is a reduction relative to soil, e.g. in a mound of *Odontotermes redemanni* (Joachim and Kandiah, 1940). The chemical constitution of soils changes from horizon to horizon down the soil profile, so unless the horizon from which construction materials are derived can be

TABLE 21

Exchangeable Cation and Organic Carbon Contents of Some Termite Structures Compared with Those of Adjacent Soil Samples

Termite species	Type of structure	Termite mound or other structure						Soil							Reference
		Exchangeable cations (m.e.%)					Organic carbon %	Sample depth (cm)	Exchangeable cations (m.e.%)					Organic carbon %	
		T.E.C.	Ca	Mg	K	Na			T.E.C.	Ca	Mg	K	Na		
Macrotermes bellicosus	Mound (outer casing)	1.28	0.13	–	0.08	0.09	0.17	45–95	0.98	0.05	–	0.01	0.08	0.23	Stoops (1964)
	Mound (central nest)	2.10	0.31	–	0.37	0.09	0.54								
Macrotermes bellicosus	Mound (outer casing)	–	3.8	0.9	0.41	0.35	0.58	30–75	–	3.6	1.0	0.38	0.35	0.25	Nye (1955)
	Mound (central nest)	–	4.0	1.3	0.41	0.38	0.91								
Cubitermes sankurensis	Mound	9.45	1.60	–	0.60	0.13	3.75	0–12	2.35	0.65	–	0.10	0.08	2.79	Stoops (1964)
								30–50	1.00	0.08	–	0.03	0.08	0.68	
Odontotermes	Galleries	14.48	8.78	0.012	1.79	–	0.58	–	14.81	9.36	0.015	1.39	–	0.54	Shrikhande and

Odontotermes	Mound	[illegible]	[illegible]	[illegible]			[illegible]		[illegible]	[illegible]				[illegible]	
redemanni	Mound	12.2	10.36	–	–	–	1.12	–	9.17	7.48	–	–	–	1.93	Kandiah (1940)
Schedorhinotermes intermedius actuosus	Soil sheath on log	23.0	12.0	2.8	0.82	0.17	7.4	30–50	9.2	4.7	1.9	0.73	0.08	0.6	Lee and Wood (in press)
Coptotermes acinaciformis	Mound (outer (casing)	20.0	8.2	3.5	1.0	0.15	2.7	0–10	16.0	8.0	2.8	1.0	0.10	2.1	Lee and Wood (in press)
	Mound (outer (casing)	15.0	0.7	2.1	0.28	0.04	2.4	20–40	7.3	0.3	1.4	0.09	0.10	0.4	
Drepanotermes	Mound	8.1	5.7	1.8	0.50	0.05	1.4	20–30	3.6	2.1	0.8	0.30	0.02	0.2	Lee and Wood
rubriceps	Subterranean nest	12.0	7.2	2.4	1.4	0.20	0.8	0–2.5	6.1	3.7	1.7	1.10	0.11	0.4	(in press)
Nasutitermes exitiosus	Mound (outer casing)	11.0	2.1	2.2	0.68	0.18	2.8	55–70	7.3	0.3	2.7	0.77	0.17	0.3	Lee and Wood (in press)
	Mound (outer casing)	25.0	5.6	3.7	0.42	0.34	6.6	25–30	12.0	2.1	3.2	0.33	0.22	0.8	
Nasutitermes triodiae	Mound (outer galleries)	11.0	0.2	3.2	1.00	0.04	2.7	40–50	4.3	0.1	0.8	0.06	0.04	0.2	Lee and Wood (in press)
	Mound (nursery chamber)	28.0	7.5	6.9	1.60	0.09	10.0								
Tumulitermes pastinator	Mound (outer galleries)	13.0	4.2	5.3	0.29	1.10	3.7	0–8	4.4	0.1	0.7	0.05	0.08	0.8	Lee and Wood (in press)

positively identified, all comparisons of the composition of termite structures with surrounding soils are dubious. It is well established that the large mounds of *Macrotermes* spp. are built of subsoil (see Hesse, 1955), so comparison of mound samples with deep soil samples (Table 21) is legitimate. *Cubitermes* spp. are humus feeders, so it is most likely that *C. sankurensis* mounds are built of topsoil. The origin of soil for mounds of *Odontotermes redemanni* and galleries of *Odontotermes* sp. is uncertain. For all remaining species in Table 21 (from Lee and Wood, in press) the origin of the soil in mounds, etc., has been identified with some certainty, and soil analyses given are for the soil horizons involved.

The figures listed for total exchange capacity exceed the sum of those for exchangeable calcium, magnesium, potassium, and sodium, often by a large margin. The difference is probably due, in most cases, to hydrogen ions as most of the samples listed have acid pH's. In some cases, where pH is relatively high, the difference may be due to the presence of ammonium ions derived from microbial decomposition of organic matter. Nye (1955) measured exchangeable hydrogen in mounds of *Macrotermes bellicosus* and found levels comparable (in m.e. %) to those for exchangeable calcium and magnesium.

We have found (Lee and Wood, in press) that increases in exchangeable cations in termite-modified soils are roughly correlated with increased organic matter content relative to surrounding soils, and have concluded that the increases are due to incorporation of faecal or salivary materials with soil during construction.

Analyses of samples of mounds of *Macrotermes bellicosus* and *Cubitermes* spp. compared with adjacent soils led Stoops (1964) to conclude that the more soil was reworked by the termites during mound construction the higher was the exchangeable cation concentration. This is illustrated by comparison of Stoops' samples from the central nest with that from the outer casing of a mound of *M. bellicosus* (Table 21). The central nest material is extensively reworked and has a higher exchangeable cation content (2.10) than the outer casing (1.28), which is not so reworked. It is further illustrated by comparison of samples (Table 21) from the nursery chamber of a mound of *Nasutitermes triodiae*, which is reworked and contains 10.0% organic carbon (T.E.C. 28.0), with that from the less worked material of outer galleries (2.7% organic carbon, T.E.C. 11.0).

We have found (Lee and Wood, in press, and Table 21) in our investigations of Australian termites that exchangeable calcium, magnesium, and potassium are generally much higher in termite-modified samples than in unmodified samples. Increase in exchangeable calcium often accounts for most of the differences in exchangeable cations measured and also for most of the increases in total calcium content. Calcium, magnesium, and potassium are constituents of plant tissue, and this must be the origin of the increased content in termite structures. Nye (1955), Sys (1955), Robinson (1958), and Stoops (1964) found similar increases, especially in exchangeable calcium, in mounds of some African termites; Griffith (1938) analysed samples from mounds (probably of *Macrotermes* spp.) in Uganda, and found total exchange capacity and exchangeable calcium sometimes higher and sometimes lower than in adjacent soils, while Joachim and Kandiah (1940, and Table 21) found similar variations in mounds of *Odontotermes redemanni*; Shrikhande and Pathak (1948, and Table 21) found a decrease in exchangeable cations, especially exchangeable calcium, in galleries of an Indian *Odontotermes* sp. Apparent inconsistencies may be due to failure to identify the soil horizon from which construction materials were derived.

E. AVAILABILITY OF NUTRIENTS FOR PLANT GROWTH

Structures built by termites on or above the ground are continuously eroded, and the materials they contain are returned to the soil surface. Thin sheets of soil covering logs and tree trunks contain comparatively little soil, but mounds and soil packed in galleries in logs sometimes comprise a significant proportion of the total soil. The soil they contain and its included plant nutrients are withheld from circulation in the plant-soil system until the mounds, etc., are finally abandoned and eroded away.

We have calculated (Lee and Wood, in press) the proportion of plant nutrients contained in mounds of some Australian termites as a percentage of the total nutrients in the A horizon and the mounds. At one site, in savanna woodland near Adelaide River, Northern Territory, the weight of mounds of *Nasutitermes triodiae* was 23 100 kg/ha, or 2% of the total weight of soil in the A_1 horizon (0-8 cm) and the mounds. But the mounds included 9.6% of the total organic carbon, 5.3% of the total nitrogen, 5.0% of the total phosphorus, 11.6% of the total calcium, 6.4% of the total potassium, 9.1% of the exchangeable calcium, 22.0% of the exchangeable magnesium, 13.1% of the exchangeable potassium, and 2.7% of the exchangeable sodium in the mound/A_1 horizon system.

At another site, near Larrimah, Northern Territory (Fig. 3, p. 20), there were five mound-building species, *Drepanotermes rubriceps, Drepanotermes* sp., *Amitermes vitiosus, Nasutitermes triodiae,* and *Tumulitermes hastilis.* Mounds of the five species together comprised 62 500 kg/ha, or 4.8% of the total weight of soil in the mound/A_1 horizon (0-10 cm) system. No chemical analyses are available for mounds of *D. rubriceps, Drepanotermes* sp., and *N. triodiae,* so we were able to estimate only the proportion of nutrients contained in mounds of *A. vitiosus* and *T. hastilis,* which together comprised 3.1% by weight of the mound/A_1 horizon system (about 65% of the total weight of mounds). The mounds of *A. vitiosus* and *T. hastilis* together included 6.3% of the total organic carbon, 4.6% of the total nitrogen, 3.0% of the total phosphorus, 3.2% of the total calcium, 3.5% of the total potassium, 5.2% of the exchangeable calcium,

5.2% of the exchangeable magnesium, 6.6% of the exchangeable potassium, and 3.5% of the exchangeable sodium in the mound/A_1 horizon system.

There are no other chemical analyses of termite mounds and soils, together with information on mound density and weight, that would enable similar calculations to be made of the total nutrients held in mounds. The two examples show that mounds may contain a disproportionately large amount of the total and available plant nutrients, but further data for other species and localities are necessary before any practical significance could be assessed.

III. Clay Mineralogy

Boyer (1948) has reported that workers of *Macrotermes subhyalinus*, if they are short of clay for mound construction, sometimes take particles of mica (especially muscovite) and work them in their mandibles until they have properties similar to illite; the material is then used as a substitute for naturally-occurring clay in mound construction. There is no evidence that any other species of termite actively influences the kinds of clay in soils. The clays in mounds can be taken to be those of the soil horizon or horizons from which material for construction is obtained, and usually provide the best basis for matching of mounds with soil materials and assessment of the effects of termites on soils (Lee and Wood, in press).

In old mounds of African Macrotermitinae, the internal structure of the mounds and microrelief sometimes differ sufficiently from surrounding soils that pedogenetic processes result in differences in the chemical properties of the clays in mounds. Leenheer *et al.* (1952) found that the clays of such mounds in the Yangambi area of the Congo are characterized by lower ion absorption capacity than those of adjacent soils. Watson (1962) described concentric cones of whitened soil beneath a large unoccupied termite mound in an area of leached ferrallitic soils at Umtali, Rhodesia. The whitened zone extended down to a depth of about 6 m, and the pale colour was due to finely divided carbonates, reaching a concentration up to 4%. Under the mound pH attained a maximum of 9.2 at about 3-5 m depth, due to concentration of sodium salts, compared with a maximum pH of 5.9-6.8 at 5-6 m depth in adjacent soil. It might be expected that some sodium-saturated clays would be found in such circumstances, but the clay minerals were not identified. Fripiat *et al.* (1957) reported montmorillonite in termite-affected soil profiles, contrasting with absence of this clay mineral in adjacent unaffected soils, near Elizabethville. Montmorillonite was associated with accumulation of calcium carbonate concretions at the base of mounds, and was found even in soils where weathering of soil profiles had proceeded to an extreme stage and the predominant clay minerals were kaolin and gibbsite. Clay minerals from other calcium-rich mounds have not been reported.

TABLE 22

Particle Size Analyses of Material Deposited on Soil Surface by Termites, Ants and Earthworms, and of Soil Samples from the same site, near Ibadan, Nigeria (Data from Nye 1955)

Sample	Size fraction	Gravel %		Coarse sand %			Fine sand %	Silt %	Clay %
	Particle size (mm)	7-4	4-2	2-1	1-0.5	0.5-0.2	0.2-0.02	0.02-0.002	<0.002
Red earthen sheath on twigs, due to termites		0	0	4	8	28	35	10	15
Red earth piled loosely by large ant		0	5	22	18	32	14	4	5
Brown earth piled loosely by small ant		0	0	10	7	18	42	9	13
Casts of *Hippopera nigeriae*		0	0	0	1	15	45	14	25
Adjacent soil									
Horizon Depth (cm)									
Cr W 0-2.5		1	3	12	10	29	26	7	13
Cr T 2.5-15		2	7	23	19	26	13	5	7
Cr G$_1$ 15-30		10	16	19	14	22	14	6	9

IV. Comparison with Other Soil Animals

Direct comparisons between the physical and chemical effects of termites and those of other animals on the same soil have been made by only a few workers. These comparisons are discussed here; in Chapter 10 more comprehensive comparisons are made between the effects on soils of termites and other soil animals, especially earthworms.

Nye (1955) compared particle size analyses of red earth formed into thin sheets over fallen twigs by termites, similar material piled loosely on the surface by large ants, brown earth piled loosely by small ants, casts of the earthworm *Hippopera nigeriae* Taylor, and soil from the same site, near Ibadan. Results of Nye's analyses are in Table 22. They illustrate very clearly the difference between the size fractions preferentially affected by animals that swallow soil and pass it through their gut (in this case only earthworms) and those preferentially affected by animals (termites and ants in this case) that carry soil, without swallowing it. *Hippopera nigeriae* is a large animal compared with termites and ants, but its casts, which are material that has been ingested and passed through the alimentary canal, contain only 16% of material larger than 0.2 mm, and none larger than 1 mm, while the termite-transported material

TABLE 23

Chemical Analyses of Samples from Termite Galleries (*Odontotermes* sp.), Ant Hills, Earthworm Casts, and Soil from Kanpur, India (Data from Shrikhande and Pathak, 1948)

Determinations	Termite galleries	Ant hills	Earthworm casts	Soil
pH	7.83	7.51	8.15	7.30
Organic C %	0.576	0.880	1.980	0.536
Total N %	0.102	0.126	0.192	0.087
Ratio C/N	5.63	6.98	10.32	6.19
Total Ca %	0.72	1.03	1.38	0.83
Total Mg %	0.44	0.26	0.28	0.35
Total K %	0.61	0.37	0.39	0.48
Total P %	1.20*	0.058	0.061	0.041
Exchangeable cations (m.e.%)				
T.E.C.	14.48	16.83	21.51	14.81
Ca	8.78	10.56	13.56	9.36
Mg	0.012	0.009	0.034	0.015
K	1.79	1.62	2.02	1.39

* Total P is calculated from the result (2.75% P_2O_5) given in a Table by Shrikhande and Pathak (1948). No special mention is made by these authors of this very high P content, and we consider that the figure in the original Table is probably incorrect.

includes 40% >0.2 mm, and 4% >1 mm, the material transported by the small ant includes 35% >0.2 mm, and 10% >1 mm, and that transported by the larger ant includes 77% >0.2 mm, 27% >1 mm, and 5% >2 mm. Differences in the proportions of larger particle sizes in the materials transported by the termite and ants must be due to differences in these animals' physical size and capacity to carry larger soil particles.

Watson (1960) compared particle size analyses of a mound built by *Cubitermes* sp. with a mound built by an ant, *Plagiolepis custodiens* (Smith), in forest near Salisbury in Rhodesia. As in the samples compared by Nye (1955) ants used a higher proportion of coarse material than termites, especially in the outer covering of the mound which included 89% coarse sand (2-0.2 mm particle size), compared with 55% in the outer casing of the termite mound.

Chemical analyses of termite (*Odontotermes* sp.) galleries, ant hills, and earthworm casts were compared with analyses of soil samples from a garden at Kanpur, India, by Shrikhande and Pathak (1948). Results of the analyses are in Table 23. It is very difficult to assess the validity of the comparisons. Only one set of analyses is given for undisturbed soil, and this would supposedly be taken from one soil horizon. No evidence is offered to show that the soil horizon sampled was the source of materials for all (or any) of the animal-modified materials. Our experience in Australia would lead us to doubt that termites, ants, and earthworms are all likely to work in the same soil horizon.

CHAPTER 6

Effects on Decomposition of Organic Matter and its Incorporation in the Soil

The food of termites has been discussed in Chapter 1. Most of their energy is derived from the digestion of polysaccharides (especially cellulose and hemicelluloses); some species are also apparently able to digest lignin, at least to a limited extent. Ability to digest these materials, which are the principal structural components of plant tissue, sets termites apart as a specially significant group of soil animals.

Previous work on the contribution of soil animals to the decomposition of plant debris and the cycling of energy and plant nutrients in soils has been done largely in regions where termites are rare or absent. Nielsen (1963), discussing the part played by soil animals in the organic cycle in the light of his findings on the enzymes possessed by a wide variety of soil animals, considered that primary decomposition—in this context the transformation of complex plant structural polysaccharides—is largely a function of the soil microflora, since soil animals generally lack the necessary enzymes. He concluded, "It is obvious that unimpeded exploitation by animals of plant structural polysaccharides would open up tremendous stores of energy to the animal kingdom but, somehow, evolution along these lines has met with little success. On the other hand, it is likely that had this enzyme barrier not existed, it might have led to an entirely different balance between producers and consumers than the one with which we are familiar in our immediate environment, since the buffering capacity of the stored plant structural polysaccharides would become partly destroyed. The main reason why these polysaccharides may act as stabilizers of the ecosystem is, apparently, that virtually all must pass through the bottleneck of microbial decomposition before recirculation can take place." Of the animals studied by Nielsen, only snails and slugs, which are not often dominant soil animals, could be regarded as decomposing significant quantities of cellulose.

Where termites are dominant soil animals, as in much of the warm temperate and tropical regions of the world, the organic cycle as it is generally presumed to function is drastically modified. Large quantities of plant tissue are taken from fallen litter or sometimes from living plants, often moved to a central storage point in a nest or mound, and intensely degraded so that the residue may contain little that is useful to other organisms. The resulting effects on soil formation, chemical and physical properties of soils are discussed in other sections of this work. In the following pages some attempt is made to summarize the knowledge that is available and to assess the contribution of termites to organic matter decomposition.

I. Digestive Processes of Termites

To a large extent termites are dependent on symbiotic flagellates and probably bacteria for digestion of polysaccharides, and perhaps other classes of organic compounds. However, they may not always be entirely dependent on symbionts.

Rao (1960) demonstrated the presence of proteolytic enzymes in the mid-gut and hind-gut of *Heterotermes indicola*; he compared defaunated termites with those having a normal gut microfauna, and concluded that the enzyme cathepsin was probably a product of the symbiotic protozoa while other proteolytic enzymes were produced by the termites themselves. These enzymes could, however, have been produced by symbiotic bacteria. Uttangi and Joseph (1962) attributed the digestion of starches to amylases produced in the fore-gut and that of proteins to proteases produced in the mid-gut. Hungate (1938) showed experimentally that in *Zootermopsis angusticollis* defaunated termites were capable of digesting about one-third of the amount of wood digested by termites with their symbiotic microfauna. The components of wood digested by defaunated termites were not identified, and the possibility that bacterial symbionts remained in the gut was not eliminated. Noirot and Noirot-Timothée (1969) reviewed the evidence for cellulase production by termites themselves, and concluded that there is as yet no convincing evidence that any termite produces significant quantities of cellulase.

A. SYMBIOTIC ORGANISMS

1. *Protozoa*

Honigberg (1970) has recently discussed protozoa associated with termites, and their role in digestion. Although protozoa have been found in the hind-gut of representatives of all termite families, Honigberg pointed out that the unique genera and species of oxymonad, trichomonad, and hypermastigote flagellates that ingest wood particles are restricted to the five families of lower termites, Mastotermitidae, Hodotermitidae, Kalotermitidae, Rhinotermitidae, and Serritermitidae. These protozoa, which are able to digest sound wood, appear to be indispensable for the survival of the insects and the relationship between them and their hosts represents true mutualism (Honigberg, 1970).

Cleveland (1923) listed 79 species of termites known to harbour protozoa, and 58 species (all Termitidae) known to lack protozoa, and listed 69 protozoan species of 40 genera together with the termite species with which they were associated. Allee *et al.* (1949, p. 717) stated that 528 species of termites were known to harbour symbiotic flagellates, and from them about 250 flagellate species were known. Honigberg (1970) doubted the reliability of estimates of numbers of flagellate species, because there is a need for critical revision of the taxa. A significant correlation can be found between many genera and species of flagellates and their host termites (Honigberg, 1970), but there does not appear to be rigid host specificity.

Most of the flagellates are concentrated in a bulbous, thin-walled enlargement of the hind-gut. They may be so tightly packed that individuals are plastically deformed, and may make up one-seventh to one-third of the insects's total weight (Brooks, 1963). Transmission of flagellates to young termites apparently results from proctodaeal feeding (see p. 5).

The possibility of wood digestion by intestinal protozoa in Termitidae was discussed by Honigberg (1970). He concluded that most of the small species found in Termitidae do not ingest wood, but some of the larger amoebae (*Endomoeba* spp. and *Endolimax* spp.) do, and it is possible that their metabolic activity contributes to the nutritional needs of their hosts. It has been stated (e.g. by Cleveland, 1926) that Termitidae do not usually feed solely on wood, and when they do eat wood it is usually much more decayed than that eaten by termites of other families. This is not borne out by evidence from the food preferences of Australasian termites. Of 53 species of Termitidae whose food preferences are listed in Table 1 (p. 12), 32 eat sound dead wood, and of these some species (*Amitermes* spp., *Microcerotermes* spp., *Nasutitermes* spp.) rarely, if ever, eat other food. Table 1 shows that wood is eaten by a higher proportion of species in the lower termites (of 32 species listed, 28 eat sound dead wood and 17 sound living wood), but it cannot be claimed, at least for Australasian species, that it is unusual for termitids to feed solely or largely on sound wood, thus explaining their lack of symbiotic flagellates.

2. *Bacteria*

A wide variety of bacteria has been isolated from the gut contents of termites. The work of Hungate (1943, 1946a), Dickman (1931), Beckwith and Rose (1929), and others indicates that they have little or no significance in cellulose digestion in Hodotermitidae, Rhinotermitidae, and Kalotermitidae. Among the Termitidae, Hungate (1946b) isolated anaerobic cellulose-digesting bacteria (*Clostridium* sp.) and an actinomycete (*Micromonosporium propionici* Hungate) from the gut contents of *Amitermes minimus* and considered that they were probably responsible for cellulose digestion in this species. *A. minimus* is a wood-eating species, and Hungate (1946a) concluded that cellulose digestion in other wood-eating Termitidae may similarly be due to bacteria. Pochon *et al.* (1959) showed that bacteria from the gut of *Sphaerotermes sphaerothorax* could digest cellulose, and Misra and Ranganathan (1954) demonstrated that cellulase and cellobiase are produced by bacteria in the gut of *Odontotermes obesus*. Noirot and Noirot-Timothée (1969) accepted that bacteria have a role in Termitidae analogous to that of flagellates in other termite families, but Honigberg (1970) concluded that, although observations indicate that bacteria have some significance, there is no incontestable evidence for any particular mechanism for cellulose digestion in Termitidae.

3. Associations of flagellates and bacteria

The possibility that flagellates and bacteria are sometimes simultaneously involved in cellulose digestion has been suggested. Hungate (1946a) considered this likely in *Kalotermes tabogae* and *Neotermes holmgreni*, which survived on a diet of wood after defaunation.

Complex associations involving bacteria living within the cytoplasm of symbiotic flagellates have been described, e.g. by Kirby (1941) and Hungate (1955). Pierantoni (1935) suggested that such bacteria may provide cellulase for wood digestion by the flagellates, but there is no definite proof that this is so. A very complex association found in the termite *Mastotermes darwiniensis* involves a symbiotic flagellate (*Mixotricha paradoxa* Sutherland), to the outer surface of which are attached large numbers of spirochaetes, mostly of one species but some of a second species, each spirochaete being attached by its anterior end to thé posterior surface of one of a large number of small brackets on the body surface of the flagellate. Anterior to each bracket a short rod-like bacterial cell adheres to the flagellate's surface, and bacteria of a different type are found within the flagellate cell. The details of this association were described by Cleveland and Grimstone (1964).

4. Fungi

Fungi are found in the gut contents of termites, and several workers (e.g. Cleveland, 1924; Hungate, 1936) have investigated the possibility that they contribute significantly to cellulose digestion. It seems unlikely that they do. The possible importance of the fungi of fungus combs built by Macrotermitinae was pointed out by Grassé and Noirot (1957, 1958a) who considered that a kind of "double symbiosis" may be practised by Macrotermitinae. Fungi are grown on the fungus combs, which these authors considered to be constructed of macerated plant tissue, mainly wood (see p. 143). It was proposed that the fungi attack lignin-cellulose complexes which are generally thought to be inaccessible to termite digestion, decompose lignin, and thus expose cellulose. The termites subsequently eat the fungus combs, especially at times when food supplies outside the mound are in short supply, and with the assistance of their intestinal symbionts are able to digest cellulose that would otherwise have been unavailable. Much fungal tissue is probably eaten at the same time. Kalshoven (1936) had shown for some Macrotermitinae, that fungus combs were eaten from below by termites and replaced by addition at the top. Sands (1969) considered that there could be no doubt that a symbiotic relationship like that proposed by Grassé and Noirot exists between termites and the fungi of fungus combs, that the fungi probably decompose lignin, and may also themselves provide a source of nitrogen and perhaps of vitamins.

In termites that have symbiotic protozoa, much of the digestive process is probably intracellular. Cleveland and Grimstone (1964) found that wood particles are taken in at an ingestive area by *Mixotricha paradoxa* in amoeboid fashion, pseudopodia flowing out and surrounding the fragments in vacuoles limited by a three-layered membrane similar in appearance to the plasma membrane. Enzymes could be present in high concentrations in intracellular vacuoles, but nothing is known of the chemistry of the vacuolar contents. Uttangi and Joseph (1962) stated that particles of wood are ingested by the flagellate cytoplasm and digested in the endoplasm without being enclosed in a vacuole; this seems unlikely, but if it is so reactions at the surface of the wood particles might be even more intense than in the vacuoles of *M. paradoxa*. In termites that lack symbiotic protozoa, where digestion is apparently due to the termite's own enzymes or to those of symbiotic bacteria, it must take place extracellularly. The efficiency of digestion has been investigated in comparatively few termites, but of those examined the most efficient at cellulose and lignin digestion (Seifert and Becker, 1965) are *Reticulitermes lucifugus* var. *santonensis,* of the family Rhinotermitidae which have symbiotic protozoa, and *Nasutitermes ephratae,* of the family Termitidae which lack symbiotic protozoa (see discussion on pp. 135–139 and Table 25).

B. PATHWAY OF CELLULOSE DIGESTION

Hungate (1946a) discussed the possible pathways by which decomposition of cellulose by symbiotic protozoa (in *Zootermopsis*) might proceed, to yield end-products that would provide an energy source for the termites. He concluded from results of experiments with *in vitro* cultures (Hungate, 1939, 1943) that the protozoa initially hydrolyse cellulose anaerobically, producing glucose. Some glycogen is synthesized and retained by the protozoa, but the majority of the glucose is anaerobically fermented by the protozoa, producing carbon dioxide, hydrogen and acetic acid. Production and evolution of hydrogen had previously been demonstrated by Hungate (1939). The energy requirements of the protozoa would be provided by the fermentation while the acetic acid, excreted by the protozoa, would be oxidized to provide energy for the termite. From the results of his experiments and those of Cook (1932), Hungate estimated the amount of acetic acid that would be produced by intact termites, and showed that the amount of oxygen necessary to oxidize the estimated amount of acetic acid agreed fairly closely with measurements of oxygen consumption by the termites. Further evidence in support of this metabolic pathway was provided by demonstrating the presence of acetic acid in gut contents of *Zootermopsis* and its absence in wood used as food and in faecal pellets, and by finding (Hungate, 1943) that the wall of the hind-gut was permeable to acetic acid. No glucose could be detected in the gut contents of *Zootermopsis*, nor in the culture medium of *in vitro* cultures of protozoa (Hungate, 1943), but Trager (1932) had found glucose in an extract of the protozoan cells. Some evidence conflicting with Hungate's conclusions came from a further test (Hungate, 1946a) in which defaunated termites were fed on calcium acetate, and another (Cook, 1943) using sodium acetate; in both cases termites failed to survive for significantly longer than did defaunated controls fed on wood.

Termites that lack symbiotic flagellates and apparently rely on symbiotic bacteria for digestion of cellulose do not seem to show any radical difference from those that have protozoa (Noirot and Noirot-Timothée, 1969). Pochon *et al.* (1959) demonstrated anaerobic decomposition of cellulose by bacteria isolated from the gut of *Sphaerotermes sphaerothorax*, with formation of acetic and butyric acids. Noirot and Noirot-Timothée (1969) stated that Kovoor found propionic and butyric acids in the hind gut of *Microcerotermes edentatus*.

C. DIGESTION OF LIGNIN

The decomposition of a large proportion of the lignin from wood by some termites (see discussion of experiments of Seifert (1962d) and Seifert and Becker (1965) on p. 135 and Table 25) is not easily explained. The initial stages of hydrolysis and fermentation of cellulose take place anaerobically and intracellularly within protozoa in those termites that have symbiotic protozoa, or anaerobically and apparently extracellularly within the gut of Termitidae which have bacterial symbionts but lack protozoa. Lignin decomposition, on the other hand, is generally believed to take place aerobically. Schubert (1965), concluded that white-rot fungi initially attacked softwood lignin by extracellular oxidases requiring aerobic conditions. Unless the degradation of lignin by termites proceeds by an entirely different pathway from that followed in fungal decay, it must be possible for anaerobic fermentation and aerobic lignin decomposition to take place simultaneously in the gut of some termites. Either there must be aerobic sites in a predominantly anaerobic milieu, or the digestion of lignin is effected in a different aerobic, portion of the alimentary canal from cellulose digestion in the anaerobic hind-gut, or the pathway of lignin decomposition in termites differs from that in other lignin-decomposing organisms. Whichever is the case, there is a need for detailed investigation of the lignin-decomposing mechanism. Noirot and Noirot-Timothée (1969) considered that symbiotic organisms must be responsible, but if so the pathway of digestion must differ from that known in the white-rot fungi. They regarded it as unlikely that the animals could themselves digest lignin, claiming that lignin digestion is not known in any other animals, although Seifert (1962c) showed that about 5% of the lignin in pine wood was decomposed during wood digestion by *Hylotrupes bajulus* L. (Coleoptera: Cerambycidae).

D. COMPARISON WITH DIGESTION IN RUMINANTS

There is an obvious parallel between the symbiotic processes that aid digestion of plant material in termites and the rather similar, but not exactly comparable, processes of digestion in ruminants. Hungate (1946a) discussed similarities and differences between these two vastly different groups of animals.

There are many species of bacteria in the rumen flora. Some of these bacteria anaerobically ferment cellulose and similar materials, producing various volatile fatty acids (which are utilized by the host animal), carbon dioxide, and hydrogen. A second fermentation, due to methane bacteria, produces methane from hydrogen and carbon dioxide. Termites also have complex associations of bacteria in their gut (Noirot and Noirot-Timothée, 1967), but they do not appear to possess methane bacteria, and produce hydrogen as a gaseous end product (Hungate, 1939). The bacterial flora in the rumen multiplies continuously, and vast numbers of bacterial cells pass into the intestine where they are digested and constitute an important part of the animal's diet. Hungate (1963) described the ruminant as a plankton feeder which cultivates its own plankton under highly productive conditions, and in which planktonic cells together with the wastes from their fermentation of carbohydrates are absorbed and utilized. Termites may digest some bacterial cells, and these may be an important source of protein, and other dietary requirements such as vitamins, but there is no evidence that the cells of symbiotic bacteria are as important nutritionally as they apparently are in ruminants.

The protozoan fauna of the rumen includes flagellates and ciliates. Little appears to be known of the flagellates, but the ciliates have received considerable attention. Ruminants can live and grow in the absence of rumen ciliates, but their presence is apparently important, at least for some ruminants. Coleman (1963) has summarized various points of view on rumen ciliates. There is evidence that they contribute to cellulose fermentation, producing similar compounds to those produced by rumen bacteria, and that they may elaborate their own nitrogen compounds from ammonia. It seems likely that they feed, at least in part, on rumen bacteria, and in their turn are digested by the ruminant and may be an important source of nitrogen. The symbiotic protozoa (predominantly flagellates) of termites appear to be most important as agents of cellulose fermentation. Hungate (1946a) stated that there was little evidence of growth or multiplication of protozoa in the termite gut during the interval between moults, so symbiotic protozoan cells must have little significance as a food for the termite. However, the intestinal contents are voided at the time of moulting and are consumed by termites in the vicinity of the moulting individual (Alibert, 1965).

The symbiotic relationships of termites and their gut microfauna and microflora, though apparently complex and in no case fully understood, are possibly rather simple when compared with the array and interrelationships of organisms in the rumen.

II. Decomposition of Plant Tissue by Termites and the Nature of the End Products

Although termites feed on a wide variety of plants and plant products, only their influence on decomposition of wood and the biochemical changes resulting from wood digestion have been studied in detail. In the dicussion that follows the decomposition process and its end products are considered under the following headings:

A. The quantity of organic matter eaten and the proportion decomposed.
B. Biochemical decomposition of wood by termites.
C. The composition of carton and fungus combs, which are the two principal materials manufactured by termites from plant tissue.

A. Amount of Organic Matter Eaten by Termites

1. *In laboratory colonies*

Very little quantitative information is available on the amount of food eaten by termites.

Seifert (1962d) found that in feeding experiments, *Kalotermes flavicollis,* with a mean weight of about 7 mg/animal, ate 0.16-0.18 mg of pine sap- and heart-wood per day, i.e. 2-3% of body weight. Of the amount eaten, 61-62% was completely decomposed and dissipated, i.e. 0.098-0.11 mg/termite/day, or 13.0-15.7 mg/g termites/day. Analyses of wood and faeces showed that 94-95% of the cellulose, 60-70% of the hemicelluloses, and 3-4% of the lignin in the wood eaten was decomposed. The proportion of cellulose decomposed in sap-

and heart-wood was closely similar; for the hemicelluloses, in sap-wood hexosans were preferentially decomposed, while in heart-wood pentosans were preferentially decomposed. In experiments with *K. flavicollis* using red beech wood as a food material about 0.16 mg wood/termite/day was eaten, and of this about 59%, i.e. about 0.094 mg/termite/day, or 14.4 mg/g termites/day, were decomposed. About 90% of the cellulose, 70% of the pentosans, and 3% of the lignin of the wood were decomposed.

We (Lee and Wood, in press) have conducted laboratory feeding trials using *Nasutitermes exitiosus,* with a mean weight of 5 mg/termite, in artificial non-breeding colonies, fed on sound wood of *Eucalyptus obliqua.* For three sets of experiments, with a total of 77 colonies, mean wood consumption (oven dry weight) was 0.053 mg/termite/day, or 10.60 mg/g/termites/day. Of the amount eaten 54% (i.e. 5.72 mg/g/termites/day) was decomposed and lost from the system. The rate of food consumption and decomposition by *N. exitiosus* was less than half that measured by Siefert in *K. flavicollis.* In both cases cultures were maintained at 26°C, but the different termite species used may have affected the results, the food materials tested were different, and the culture methods used by Seifert differed in many respects from ours.

2. Quantitative significance in natural conditions

Natural populations of termites are subject to environmental conditions that are not readily simulated in laboratory feeding trials. It is particularly difficult to assess the amount of food consumed by natural populations, but some indication of their quantitative significance in organic matter breakdown may be obtained by extrapolation from the results of feeding trials.

In an area of dry sclerophyll forest (*Eucalyptus obliqua–E. baxteri* (Benth.) dominant) near Adelaide, we have estimated populations of *Nasutitermes exitiosus,* measured litter fall and separated this into sticks and logs, and other plant material, over a period of three years (Lee and Wood, in press). *N. exitiosus* feeds on sound dead wood; there are approximately 600 *N. exitiosus*/m², with a biomass of 3 g/m²; total litter fall is approximately 230 g/m²/year, and of this stick and log fall totals approximately 70 g/m²/year. Applying the results of laboratory feeding trials, described above, 3 g of *N. exitiosus* would eat 31.8 mg wood/m²/day, or 11.6 g/m²/year. This is 16.6% of the total estimated annual fall of sticks and logs, or 4.9% of the total estimated annual litter fall. Further, the laboratory feeding trial showed that 54% of the weight of wood eaten, i.e. 6.27 g/m²/year, was decomposed and dissipated through the termites' digestive processes, leaving the remainder as faeces.

In the experimental area there are at least nine species of termites which are listed, with information on their habitats and apparent feeding preferences, in Table 24. Information in the table is derived from systematic searching of 18

TABLE 24

Termites Collected from an Area of Dry Sclerophyll Forest near Adelaide, South Australia (Lee and Wood, unpublished data)

| Termite species | Habitats and probable food | | | | |
| | Probable food — Dead wood | | | Probable food — Leaf litter, grass and/or humus | |
	Habitat — Sticks and logs	Habitat — Stumps	Habitat — Under stones	Habitat — Under stones	Habitat — Soil
Porotermes adamsoni	x				
Heterotermes ferox	xx		x		
Heterotermes sp.	x		x		
Coptotermes frenchi		x			
Amitermes neogermanus	x			xx	xx
Amitermes xylophagus				x	
Amitermes sp.				xx	
Microcerotermes implacidus	x	x			
Microcerotermes newmani	x				
Microcerotermes sp.	x		x		
Nasutitermes exitiosus	xx	xx			
Nasutitermes fumigatus		x			

xx = Commonly found in this habitat.
x = Occasionally found in this habitat.

plots each of 100 m^2, together with other sampling over a three-year period. Although *N. exitiosus* is the most common dead-wood-feeding termite in the area it is probably responsible for only a small proportion (probably less than 20%) of the total consumption of organic matter by termites.

Maldague (1964) attempted to estimate the amount of organic matter consumed by all termites in shadowy *Brachystegia* forest near Yangambi (Congo). He estimated the total termite population as approximately 1000/m^2, and their biomass as 11 g/m^2, which is a quite moderate population (see population figures on p. 91). Using Zeuthen's (1953) estimates of oxygen consumption in relation to body weight he calculated that the termites would require for metabolic purposes about 70 litres of O$_2$/m^2 ground surface/year. He assumed that termites obtain all their energy by decomposing cellulose, and calculated that they would therefore consume 170 g cellulose/m^2/year. Taking the average cellulose content of plant material as 30%, and assuming that all the cellulose in the food is fully decomposed, he calculated that the termites would consume 570 g plant material/m^2/year, which is approximately half of the total estimated litter fall. There are several errors in this series of calculations. Assuming that all the oxygen is used in the oxidation of cellulose or products derived from cellulose, 70 litres of oxygen is sufficient to oxidize only 84.37 g of cellulose, not 170 g. It has been shown by Seifert (1962d), Seifert and Becker (1965) and by the authors that in a variety of termite species the proportion of ingested food material decomposed is not less than 50% and may be as high as 89% (figure from Seifert and Becker (1965) for *Reticulitermes lucifugus* var. *santonensis*). Taking a minimum figure of 50% of the food material as the proportion decomposed, and assuming that this material is all cellulose or related compounds, Maldague's estimate would be reduced to about 169 g plant material/m^2/year, i.e. about 15% of the total estimated litter fall. Zeuthen (1953) claimed only that, using his methods, from the weight of an animal it was possible to predict its basal metabolic rate to the two nearest powers of ten. We have indicated (p. 91) that, in comparison with Hébrant's (1964) direct measurements of oxygen consumption, Maldague has overestimated by a factor of about ten times. Taking oxygen consumption from Zeuthen's curves and using this to assess the probable consumption of plant tissue by *Nasutitermes exitiosus*, in the same way as Maldague did, we have calculated that in our experimental area near Adelaide a biomass of 3 g/m^2 *N. exitiosus* would decompose 77.04 g plant material/m^2/year (assuming that 54% of the food ingested is decomposed). This is approximately 10% more than the total annual fall of sticks and logs, upon which *N. exitiosus* and at least six other species of termites, together with a variety of other insects, micro-organisms, etc. are known to feed. In addition, an almost equal amount (46% of food consumed) would remain as termite faeces. At least for *N. exitiosus*, using Zeuthen's formula in this way obviously leads to a gross overestimate of food consumed.

The termite population at the authors' experimental site near Adelaide is low, and seasonally (in winter) relatively inactive, compared with that of much of northern Australia and many other tropical and subtropical regions. In these latter regions termite populations may approach 10 000/m^2, are active for most or all of the year, and must be major contributors to the decomposition of organic matter. Much more work is necessary on this important aspect of termite biology.

B. BIOCHEMICAL DECOMPOSITION OF WOOD

1. Lignin and cellulose

The principal component of wood that is decomposed during digestion by termites is cellulose (together with related polysaccharides and oligosaccharides). Lignin is also decomposed, but its digestibility apparently varies widely, both between various plants and between various termite species.

Becker and Seifert (1962) fed *Kalotermes flavicollis* on wood from nine tree species and compared the lignin content of faeces with that of the wood used as food. They found that the proportion lignin in faeces : lignin in wood varied from 1.6 : 1 (wood of *Toona sinensis* (A. Juss.) M. Roem.) to 2.4 : 1 (wood of *Pinus sylvestris* L. and *Fagus sylvatica* L.).

Controlled feeding experiments with several species of termites, feeding on wood from various species of trees, were conducted by Seifert (1962d) and Seifert and Becker (1965).

Seifert (1962d) fed *Kalotermes flavicollis* on sound sap- and heart-wood of *Pinus sylvestris,* sap-wood of *P. sylvestris* that had been exposed before the feeding trials to decomposition for 28 days by the brown-rot fungus *Coniophora cerebella* Pers., and sound wood of *Fagus sylvatica.* Samples of the wood and termite faeces from the feeding trials were analysed and compared. Sound sap- and heart-wood of *P. sylvestris* were eaten in approximately the same quantities. The cellulose content of wood in both cases was about 45%, of faeces 5-6%; 60-70% of the hemicellulose was digested, but in sapwood hexosans were preferentially hydrolysed while in heartwood pentosans were preferred. The lignin content of faeces was 65.03% for termites feeding on sap-wood, 65.44% for those feeding on heart-wood, compared with 25.44% and 26.70% respectively in the original wood. A small proportion (3-4%) of the lignin was decomposed. Demethoxylated cleavage products of lignin were detected in ether extracts of faeces by thin-layer chromatography; a substance identical with protocatachualdehyde, not present in sound pine wood was identified. Alkali-soluble material in faeces derived from digestion of sap- and heart-wood, was 32% compared with about 12.5% in undigested wood. Wood partially decomposed by *Coniophora cerebella* differed from sound wood chiefly in its lower cellulose content (36.38%) and increased "hexosans" (26.56% compared with 19.86% in sound wood) which include cellodextrin and lower carbohydrates derived from cellulose by the fungus. Faeces derived from the partially decomposed wood differed little from those from sound wood except for an increase (to 38.45%) in alkali-soluble material. The total decomposition due to termites alone for sound wood and for fungus and termites together for the partially decomposed wood was approximately the same. In all cases some cellulose remained in the faeces, apparently at least partially in the form of a lignin-cellulose complex, since the cellulose extracted from faeces always contained about 10% lignin. Digestion of the individual components of *Fagus sylvatica* wood differed little from that of pine wood. About 90% of the cellulose was decomposed, compared with about 95% of that of pine wood; about 3% of the lignin was decomposed.

Seifert and Becker (1965) conducted feeding trials with four species of termites, feeding on six varieties of wood. The termites (see Table 25) included a "dry-wood" species of *Kalotermes*, two "moist wood" species of the genera *Heterotermes* and *Reticulitermes*, and a carton-nest building species of *Nasutitermes*. Hard woods and soft woods, with a range of cellulose and lignin content, were included in the trials (Table 25). Lignin and cellulose determinations were made on wood samples and on faeces of the termites. The ratios lignin : cellulose for wood and faeces are summarized in Table 25, together with the percentage of each of these wood constituents decomposed by the termites' digestive processes. *R. lucifugus* var. *santonensis* failed, in trials with three wood varieties, and *N. ephratae*, with two varieties, to survive for long enough for satisfactory faecal samples to be obtained.

Cellulose was vigorously attacked by all species. Differences are apparent between the extent of cellulose decomposition in the six wood varieties by individual termite species. Pine cellulose was most vulnerable, and was almost completely destroyed by *R. lucifugus* var. *santonensis*, but no consistent pattern of vulnerability was shown for the cellulose of the other woods. *R. lucifugus* var. *santonensis* and *N. ephratae* decomposed more of the ingested cellulose for all wood varieties eaten than did *K. flavicollis* and *H. indicola*, and Seifert and Becker considered that this might be due to re-ingestion of faeces.

Except in the case of *K. flavicollis* feeding on beech wood, lignin decomposition was unexpectedly high. The mechanism of lignin digestion in termites is not known. There was no consistent pattern in the proportion of lignin from the different wood samples decomposed by individual termite species except that *N. ephratae* and especially *R. lucifugus* var. *santonensis* decomposed more lignin than did *K. flavicollis* and *H. indicola*. Lignin includes a range of chemically similar materials that vary from one plant species to another, and vary also in their structural relationship with cellulose in plant tissue. This variability, together with variations in the ability and possibly even in the

TABLE 25

Lignin : Cellulose Ratio in Wood Samples and Faeces of Termites Used in Feeding Trials, together with Percentages of Lignin and Cellulose of Original Wood Decomposed by Termite digestion (Data from Seifert and Becker, 1965)

| Wood | | Faeces | | | | | | | | | | | |
| | | Kalotermes flavicollis | | | Heterotermes indicola | | | Reticulitermes lucifugus var. santonensis | | | Nasutitermes ephratae | | |
Species	Ratio L : C*	Ratio L : C*	Lignin % decomposed	Cellulose % decomposed	Ratio L : C*	Lignin % decomposed	Cellulose % decomposed	Ratio L : C*	Lignin % decomposed	Cellulose % decomposed	Ratio L : C*	Lignin % decomposed	Cellulose % decomposed
Ulmus campestris L. (elm)	0.82	2.7	19.3	73.8	2.6	32.0	77.9	–	–†	–†	4.9	43.4	90.7
Acer pseudoplatanus L. (maple)	0.75	3.8	22.8	85.3	4.0	25.7	86.5	–	–†	–†	6.7	42.4	93.9
Betula verrucosa Ehrh. (birch)	0.54	3.0	15.1	84.7	3.3	30.9	88.3	–	–†	–†	–	–†	–†
Fagus sylvatica L. (beech)	0.39	4.3	1.7	88.5	2.6	28.1	86.4	2.8	83.1	97.1	10.1	48.5	97.4
Populus sp. (poplar)	0.79	4.6	35.6	89.0	3.5	40.5	86.9	4.3	78.2	96.0	5.7	51.5	93.2
Pinus sylvestris L. (pine)	0.70	6.7	18.8	91.4	5.3	14.5	88.6	15.7	70.0	98.7	–	–†	–†

*Ratio L : C = Ratio lignin : cellulose on dry weight basis.
†Termite cultures failed to survive on this food.

biochemical mechanism adopted to digest lignin between termite species probably accounts for the inconsistencies of lignin decomposition shown by the experiments.

2. Alkali-soluble and water-soluble materials

(a) *Alkali-soluble material.* In the experiments of Seifert (1962d) sound pine sap-wood contained 12.31% alkali-soluble material, sound pine heart-wood 12.48%, pine wood after partial decomposition by fungi 27.19% and beech wood 19.12%, while termite faeces derived from digestion of these materials contained respectively 31.99%, 32.00%, 38.45%, and 35.77% alkali-soluble material. Cohen (1933) analysed material from samples of mounds of *Nasutitermes exitiosus* and found that the outer region of the carton wall contained 36.9% alkali-soluble material, the inner region of the wall 43.6%, and the nursery 46.1%. Lee and Wood (1968) reported values for *N. exitiosus* mounds of only 8.1% from outer wall material and 15.3% from inner wall material.

Carton material from the nursery of a mound of *N. exitiosus* was extracted in the authors' laboratory* (Lee and Wood, in press) with cold 0.5 N NaOH in an atmosphere of nitrogen, and purified by the conventional methods used with soil humic acid extracts, i.e. the acid insoluble-alkali soluble components were isolated, and these constituted 5.8% (uncorrected for ash content) of the original material. Fractionation of the material on Sephadex columns showed a higher proportion of low molecular weight components than in most soil humic extracts (nominal molecular weight of carton extract: >5000, 74%; >10 000, 64%; >100 000, 62%; figures based on absorbance at 260 mμ). The absorbance (at 260 mμ) of a 1 mg/ml solution of the extract was 22.50, which is lower than most soil humic acid extracts. The material extracted showed some similarities to alkali-soluble humic materials extracted from soils.

(b) *Water-soluble material.* Carton from the nursery of a mound of *N. exitiosus,* collected by the authors near Adelaide, was extracted in cold distilled water, purified by dialysis and cation exchange chromatography, and freeze dried. The final yield of freeze dried extract was 0.33% of the original material.

The chemical and physical properties (Table 26*) of the material were comparable with those of humic acid and fulvic acid components of the alkali-soluble material extracted from a podzolic soil and subjected to the same series of tests. The termite carton material had more carbohydrate than humic acid (1.33%) or fulvic acid (4.79%), more amino-acid N than humic acid (0.26%)

---

* The authors gratefully acknowledge the assistance of Dr. J. N. Ladd in carrying out this work.

TABLE 26

Some Chemical and Physical Characteristics of a Water-soluble Extract of Carton Material from the Nursery of a Mound of *Nasutitermes exitiosus* (Lee and Wood, unpublished data)

Ash %	4.60	Nominal molecular weight distribution by Diaflo
Carbohydrate %	13.00	ultrafiltration (based on absorbance at 450 mμ)
Nitrogen %	1.22	MW < 10 000 24.0%
Amino-acid nitrogen %	0.44	MW 10 000–30 000 66.4%
Carboxyl m.e./g.	3.42	MW > 30 000 9.6%
		Optical density of 1 mg/ml solution
		O.D. at 260 mμ 12.64
		O.D. at 450 mμ 1.04
		Ratio $\dfrac{\text{O.D. } 260 \text{ m}\mu}{\text{O.D. } 450 \text{ m}\mu}$ 12.2

and less than fulvic acid (1.15%), a little less carboxyl than humic acid (4.45 m.e./g) and less than fulvic acid (7.48 m.e./g). It resembled fulvic acid in its molecular weight distribution and differed from humic acid (fulvic <10 000, 24.5%; 10 000-30 000, 69,5%; >30 000, 6.0%; humic <10 000, 11.0%; 10 000-30 000, 58.0% >30 000, 31.0%). It more closely resembled fulvic acid than humic acid in the ratio of optical density at 260 mμ to that at 450 mμ (fulvic 15.1, humic 6.5).

It is apparent that digestion of wood by termites leads to the formation of small quantities of material closely resembling the humic materials extractable from soil organic matter. In the case of *N. exitiosus* there is some evidence that this material is inhibitory to microorganisms (see p. 149), and may have considerable importance in determining the course of subsequent breakdown of the residual organic matter excreted by the termites. Further work, with *N. exitiosus* and other species of termites, must be done before the significance of termites in the formation of humic compounds can be assessed.

C. COMPOSITION OF CARTON AND FUNGUS COMBS

1. *Carton*

The carton material that makes up all or part of the nests or mounds of many termites consists of excreta, often mixed with mineral soil particles, and occasionally with undigested, comminuted plant tissue. Similar material is frequently used to cement mineral particles in mounds constructed principally of mineral soil, and to line and strengthen the walls of subterranean galleries and covered runways. Digested organic matter is excreted in a semi-liquid form and is moulded to form galleries and chambers, either alone or mixed with mineral material (see Chapter 2). There is a continuous gradation between carton structures made entirely of organic matter, through mixtures of organic and mineral material, to mounds and their associated galleries composed almost entirely of soil but stuck together with carton-like material.

The principal organic constituents of carton are lignin and carbohydrates (especially cellulose). Much of the cellulose is probably in the form of lignin-cellulose complexes, and inaccessible to digestion by termites. Becker and Seifert (1962) determined the lignin and carbohydrate contents of carton from a wide variety of termite nests, galleries, and faecal material. Similar determinations of lignin and carbohydrates in carton have been made by Cohen (1933), Holdaway (1933), Leopold (1952) and Lee and Wood (1968, in press). The ratios lignin : carbohydrate in some carton and carton-like materials analysed by these authors are listed in Table 27.

There is great variation in the lignin : carbohydrate ratios listed. Coarsely comminuted plant tissue, in which cellular structure is still visible, is incorporated in carton structures of some termites, e.g. *Coptotermes acinaciformis* (see p. 36, and Fig. 13). Where ratios are low this could be the explanation, but it is also likely that efficiency of carbohydrate digestion varies between species and for different types of food. Gay *et al.* (1955) found that *Nasutitermes exitiosus* survived when fed carton of *Coptotermes lacteus,* which contains minute fragments of undigested plant tissue, while *C. lacteus* died when fed carton of *N. exitiosus.* Table 27 shows a general tendency for ratios to be higher for species of the family Termitidae than for species of other families. Of the 21 carton samples from structures of Termitidae in the table, one has a lignin : carbohydrate ratio >5, four >4, eleven >3, and the remaining ten <2. For samples of structures and faeces of other families (lower termites), of 20 samples, one has a ratio >5, two >4, two >3, six >2, and the remaining fourteen <2. This difference is the more remarkable as only the lower termites are known to have intestinal flagellates which digest cellulose, and only the lower termites habitually practise proctodaeal feeding (p. 5), which implies redigestion of plant tissue already partially digested by the termites. The generally lower lignin : carbohydrate ratios of carton of lower termites could be due to less efficient comminution and digestion of plant tissue, resulting in the presence in carton of more undigested material than in the carton of Termitidae; this is so in *Coptotermes acinaciformis* and to a lesser extent in *C. lacteus,* but there is little evidence that such differences are general. A more likely explanation is that carbohydrate digestion is more efficient and thorough in Termitidae than in lower termites. If the latter explanation is true it emphasizes the need for more thorough investigation of the mechanism of carbohydrate digestion by Termitidae. Although Termitidae do not practise proctodaeal feeding some species (e.g. *Nasutitermes exitiosus*) re-ingest carton during nest construction, and may digest some of the carbohydrates not decomposed

TABLE 27

Proportions of Lignin to Carbohydrates (and Similar Materials) in Carton, Galleries, and Faeces of Various Termites

Termites		Material tested	Lignin : Carbohydrate ratio (dry weight basis)	Author and reference
Family	Species			
Mastotermitidae	*Mastotermes darwiniensis*	Galleries	5.39	Lee and Wood (in press)
Kalotermitidae	*Kalotermes flavicollis*	Galleries	2.00*	Becker and Seifert 1962
	Cryptotermes brevis	Faeces	2.11*	Becker and Seifert 1962
	Cryptotermes brevis	Faeces	4.58	Leopold 1952
Hodotermitidae	*Zootermopsis nevadensis*	Galleries	1.38*	Becker and Seifert 1962
	Zootermopsis nevadensis	Faeces	1.34	Becker and Seifert 1962
Rhinotermitidae	*Heterotermes indicola*	Galleries	1.52*	Becker and Seifert 1962
	Heterotermes indicola	Filled in galleries	1.87	Becker and Seifert 1962
	Reticulitermes flavipes	Galleries	0.15–1.73	Becker and Seifert 1962
	Reticulitermes hesperus	Galleries	0.84*	Becker and Seifert 1962
	Reticulitermes lucifugus	Galleries	1.89*	Becker and Seifert 1962
	R. lucifugus var. *santonensis*	Galleries	0.31–1.30	Becker and Seifert 1962
	Reticulitermes tibialis	Galleries	0.55–1.72	Becker and Seifert 1962
	Coptotermes acinaciformis	Nest	1.19*	Becker and Seifert 1962
	Coptotermes acinaciformis	Nest wall	2.35	Lee and Wood (in press)
	Coptotermes acinaciformis	Nest	1.64	Lee and Wood (in press)
	Coptotermes crassus	Nest	1.65	Becker and Seifert 1962
	Coptotermes lacteus	Nest	1.24*	Becker and Seifert 1962
	Coptotermes lacteus	Galleries	1.73	Becker and Seifert 1962
	Coptotermes lacteus	Nest	2.06*	Lee and Wood (in press)
Termitidae	*Amitermes* sp.	Galleries	5.10	Lee and Wood (in press)
	Microcerotermes cameroni	Nest	1.23*	Becker and Seifert 1962

TABLE 27—*cont.*

Termites		Material tested	Lignin : Carbo-hydrate ratio (dry weight basis)	Author and reference
Family	Species			
Termitidae —*cont.*	*Microcerotermes nervosus*	Nest	4.10	Lee and Wood (in press)
	Cubitermes fungifaber	Mound	0.49*	Becker and Seifert 1962
	Termes panamaensis	Nest	1.24	Becker and Seifert 1962
	Nasutitermes beckeri	Nest	0.66*	Becker and Seifert 1962
	Nasutitermes ekunduensis	Nest	1.62	Becker and Seifert 1962
	Nasutitermes ephratae	Nest	1.50*	Becker and Seifert 1962
	Nasutitermes ephratae	Nest wall	1.81*	Becker and Seifert 1962
	Nasutitermes ephratae	Galleries	1.75*	Becker and Seifert 1962
	Nasutitermes exitiosus	Nest	1.89	Becker and Seifert 1962
	Nasutitermes exitiosus	Nest	3.7	Holdaway 1933
	Nasutitermes exitiosus	Nest	3.07*	Lee and Wood (in press)
	Nasutitermes exitiosus	Outer nest wall	4.8	Holdaway 1933
	Nasutitermes exitiosus	Inner nest wall	4.3	Holdaway 1933
	Nasutitermes exitiosus	Inner nest wall	3.02	Lee and Wood (in press)
	Nasutitermes magnus	Nest	3.17	Lee and Wood (in press)
	Nasutitermes nigriceps	Nest	1.58	Becker and Seifert 1962
	Nasutitermes triodiae	Nest	3.60	Lee and Wood (in press)
	Tumulitermes comatus	Galleries	3.30	Lee and Wood (in press)
	Tumulitermes pastinator	Nest	3.41	Lee and Wood (in press)

*Means of analyses of two or more samples.

previously. Some differences shown in Table 27 are probably related to differences in the original lignin and carbohydrate contents of the food, as some species feed mainly on grass, some on wood, and at least one (*Cubitermes fungifaber*) is humivorous.

2. *Fungus combs*

The fungus combs constructed by termites of the sub-family Macro-termitinae, apparently as a substrate for the growth of fungi, were described by Grassé (1949) as consisting of macerated but undigested plant material, usually wood. They are constructed, according to Grassé's description, from a paste of finely divided wood, chewed for a long time by the workers and shaped into small balls by rolling in the mouth parts, then built up by packing the balls side by side to form a granular structure, stuck together with some of the wood paste. Coaton (1947) and Sands (1969), on the other hand, claimed that the combs are constructed from faecal pellets.

Very little is known of their chemical composition, but the available analyses indicate that although, like carton, they consist mainly of lignin and cellulose (Bachelier, 1963), they do not in their detailed composition resemble carton, which is undoubtedly composed, except in a few exceptional cases, principally of faecal material. Joachim and Kandiah (1940), Hesse (1957), and Becker and Seifert (1962) have analysed fungus combs constructed by several East African species of *Macrotermes* and Indian species of *Odontotermes*. It is difficult to compare the analyses as different determinations were made. However, ash content (mineral material) varied from 10.7% for *O. redemanni* (Becker and Seifert, 1962) to 23.9% for *M. falciger* (Hesse, 1957); Hesse found that the pH of fungus combs of *M. falciger* was 4.3, of *M. bellicosus* 4.4, and of *M. subhyalinus* 4.5; Becker and Seifert found that the lignin : cellulose ratio in fungus combs of *M. natalensis* was 0.20, of *O. obesus* 0.55, and of *O. redemanni* 0.49; the nitrogen content of combs of *M. falciger* was 1.5%, of *M. bellicosus* 1.1%, of *M. subhyalinus* 2.0% (Hesse, 1957) and of *O. redemanni* 1.22% and 1.44% (Joachim and Kandiah, 1940). The lignin : cellulose ratios are in the range normally found in fresh plant tissue and are quite different from those reported for carton (Table 27). Samples of carton structures from the mounds of various Australian termites had nitrogen contents between 0.38% and 0.80%, but their pH and ash contents extended over the range measured in fungus combs (Lee and Wood, in press).

Sands (1960a, 1969) observed comb construction in *Ancistrotermes guineensis*, and stated that the comb was built from faecal pellets, without additions of masticated wood. Grassé (1959b) showed that newly constructed comb and faeces have staining reactions that are strongly lignin-positive, and contain little cellulose. Sands (1969, and personal communication) considers that the outer, newly deposited layer of the comb differs from the main mass of the comb, which is older and has had much of its lignin decomposed by basidiomycetes. Becker and Seifert (1962) analysed samples from whole combs of species other than *A. guineensis,* but Sands considers that their results are influenced by the large proportion of the comb from which lignin has been removed by the fungi, and consequently show lignin : cellulose ratios more closely resembling those of plant tissue than those characteristically found in the faecal material of termites. The conflict might best be resolved by separate analyses of outer and inner comb material, and by microscopic examination of thin sections of combs. It may be that combs are constructed from undigested plant material in some species and from faeces or mixtures of the two materials in other species, as is certainly the case with carton (see p. 35). Whether or not fungus combs are constructed entirely or only partly of excreted material, a striking feature of the nests of Macrotermitinae is the lack of excreta (on gallery walls, etc.) in the main bulk of the nest (see pp. 27, 30, and personal observations). Any excreta in the combs is apparently partially decomposed by the fungi; the termites then eat the older parts of the combs, together with the fungi they contain, and further decompose the organic matter. The end result would appear to be almost complete degradation of the plant tissue originally collected by the termites, leaving very little residue. Research on the biochemical processes involved in this system could make a significant contribution to knowledge of decomposition processes, particularly the decomposition of lignin.

Various functions have been attributed to fungus combs, including provision of a substrate for growth of fungi for food (p. 64), as sites for fungal pre-digestion of the substrate to provide accessible cellulose for the termites (p. 127), as temperature regulating devices (p. 59), or humidity regulating devices (p. 65). There is evidence for all these functions and, like many other structural features of termite mounds and nests, fungus combs may have several functions, whose relative importance may vary from one species to another, and even from time to time in one species.

III. Comparison of Termites with Other Wood-feeding Organisms

Seifert (1962a) reviewed the literature on the chemical decomposition of wood and similar materials by bacteria, fungi, insects other than termites, molluscs, and crustaceans, but because of variations in the methods used, it is difficult to make any direct comparison with results obtained from studies on termites.

Seifert (1962b, c) has studied the biochemical degradation of pine wood by the fungus *Coniophora cerebella* and by larvae of the cerambycid beetle *Hylotrupes bajulus,* and of alder wood by larvae of the anobiid beetle *Anobium punctatum* de Geer, all of which are destructive pests of timber. The methods used enable direct comparisons to be made between the results of these experiments and the results of similar experiments with termites (Seifert, 1962d, Seifert and Becker, 1965).

Degradation of pine wood by *Coniophora cerebella* was characterized by an initial rapid breakdown of cellulose, then a period of slower breakdown, with eventual decomposition of about 75% of the initial cellulose content. About 60-65% of the hemicelluloses were decomposed, and about 10% of the lignin. The degree of decomposition produced by *C. cerebella* was comparable to that produced by many termites, but the fungus took up to 270 days to produce an advanced level of wood decay. Termites are able to produce comparable or even more severe degradation of wood during one passage of wood through the gut. Noirot and Noirot-Timothée (1969) quoted observations by Kovoor, who found that food passes through the gut of *Microcerotermes edentatus* in about 24 h (at 25-30°C).

Neither *Hylotrupes bajulus* nor *Anobium punctatum* has a symbiotic gut microfauna or microflora like those of termites. The beetles themselves produce cellulase, and though it has not been demonstrated in *H. bajulus*, it is known that tyrosinase, an enzyme associated with lignin decomposition, is produced in the intestine of cerambycids. Seifert's studies showed that about 35% of the cellulose in wood is decomposed by both beetles. This is very much less than the proportion of cellulose decomposed by termites (see Table 25, p. 137). Cellulose is decomposed to form oligo- and mono-saccharides, which are apparently used directly by the insects; in termites hydrolysis products of cellulose undergo a microbial fermentation before they become available to the insects. Faeces of *H. bajulus* contain much undigested mono- and oligo-saccharides. The rate of consumption of wood by *H. bajulus* was about 25-33% of the weight of the animal per day, and its digestive efficiency was low; termites (*Nasutitermes exitiosus*) kept in the authors' laboratory consumed about 1% of their weight per day, but digested more than 90% of the cellulose, as well as other wood constituents. *H. bajulus* was shown to decompose about 5% of the lignin of the wood eaten, while *A. punctatum* was also shown to decompose a small proportion of lignin. Capacity to digest lignin varies greatly among termites, but sometimes reaches very high levels (Table 25).

IV. Microbial Decomposition of Organic Materials in Mounds and Nests

Large quantities of organic matter are commonly found in mounds and nests, and a variety of microorganisms, including some actively feeding on the organic matter and some inactive spores, is always present. For as long as termites occupy their mounds, nests, or other structures they continuously modify and maintain them. Although some microbial decomposition must proceed continuously, massive growth of microorganisms is kept under control, since most, if not all, termites eat fungi and might also digest some bacterial cells when mound material is re-ingested during reconstruction.

A. MICROORGANISMS REPRESENTED IN MOUNDS AND NESTS

Knowledge of the microflora of termite mounds and nests, compared with that of adjacent soils, is confined mainly to studies of the large mounds of African Macrotermitinae, and to previously unpublished results of a study of mounds of *Nasutitermes exitiosus*, by J. D. Stout, in the authors' laboratory.

Meikeljohn (1965) examined the microflora of 32 pairs of samples collected from mounds of *Macrotermes* spp. and adjacent soils in Rhodesia. She estimated populations of cellulose decomposers, denitrifiers, aerobic and anaerobic nitrogen fixers (Clostridia), ammonifiers and nitrifiers. She found that all groups of organisms investigated were more numerous in mounds than in soils, except for nitrogen fixing bacteria of the genera *Beijerinckia* (aerobic) and *Clostridium* (anaerobic). Mean numbers of the various groups in mounds and soils are listed in Table 28. From the much greater numbers of cellulose decomposers and

TABLE 28

Mean Numbers of Bacteria in Samples from Mounds of *Macrotermes* spp. and Adjacent Soil Samples (0–10 cm) from Rhodesia (Data from Meikeljohn, 1965)

Bacteria	Nos./g dry weight		Significance of difference
	Mound samples	Soil 0–10 cm	
Cellulose decomposers	6913 ± 999	1504 ± 578	P = 0.001
Denitrifiers: *Pseudomonas* spp. (×10³)	159 ± 54	4.6 ± 1.3	P = 0.01
Denitrifiers: *Bacillus* spp. (×10³)	356 ± 69	196 ± 44	n.s.
Beijerinckia spp.	156 ± 46	393 ± 121	n.s.
Clostridium spp. (×10³)	197 ± 55	474 ± 146	n.s.
Ammonifiers (×10⁶)	37.7 ± 4	24.6 ± 4	P = 0.05
Nitrifiers: Ammonia-oxidizers	4808 ± 858	938 ± 305	P = 0.001
Nitrifiers: Nitrite-oxidizers	943 ± 423	13 ± 6	P = 0.05

denitrifiers (which depend on easily-decomposable organic compounds) Meikeljohn concluded that the general biological activity was greater and organic matter decomposed faster in mounds than in adjacent soils. The mound samples had more organic matter, nitrogen, calcium, magnesium, and phosphate than adjacent soils, and these factors might account for the large numbers of cellulose decomposers, denitrifiers and ammonifiers. Higher pH, more calcium and greater nitrogen supply in mounds might account for the high numbers of nitrifiers. Most of the termite mounds supported trees and shrubs, while surrounding soils had a grassland vegetation. Meikeljohn considered the differences in microbial numbers to reflect rather the extreme poverty of most Rhodesian soils than extremely high populations in mound soils.

Boyer (1955, 1956a) examined mounds of Macrotermitinae in the Congo and Ivory Coast. He also found high populations of aerobic cellulose decomposers, aerobic and anaerobic nitrogen fixers. Fungus gardens were found to have a specialized nitrogen fixing flora, including two species of *Beijerinckia*, and a dominance of oligonitrophiles. In the nests of forest-dwelling "humivorous" (*Thoracotermes* sp.) and rotten wood-feeding (*Sphaerotermes sphaerothorax*) termites there were no aerobic nitrogen-fixers apart from oligonitrophiles. Pathak and Lehri (1959) examined microbial activity in mounds of *Odontotermes obscuriceps* in India, and reported that the rates of nitrification and nitrogen-fixation were higher than in adjacent soils. From the amount of nitrogen fixed and carbon consumed they concluded that the efficiency of microbial decomposition was higher in mounds than in adjacent soils.

The mounds and nests of Macrotermitinae are constructed very largely of mineral soil. Those of *Nasutitermes exitiosus* are composed mainly of carton, with a thin, relatively unconsolidated, outer coating composed largely of mineral soil. When the colony dies and the mound is deserted, the soil covering is quickly washed off by rain, leaving the carton interior exposed. J. D. Stout (personal communication) has examined the microflora of occupied and abandoned mounds in dry sclerophyll forest near Adelaide. Results of his investigations are summarized in Table 29. The soil capping of an occupied mound and the eroded surface material of an abandoned mound had populations comparable with or higher than those of adjacent soil samples. The outer wall and nursery of both occupied and abandoned mounds had very low populations. The low pH of the wall and nursery material may partially account for the low bacterial numbers, and for the high population of acid-tolerant aerogenic fermenters in the eroded surface material of the abandoned mound, which was actually inner wall material exposed to the air. The dominant organisms in the very small populations of the inner wall and nursery material of the occupied mound were spore-forming fungi and streptomycetes. These may have been present in the original samples largely as inactive spores, possibly carried in on the bodies of the termites. Non-spore-forming bacteria were numerous only in samples from the nursery of the abandoned mound. The nursery of this mound was partially below ground level, and the bacteria isolated from this region were probably invading from the surrounding soil.

There is a remarkable contrast between the microflora of the African macrotermitid soil mounds, which is much richer than that of adjacent soils, and that of the carton mounds of *N. exitiosus,* with their impoverished microflora. Abandoned mounds of *N. exitiosus* are known to decompose very slowly. Mounds unoccupied for up to 11 years have been examined in our laboratory and, apart from the loss of their outer soil capping, show little physical and chemical difference from adjacent occupied mounds (Lee and Wood, 1968).

TABLE 29

Mean Numbers of Microorganisms from Soil (0–5 cm) and Mounds of *Nasutitermes exitiosus* at Engelbrook, South Australia (J. D. Stout, personal communication)

| | | *N. exitiosus* mounds | | | | | |
| | | Occupied mound | | | Abandoned mound | | |
	Soil (0–5 cm)	Soil capping	Outer wall	Nursery	Eroded surface	Outer wall	Nursery
pH	6.2	5.6	4.1	3.7	4.8	3.2	5.1
Bacteria (no./g dry weight)							
Total plate count ($\times 10^5$)	33	181	0.06	0.005	53.5	0.12	4.07
Bacillus spp. ($\times 10^3$)	333	181	n.d.	n.d.	26.8	n.d.	n.d.
Clostridium spp. ($\times 10^3$)	800	36	n.d.	n.d.	<1.0	n.d.	n.d.
Aerogenic fermenters ($\times 10^3$)	20	2.4	0.004	0	197	0.005	0.052
Streptomyces ($\times 10^5$) (no./g dry weight)	6.7	3.6	<0.001	<0.001	<0.01	0.35	7.0
Fungi ($\times 10^5$) (no./g dry weight)	4.0	6.0	0.02	0.006	3.6	0.08	1.16

n.d. = not determined

B. Toxicity of Carton Material from Mounds of Nasutitermes exitiosus

Microbial respiration in samples from occupied and abandoned mounds of *N. exitiosus* and adjacent soils was measured by J. D. Stout, in the authors' laboratory, using Warburg techniques. Rates of carbon dioxide evolution of samples from the inner nest wall and nursery of occupied and abandoned mounds were so low that they could not be reliably measured, and results were obtained only for the soil capping of the occupied mounds, surface material from an abandoned mound, and samples of adjacent soils. Results of the tests are summarized in Fig. 29. After determining the initial respiratory rate, a solution

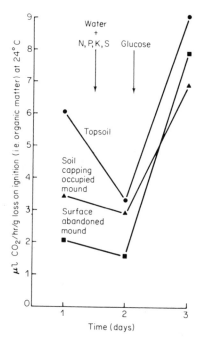

Fig. 29. Respiration of topsoil, soil capping of occupied mound, and surface layer of abandoned mound of *Nasutitermes exitiosus.* See text for explanation. (Data provided by J. D. Stout.)

of potassium phosphate and ammonium sulphate was added to the samples to determine whether metabolism was limited by major nutrient deficiencies; the result was a depression of respiratory rate in all cases. Glucose was then added, and resulted in an increase in respiratory rate to levels much higher than in the original samples; apparently microorganisms were present in an inactive state, and began active growth when a readily utilized substrate was available.

However, the experiments indicated an inverse relationship between the organic matter content of the mound material tested and the carbon dioxide produced, which may be due to the presence of toxic components in the organic matter.

As a test of toxicity, the effects of water-extracts of organic matter from a *N. exitiosus* mound on the activity of several enzymes were determined.* The extract used was the same as is described on p. 138, brought to pH 7. Effects of the extract on the activity of the enzymes pronase, carboxypeptidase, trypsin, and papain, were examined and compared with those of fulvic acid and humic acid derived from an alkaline extract of a podzolic soil, and with standards without test materials, using methods described by Ladd and Butler (1969), and Butler and Ladd (1969). Results of the tests are summarized in Table 30. The

TABLE 30

Effects on the Activity of Enzymes of a Water-extract of Organic Matter from the Nursery of a *Nasutitermes exitiosus* Mound, Compared with Those of Fulvic and Humic Acids from a Podzolic Soil. Enzyme Activity is Expressed as a Percentage of That Measured in Standards, Lacking Test Materials (Lee and Wood, unpublished data).

Enzyme	Concentration of test material (μg/ml)	% Activity of enzyme in presence of		
		Mound extract	Fulvic acid	Humic acid
Pronase	10	89	104	86
	200	75	74	54
Carboxypeptidase	20	92	95	64
	400	73	63	42
Trypsin	10	84	83	53
	200	30	24	13
Papain	18	124	79	191
	364	216	122	—

mound material depressed the activity of pronase, carboxypeptidase, and trypsin and stimulated the activity of papain, to an extent fairly closely paralleled by fulvic acid, and to a lesser extent than humic acid. Further tests were made to assess the similarities of the mound material to soil humic compounds. Methylation with diazomethane destroyed the material's ability to inhibit trypsin activity, addition of sodium chloride or magnesium chloride lessened its ability to inhibit pronase and carboxypeptidase, both effects paralleled by soil humic compounds. Acid hydrolysis of the material resulted in increased

---

* The authors are grateful to Dr. J. N. Ladd for his assistance in conducting and interpreting the results of these tests.

inhibition of the activity of trypsin, carboxypeptidase, and pronase, and increased stimulation of papain, unlike the effects of acid hydrolysis of soil humic materials.

It is not suggested that the results obtained with enzymes entirely explain the apparent inhibition of microbial activity in *N. exitiosus* mounds, but enzyme inhibition by materials similar to soil humic compounds may be a partial explanation. Other factors that may contribute to the slow breakdown of carton from this species' mounds are its low pH, which would tend to inhibit bacteria, its very high carbon : nitrogen ratio (55-85), very high lignin (*ca.* 30%) and low carbohydrate (*ca.* 8-10%) content, the inaccessibility of much of the carbohydrate, which appears to be in the form of ligno-cellulose complexes, and probably the relative concentration of resins, phenol, and other resistant wood components resulting from preferential degradation by the termites of the more readily accessible components of plant tissue.

The very slow breakdown of organic matter in abandoned mounds of *N. exitiosus* contrasts with the relatively rapid decomposition of carton in abandoned mounds of *Coptotermes lacteus,* which is a common wood-feeding species in eucalypt forests in south-eastern Australia and builds somewhat similar mounds, with a soil outer capping and predominantly carton interior. Analyses (Lee and Wood, in press) showed that five samples of carton from *C. lacteus* mounds contained between 16.7% and 26.4% carbohydrate, while five samples of carton from *N. exitiosus* mounds contained between 7.7% and 14.5% and one contained 23.9% carbohydrate. Apparently there is a generally lower content of carbohydrate in *N. exitiosus* than in *C. lacteus* carton. This probably contributes to the difference in rate of decomposition, since carbohydrates provide a substrate for growth of many microorganisms. Much of the small amount of carbohydrate in *N. exitiosus* carton may be combined with lignin (see p. 140), and thus may be accessible only with difficulty to further decomposition; microscopic examination of thin sections of carton of *C. lacteus* (p. 36) shows that it includes much finely divided but apparently undigested wood, which would provide a suitable substrate for microorganisms. Further investigation of the biochemical composition of carton from a variety of species is necessary to elucidate the differences that undoubtedly exist.

CHAPTER 7

Modifications of Soil Profile Morphology

Modifications of soils attributed to termites that affect the morphology of soil profiles may be summarized as follows.

I. Physical disturbance and overturning of profiles, especially the removal of fine materials from deep soil horizons to the surface, where they are used for the construction of mounds and surface runways, or packed in eaten-out feeding galleries in living trees, logs, stumps, timber structures, etc. In some cases subsurface gravelly or stony horizons (stone lines) are attributed to burial of stony, former surface, horizons or to removal of fine materials from subsurface horizons containing a high proportion of gravel or stones.

II. Formation of laterite in abandoned gallery systems, or alternatively changes in pedogenetic processes resulting in decomposition of previously formed laterite.

III. Changes in the distribution and quantity of organic matter in soils.

IV. In-filling of deep galleries and burrows with material washed down from overlying soil horizons.

V. Cementing of surface soil horizons.

VI. Microrelief due to persistence of mounds, resulting in variations in pedogenetic processes.

I. Physical Disturbance of Soil Profiles

Soil materials brought to the surface from deeper horizons and used for construction of mounds, surface runways, in-filling of galleries in logs and twigs, as well as spoil from subterranean galleries and nests, are eventually redistributed by rain and wind. The majority of the material appears to be redistributed in the vicinity of the mounds or other structures, while some material is transported and incorporated elsewhere into alluvial, colluvial, or aeolian deposits. Information on the amount of soil contained in termite mounds and the proportion of ground surface covered by mounds in some Australian, African, and Asian regions is summarized in Table 3 (p. 44). The proportions of material eroded from mounds that are redistributed locally or transported to a distance are not known.

Nye (1955) described a catenary sequence of soils from granitic gneiss on forested rolling land near Ibadan, which he considered to show the essential features of much of the forested soils of western Africa and similar parts of the world. He distinguished two primary horizons: a surface horizon of soil creep (Cr horizon) and an underlying sedentary horizon (S horizon). He subdivided the Cr horizon into a CrW horizon formed from earthworm-cast material (dominant earthworm *Hippopera nigeriae*), a CrT horizon formed largely from material transported by termites (*Macrotermes bellicosus* dominant), and a CrG horizon of gravel accumulation. In immature profiles at the top of slopes the CrT horizon was about 10 cm thick; in more mature profiles in the middle of the slopes it was thicker (>15 cm) and varied from about 15 cm to about 60 cm throughout the remainder of the catena. The CrT horizon was overlain by the CrW horizon, which was always about 1.25-2 cm thick. The CrT horizon was a loose loamy sand, consisting of particles up to about 4 mm diameter, while the CrW horizon was a fine sandy loam with much humus. Nye considered that the material constituting the CrT horizon was derived from the CrG and S horizons, while the CrW horizon consisted mainly of fine material derived from the CrT horizon. Were it not for the activities of termites and earthworms the CrG horizon, which often has a gravel content exceeding 50%, would be exposed at the surface. The gravel-free horizon formed by the fauna promotes soil creep down slope and so inhibits the formation of an excessively leached and weathered surface horizon, and gives plant roots access to decomposing minerals as a source of nutrients.

Nye (1955) also calculated the rate of accretion of material to the CrT horizon. *M. bellicosus* mounds are built very rapidly; a mound 60 cm high was built in one month, and mature mounds 150 cm high had annual herbs, rooted in the underlying soil surface, projecting from the mound surface. Observations of mounds indicated that they grow and decay to half their original height in five to ten years. A typical mound near Ibadan, Nigeria, weighed approximately 2500 kg, and mounds numbered about 5/ha. Nye calculated that at least 1250 kg/ha/year of soil would be brought to the surface by termites at this site, resulting in the accumulation of 30 cm of soil in the CrT horizon in 12 000 years. Assuming that equilibrium conditions exist, this must also represent the minimum rate of lowering of the land surface by erosion.

Watson (1960) reported similar profile modifications near Salisbury, Rhodesia, and attributed them to termite activity. He described three-layered soil profiles, with an upper (M) horizon consisting of fine mineral material, overlying a stony (S) horizon and a deeper (W) horizon of weathered rock. He considered the M and S horizons equivalent to the Cr horizon described by Nye, with the M horizon corresponding to Nye's CrT layer and similarly derived from termite-transported material from the lower horizons.

Williams (1968) described similar profiles, with M, S, and W horizons (using the nomenclature of Watson) on deeply weathered hornblende granite slopes in Northern Territory, Australia. The M horizon averaged 15 cm deep and the S horizon 30 cm deep. He considered that termites (*Tumulitermes hastilis, T. pastinator,* and *Nasutitermes triodiae*) were responsible for the formation of the M horizon, and that the material of this horizon had been derived from fine material in quartz veins in the W horizon, resulting in the formation of the S horizon, which is essentially W horizon material lacking the finer fractions that have been removed to the surface. Williams estimated growth and decay rates of mounds built by the three termite species, and numbers and weights of mounds. Comparing the present composition of S and W horizons, and assuming that the S horizon had originally the same proportion of coarse and fine materials as the W horizon, he calculated that 6000 m^3/ha of fine material must have been removed to the surface by termites. Of this, 1500 m^3 remains in the M horizon to yield the present thickness of 15 cm, and 4500 m^3 must have been removed by erosion. At present rates of termite mound growth Williams calculated that the present stone layer and the overlying M horizon would be formed in about 12 000 years.

We have estimated (Lee and Wood, in press), on the basis of numbers and weights of occupied and abandoned termite mounds, in two areas near that studied by Williams, that fine materials from deep horizons are added to the surface by termites at rates of 0.4 mm/year and 0.08 mm/year in the two areas respectively. Assuming a rate of loss by erosion the same as that estimated by Williams, rates of accumulation would be respectively 0.1 mm/year and 0.02 mm/year.

Converting the estimates of Nye, Williams, and Lee and Wood to the same basis, rates of accumulation of surface horizons are:

Nye (West Africa)	0.025 mm/year
Williams (Northern Australia)	0.0125 mm/year
Lee and Wood (Northern Australia)	0.10 mm/year
	0.02 mm/year

Stoops (1968) examined the micromorphology of some three-layered soils from the Lower Congo. The three layers distinguished were the α-layer at the surface, a loam apparently corresponding to the CrT horizon distinguished by Nye (1955) and thought to result from accumulation of termite-transported material from deeper horizons, the β-layer, a stone-line or lateritic gravel layer apparently corresponding to Nye's CrG horizon, and the γ-layer, of soft weathered material between the β-layer and the unweathered bedrock (δ-layer), apparently corresponding to Nye's S horizon. Microscopic examination of soil sections showed small nodules of γ-layer material in the α-layer, and an increase of mica flakes from the β-layer towards the α-layer. Stoops concluded that this material must have been transported upwards by termites and considered it as positive proof that the α-layer consisted of such transported material.

Sys (1955) compared a soil profile on the site of a former termitarium with adjacent undisturbed yellow latosolic soils near Lubumbashi (Elizabethville), Republic of the Congo. The "termitarium" profile lacked sharp horizon differentiation, with a light yellowish brown (2.5 Y 6/4*) clay A horizon grading into an olive brown (2.5 Y 5/4) B horizon with some small calcium carbonate concretions, and a gradual transition to an olive brown clay C_1 horizon with numerous calcium carbonate concretions. The "normal" profile had a brown (10 YR 5/3) clay loam A horizon, brown (7.5 YR 5/6) B_1 horizon, yellowish brown (7.5 YR 5/6) friable clay B_2 horizon with well developed clod structure, and a yellowish brown (7.5 YR 5/6) very friable clay C horizon; the "normal" profile lacked calcium carbonate concretions.

Many reports of soil surveys in Africa contain references to effects of termites on soil horizon differentiation, but quantitative estimates of their effects are rare. Fölster (1964) described shallow gravel and loam deposits overlying pediments of the southern Sudanese pediplain. He considered the gravels to be a degradation residue deposited during pedimentation and the loam to be partly a product of erosion and partly a pedogenetic horizon built by termites carrying fine material to the surface. Horizontal movement of clay by surface wash was apparent, and Fölster considered termites responsible for the presence of this clay and for constantly replenishing the supply. Ollier (1959) described east African soils formed on rocks with bands of quartz in which the upper horizons consist of fine material, usually not exceeding 1 mm diameter, with a sharp boundary to lines of quartz stones. He attributed the surface horizons to termite activity, and distinguished termite-modified profiles of this kind from a variety of other layered soils, especially by the uniformity of the overlying material. Stone lines in soils near Kinshasa (Leopoldville), Republic of the Congo, were described by Ploey (1964). The stony layer was considered to have resulted from intense sheet erosion on an old soil surface during a former semi-arid climatic regime. During a subsequent period of less arid climate Ploey considered that termites had deposited fine material on the surface. Particle size analyses of samples from mounds of *Macrotermes* sp. nearby showed that the mounds were composed of sandy clay closely resembling that overlying the stone lines. Other qualitative observations of horizon differentiation due to termites are discussed below in the section on relationships of termites to laterites.

Soil is commonly packed in old feeding galleries in logs and twigs, and is used for construction of above-ground runways, which are often fragile and disintegrate quickly. We know of no quantitative data on amounts of soil moved to the surface in this way, but the quantity must often be very large, and may

*Soil colours as in Munsell soil colour charts.

well exceed that in mounds. The material used may be derived from deep soil horizons, as we have noted (Lee and Wood, in press) for soil packed in logs by *Coptotermes acinaciformis* in an area of savanna woodland in northern Queensland, and would then represent another mechanism by which soil profiles are overturned.

II. Relationships to the Development of Laterite

The term "laterite" was first used by Buchanan (1807) to describe ferruginous, vesicular material from soils in India that was soft enough to be cut into blocks, but on exposure to the air quickly hardened to a brick-like consistency and was used as a building material. Since then the term has been used to denote many things, from the original material described by Buchanan to a general name for all tropical soils (Gerasimov, 1962). Sivarajasingham *et al.* (1962) have reviewed the various uses of the term and have restricted it to include highly weathered soil materials found usually in tropical or sub-tropical regions that are (1) rich in secondary forms of iron, aluminium, or both; (2) low in humus content; (3) depleted of bases and combined silica; (4) with or without non-diagonistic substances such as quartz, limited amounts of weatherable minerals, or silicate clays; and (5) either hard or subject to hardening on exposure to alternate wetting and drying. The term is used here in this restricted sense.

Lake (1890) distinguished *vesicular laterite,* a ferruginous hardened clay, penetrated by numerous vermicular, branching and anastomosing tubes, from *pellety laterite,* consisting of small, irregular, nodular pellets, rich in iron oxides, often cemented together by similar material. Maignien (1966), in his recent review of research on laterite, recognized Lake's two forms and a third form added since Lake's description, of homogeneous or continuous structures in which the indurated elements form a continuous, coherent skeleton.

Various authors have proposed that termites contribute to the formation of laterite in soils, while others attribute to termites the decomposition of lateritic materials formed by physico-chemical processes.

A. POSSIBLE CONTRIBUTION TO LATERITE FORMATION

Nazaroff (1931) first proposed that spongy ferruginous masses (vesicular laterite), which he found in sandy soils in the uplands of Angola, resulted from deposition of iron oxides, derived from the weathering of soil minerals and transported by percolating groundwater, in the galleries of old termitaria. Nazaroff regarded the strongly ferruginized structures as sub-fossil or fossil, but he also found what he considered to be intermediate stages in the ferruginization of termitaria, and noted that near rocks rich in silica, such as quartzose sandstones and quartzites, a parallel process of silicification produced pseudomorphs of termitaria composed of silica. The ferruginous masses ranged in size from a few hundred cm^3 to several m^3.

Lateritic materials similar to those described by Nazaroff have been noted and attributed to ferruginization of termite nests and gallery systems by Erhart (1951a, b, 1953) in Sudan and Congo, Conrad (1959) in the Beni-Abbes region (north-west Sahara), Tessier (1959a, b) at Dakar, Taltasse (1957) in north-eastern Brazil, and Saurin and Roch (1958) near Saigon in Vietnam. Their formation has been associated with a variety of termite species, but the structures described are closely similar.

Formation of relatively homogeneous lateritic surface crusts has also been attributed to ferruginization of termite gallery systems with iron oxides deposited from percolating groundwater. Erhart (1951a, b, 1953) described crusts, which he called "cuirasses termitiques", in tropical forests and semi-desert areas of Sudan and also in Gabon, in which he recognized vacuolar structure and a labyrinthine framework similar to termitaria. Yakushev (1968) reported similar formations in south-western Mali, in which it was sometimes possible to identify ferruginous bodies resembling termite galleries and nests.

Griffith (1953) questioned the significance of termites in laterite formation. He studied extensive cuttings exposed during road making in Trinidad, and found a soil horizon rich in "ironstone" fragments, ranging through all degrees of hardness to completely indurated, and from small grains to fragments more than 15 cm in length. The larger fragments had grotesque shapes like those of fossil laterites described from Africa, but he attributed their shape to the irregular shape of the soft iron-rich mottles from which they were apparently formed. He proposed that further enlargement, induration, and ultimate contact and fusion of iron-rich mottles and ironstone nodules would result, after removal of the softer enclosed material, in a more or less continuous pavement of vesicular laterite. A mound-building termite *(Nasutitermes ephratae)* is found in the area, but there was no sign of termite burrows in the horizon of ironstone accumulation. Griffith concluded that termites did not contribute in any way to the formation of the nodules, and hence to the possible development of the laterite pavement.

Evidence for the formation of laterite in western Africa through the agency of termites was examined by Grassé and Noirot (1959a). They concluded that the explanation was unlikely, for the following reasons: (1) The volume of individual masses of vesicular laterite is often much greater than that of any termitaria. (2) The vesiculae of laterites, though they sometimes resemble the galleries and chambers of some termite structures, are not arranged in ways that even vaguely resemble any part of termite nests. (3) The alveolar portions of abandoned nests rapidly collapse and become filled with earth. Boyer (1959) confirmed this point. (4) Neither termitaria nor surrounding networks of galleries have a form resembling that of lateritic crusts.

The supposition that laterite structures are fossil or sub-fossil termitaria and gallery systems seems to have arisen from rather uncritical appraisal of superficial resemblances between them. The description given by Lake (1890) of vesicular laterite leaves little doubt that it is formed by physico-chemical processes. Lake stated, "the deeper we dig into the laterite and the less affected it is by the weather, the fainter becomes the distinction between the walls of the tubes and their contents, till at last it may disappear altogether, and what is laterite above is simply clay below. This shows, if it were necessary, that the peculiar structure of laterite is due to a kind of concretionary action . . ."

The possibility that, in some circumstances, the walls of abandoned termite nests and burrows may act as surfaces for deposition of ferruginous materials can not be entirely dismissed, but there is little evidence that extensive deposits of vesicular or crust-like laterite result from this process.

B. Possible Contribution to Modification and Decomposition of Laterite

Grassé (1950) considered that termites in western Africa were responsible for the burying of some laterite crusts. Many termites, especially macrotermitids, require clay for their structures and may gather it from depths up to 3-4 m, below a laterite layer, and carry it up to the surface. Grassé considered *Macrotermes subhyalinus* to be particularly important in this way, since it carries great quantities of soil to the surface, and is distributed over a vast area in Africa.

In the soils of some dry regions where laterite outcrops occupy much of the ground surface (e.g. between Odienné, Ivory Coast, and Kankan, Guinea), fine material brought to the surface to build nests by *Cubitermes* spp. results in burial of laterite and development of conditions more favourable to plant growth. During the hot dry summer the termites take refuge in deep fissures in the laterite, and from the fissures they collect fine material to build their nests at the surface.

Boyer (1959) reported soil changes, sometimes involving the disappearance of lateritic gravels and crusts, under mounds and galleries constructed by macrotermitids. He considered that the maintenance of high humidity in mounds and galleries leads to physico-chemical conditions in the underlying soil that permit solubilization of iron and manganese hydroxides, which are then subject to leaching by infiltrating water.

Tricart (1957), on the basis of observations in western Africa and Brazil, distinguished two possible effects of termites on laterite formation. First, previously-formed laterite may be broken up and destroyed by termites in the construction of mounds and galleries. Subsequently, gallery systems may be flooded by water rich in iron hydroxides, leading to a new phase of lateritization.

A sequence of stages in the degradation of exposed laterite crusts is described by Maignien (1966). A change in environmental conditions (climate) leads to establishment of herbaceous vegetation in cracks in the crust that contain fine material; gradually an organic horizon builds up, and the cementing materials are dissolved so that the surface layer of the crust is loosened and forms a juvenile soil, often enriched with earth material transported by termites. Shrubs and then trees may follow, resulting in an increase in soil organic matter and further disintegration of cemented layers, and leading finally to the formation of a gravelly soil. The time-scale is long, but by a combination of physical, chemical, and biological processes (to which termites sometimes contribute) laterite can be degraded and can contribute to the formation of new soils.

III. Changes in Distribution and Quantity of Organic Matter

In soils with large populations of mound-building or other concentrated nest-building termites their influence on the distribution and quantity of organic matter and on the cycling of plant nutrients contained in organic matter can assume considerable importance. The combination of foraging for food over a wide radius from the nest and returning it to the nest (p. 45), intense degradation of the plant tissue collected, and use of the excreted end products of digestion for mound-building resulting in their removal from participation in the plant/soil system for long periods, sets termites apart from other soil animals in their influence on soil organic matter.

Chemical degradation of organic matter is discussed elsewhere (p. 131). We have estimated (Lee and Wood, in press) that, in an area of dry sclerophyll forest near Adelaide, *Nasutitermes exitiosus* eats 16.6% of the total dead wood (logs, stumps, and twigs), that 9% is metabolized and lost from the ecosystem, and most of the remaining 7.6% is incorporated in mounds, which may be occupied for up to 50 years (Ratcliffe *et al.,* 1952) and decompose very slowly after the termites have abandoned them (Lee and Wood, 1968). Similar mounds built by *Amitermes hastatus* in South Africa were estimated by Skaife (1955) to be occupied by the termites for about 30 to 50 years. We have estimated (p. 119, and Lee and Wood, in press) the amount of organic matter and major plant nutrients contained in mounds of *Nasutitermes triodiae, Amitermes vitiosus,* and *Tumulitermes hastilis* in relation to the total contained in the mound/A_1 horizon system, and have concluded that mounds withhold a substantial proportion of the available organic matter and nutrients from circulation. The organic matter in the mounds represents only a fraction (probably less than half) of the total organic matter removed from the ecosystem; the remainder is metabolized and lost. But the quantity of organic matter in mounds is not the only significant fact. This organic matter represents the residue of food, grass and plant litter in the two cases cited, collected over a wide radius around the mound. Its accumulation in mounds involves transference of fertility from the surrounding soil to the mounds, where plants are unable to grow. In the absence of termites organic matter and its included nutrients fall to the ground surface, and in most temperate regions are decomposed on the surface or incorporated in the soil *in situ*.

Chevalier (1949) considered that some termites in West Africa, which feed on surface litter-layers, are useful in decomposing dead organic matter and incorporating nutrients in the soil, while humus-feeders such as *Cubitermes fungifaber* deplete soil organic matter by ingesting and digesting humic materials and incorporating their excreta in termitaria. Robinson (1958) drew attention to the destruction by termites of organic mulch spread on the soil surface to promote plant growth.

IV. In-filling of Deep Burrows and Galleries

Some mixing of soil from superficial horizons into deeper horizons results from in-filling of abandoned termite galleries. Watson (1960) found patches of grey soil, apparently formed in this way, at depths up to about 8.5 m in soils near Salisbury, Rhodesia, and Robinson (1958) found similar features at depths of 60-120 cm in soils of Kenyan coffee fields. We know of no estimates of the quantities of soil mixed in this way, but such features are common wherever soil-inhabiting termites occur.

V. Cementing of Surface Soil Horizons

In constructing mounds and nests, excavating galleries, and building surface runways, soil particles are sorted, repacked and cemented, often rather loosely, but some species can fabricate structures that are very hard and virtually impervious to water. In extreme cases soil development is arrested and previously formed horizons may disappear (Boyer, 1958). However, areas affected in this way are small and would not usually be of much significance in soil development. They are perhaps more important in inhibiting the establishment of plants (see p. 165).

VI. Microrelief

Termite mounds, especially when they are numerous, are prominent features of landscape microrelief. Like other microrelief features they affect the infiltration of water into the soil, promoting surface runoff on their steep sides and serving to concentrate water on the intervening soil surface. This must result in differential leaching of soil beneath mounds, compared with soil between mounds. Most termite mounds are comparatively short-lived and, though they may be prominent microrelief features, have little effect on the long-term leaching of soil materials that is responsible for horizon differentiation. Some mounds, notably those built by some African Macrotermitinae, are very large (see p. 43 for dimensions), and once built persist for very long periods, although they may be occupied by their original inhabitants for only a short time. Meyer (1960) considered such mounds now found in the central Congo basin to have been built during a former period of drier climate dating from the early Quaternary. They have their own characteristic vegetation, and the soils found within and under them may differ considerably from surrounding soils.

Accumulation of a horizon of calcareous concretions through the basal portion of macrotermitid mounds is discussed on p. 113. At Legon, in the southern grassland savanna zone of Ghana, P. H. Nye (personal communication) has observed concretions of calcium carbonate under mounds (*Macrotermes* sp.) on freely-drained soils on slopes where the profile shows no influence of ground water. He attributes the presence of calcium carbonate concretions to the "umbrella effect" of the mound in preventing or retarding leaching, combined with the transport of calcium into the mound in the food of the foraging termites. Watson (1962) described concentric cones of whitened soil extending to about 6 m depth beneath a large (macrotermitid) mound in an area of leached ferrallitic soils at Umtali, in Rhodesia. The whitened horizons beneath the mound had the same physical structure as the surrounding soils. The pale colour was due to finely divided carbonates, with a concentration of 4% in the outermost cone and 2% in the inner region. Removal of carbonates by acid treatment eliminated the pale colour and changed the soil to yellowish red, similar to the colour of surrounding soil horizons.

Leenheer *et al.* (1952) noted great differences between soil development under similar mounds, which occupied up to 30% of the ground surface in the Yangambi area (Congo), and attributed the differences to microrelief and the internal structure of the mounds.

Observations by Boyer (1959) of degradation of laterite crusts under ancient macrotermitid mounds (p. 158) may also be attributed partly to the effects of the microrelief of mounds.

CHAPTER 8

Effects on Vegetation

Termites affect the vegetation in two ways; firstly, by consuming selected components of living and dead vegetation and, secondly, by modifying certain properties of the soil that influence the growth of plants. The effects of termites' feeding on plant tissue are considered elsewhere (the food of termites p. 5; destruction of living vegetation by termites p. 169). Modifications to soils that influence plant growth can be considered under two headings—the growth of plants on termitaria and the growth of plants on termite-modified soil eroded from termitaria and spread over the surrounding ground surface.

I. Growth of Vegetation on Termitaria

Detailed studies of the vegetation associated with termite mounds in Africa have been made by Burtt (1942), Glover (1949) unpublished, in Glover *et al.* (1964), Glover *et al.* (1964) in East Africa and Glover (1937) in South Africa, Fries (1921) in Zambia, Wild (1952) in Southern Rhodesia and Morison *et al.* (1948) in south-western Sudan. In South America surveys have been made by Goodland (1965), Martyn (1931), and Myers (1936), in Guyana.

A. ENHANCEMENT OF GROWTH

"Termitensavannen" is a term proposed by Troll (1936) to describe vegetation formations in Africa consisting of discrete islands of woodland growing on large termite mounds, surrounded by sparsely timbered grassland. Earlier Fuller (1915) had recognized that the so-called "park-formation" of inland areas of Natal resulted from the growth of trees being more or less confined to termite mounds *(Macrotermes natalensis)*. In Africa the principal species building large mounds are *Macrotermes falciger, M. bellicosus, M. subhyalinus* and *M. natalensis* (Macrotermitinae). These species do not occur in primary tropical rain forest and the presence of their mounds under a closed canopy indicates the secondary nature of the vegetation, as more open, savanna woodland conditions are necessary for the mounds to be built (Harris, 1961). Large mounds in forests in southern Nigeria (Jones, 1956) and in the central

Congo basin (Meyer, 1960) are considered to have been built during climatic conditions quite different to those now prevailing; the mounds in the Congo were considered to date from the Quaternary period.

In Thailand, Pendleton (1941) noted that large termite mounds (Macrotermitinae) were occupied by a dense growth of trees and shrubs which did not grow well, if at all, on the padi or forested land around them. In contrast, Goodland (1965) noted that the species of plants occurring on termitaria in Guyana were all characteristic of the surrounding savanna; however, the species building the mounds was not specified. More precise information is available on the vegetation of the large mounds of Macrotermitinae in Africa, where the trees and shrubs on the mounds appear to be specialized types rather than concentrations of the species sparsely distributed over the surrounding savanna (Fuller, 1915; Harris, 1961; Wild, 1952). The termite mound-inhabiting species also occur in other specialized habitats in the same areas, such as rocky "kopjes" or in "gallery forest" along the borders of water courses. Wild (1952) found 72 species of plants growing on termite mounds *(Macrotermes natalensis)* in Southern Rhodesia and 53% of these species were important constituents of deciduous woodland in warmer and/or drier areas. For instance, species growing on mounds at altitudes of 1200-1500 m with annual rainfalls of 760-1020 mm occurred in 250-630 mm rainfall areas at 300-600 m altitude and 500-630 mm rainfall areas at 1350 m altitude. Two families of plants, Capparidaceae and Celastraceae, favouring hot, dry climates, included high proportions (50% and 46% respectively) of the total Southern Rhodesian flora growing on termite mounds. Wild found that a few species growing on mounds exhibited a reverse trend, being significant constituents of high rainfall (1270-1780 mm) forests. Morison *et al.* (1948) found that of 155 species of plants identified on catenary sequences in south-western Sudan, 33 species occurred characteristically on large termite mounds (species of termite not identified). On deep, eluvial soils they found that mounds supported an evergreen vegetation different from the deciduous vegetation of the surrounding soils, and presented evidence that suggested that the charactistic flora of the mounds gradually disappeared as the mounds collapsed and eroded away. Glover *et al.* (1964) found that of the 59 species of plants they identified on the Loita plains in Kenya only 10 were recorded on termite mounds (*Odontotermes* sp.) and of these six appeared to be exclusive to the mounds. The dominant species growing on these mounds were a low shrub and a prostrate, creeping grass, and the influence of mounds on the vegetation was more obvious through their indirect effects on the growth of vegetation around the mound (see below).

Wild (1952) concluded that the majority of plants characteristic of termite mounds are restricted to this type of habitat, or some other specialized locality, because they are outside the areas where climatic factors favour their optimum growth. Away from these optimum conditions they cannot compete successfully with the surrounding vegetation and are confined to specialized conditions provided by termitaria. However, other workers have suggested that, at least in certain regions, it is the grasses of the savanna that cannot compete successfully with the shrubs and trees and that special conditions favour the maintenance of grassland, which is thus a disclimax community. For instance, Morison *et al.* (1948) and Harris (1961) considered that protection from fires and from waterlogging, as well as better nutrient status, were the main factors favouring development of woodland on large termite mounds. Ghilarov (1962) reported a slightly different situation in the virgin arid deserts of Central Asia where the sites of subterranean nests of *Anacanthotermes turkestanicus* are revealed in spring by the better growth of *Poa, Malcolmia* and other plants. In this case the enhanced growth of plants is possibly due to the higher nitrogen content of the termitaria compared with the surrounding soil. Thus there appear to be many interrelated factors responsible for the occurrence of special vegetation on termite mounds. The more important of these can be summarized as follows:

(a) Protection from burning, allowing the survival of seedlings of plants that could possibly germinate on the surrounding soil but would be destroyed by fire.

(b) Absence of waterlogging, in that in poorly-drained, seasonally-flooded areas, the mounds provide well-drained, relatively dry sites.

(c) Provision of a greater depth of soil in areas with shallow, stony soils.

(d) Provision of moist soil (due to retention of water by higher content of clay) in otherwise dry, well-drained sites.

(e) Provision of soil chemically different to the surrounding soil; the principal factors appear to be higher pH and higher base-status (see p. 107).

(f) Resistance to termite attack by species growing on the mounds.

(g) Possible response by plants to substances produced by the termites. Araujo (1970) (quoting the work of Kaiser, 1953) suggested that the profuse growth of roots of various Brazilian rain-forest plants, such as *Mapouria cephalantha* Muell., in the outer layer of nests of *Anoplotermes pacificus* may be a response by these plants to special substances in the nests of the termites. In abandoned nests the roots are dead and in partially abandoned nests the roots are alive only in the areas still maintained by the termites. The roots provide the termites with food (see p. 18) and old roots inside the nest that are unable to furnish nutrients are enveloped by the termites with a papery layer of excrement. The net effect of these factors will vary according to the general climate (both past and present) of the region, the species of plants available for colonization of mounds and the nature of the mounds (i.e. the identity of the termites and the source of mound material). The latter aspect has often been neglected, which makes it difficult to compare the observations of different authors from different regions.

Harris (1961) considered that the large termite mounds in Africa played a useful role in the regeneration of vegetation after interference by man through clearing, burning, and over-grazing. Sillans (1959) in Oubangi-Chari and Thomas (1941) on the Sese Islands in Lake Victoria, have described the seral succession of vegetation on termite mounds. Initial colonization is by grasses on stable (i.e. fully grown or abandoned) mounds, followed by shrubs and finally tall trees. Where conditions are favourable these islands of woodland increase in size until they merge with each other and produce a closed canopy forest. In drier areas the spread of woodland, such as "miombo", into areas where man has obliterated the original vegetation is similarly preceded by the development of large termite mounds (Harris, 1961). However, in these drier areas there is little or no spread outwards from the immediate vicinity of the mounds.

B. RETARDATION OF GROWTH

The large termite mounds of Africa and Asia appear to be the only mounds which support a distinct vegetation. In both these continents there are many smaller mounds, such as those built by various species of *Cubitermes* and *Amitermes,* which do not support plant growth and the same is true of small mounds, such as those built by various species of *Amitermes, Tumulitermes, Coptotermes* and *Nasutitermes* in Australia. The only large mounds in Australia are those of *Nasutitermes triodiae* (Fig. 17, p. 43) and these do not support vegetation either while occupied or when abandoned and severely eroded. Similarly, Goodland (1965) noted that large, occupied mounds (species of termite not identified) in the northern Rupununi area of Guyana did not support vegetation; eroded mounds, however, did support plant growth (see above). In Africa Murray (1938) in the Transvaal, Nye (1955) in Nigeria, Glover (1949) unpublished in Glover *et al.* (1964) in Zambia noted a lack of plant growth on occupied mounds. It appears that occupied mounds under active construction do not support vegetation and lack of growth on stable (i.e. fully grown or eroded) mounds appears to be due to steep-sidedness and hardness or a combination of these factors. The hard basal core of mounds of *Nasutitermes triodiae* in northern Australia probably prevents the growth of plants on eroded mounds. Watson and Gay (1970) attributed the limitation of plant growth (for up to 30 years) on eroded areas of mulga (*Acacia* spp.) in south-western Queensland to the exposure at the surface of the hardened tops of subterranean nests of *Drepanotermes rubriceps* and *D. perniger* and their resistance to water-penetration and seed lodgement. Glover (1949 unpublished, in Glover *et al.,* 1964) regarded hardness as the factor responsible for the absence of vegetation on occupied mounds around Abercorn (Zambia). Colonization of the large mounds of certain African Macrotermitinae already referred to may not start until rain has eroded steep-sided surfaces into gentler contours.

Some mounds may actively inhibit the growth of plants. We have shown

(p. 149) that the carton material (excreta) in the mounds of the wood-eating species *Nasutitermes exitiosus* depresses microbial activity. We have also observed that eroded mounds which are no longer hard or steep-sided, such as those of *Nasutitermes magnus* in eastern Queensland, do not support vegetation, and toxic substances may be involved in such cases.

II. Growth of Vegetation Around Termitaria

Many termites construct covered runways which may be "tunnel-like" or in the form of "sheets" over the soil-surface or the base of vegetation. There is no information on the effects of this soil on plant growth, but Adamson (1943) suggested that certain epiphytes in the rain forests of Trinidad may be at least partly dependent on soil carried up into the trees by termites. There is also a lack of information on the effects of the network of subterranean galleries, concentrated in the vicinity of nests, on the growth of plants. In general, distinctive patterns of vegetation around mounds appear to result from the deposition around the mound of material eroded from the mound by rain.

Many mounds, particularly the larger ones, have their base surrounded by soil which has obviously been eroded from the mound. These areas are often bare and in Australia we have noticed such bare areas around the base of mounds of *Nasutitermes exitiosus, Coptotermes lacteus, Amitermes laurensis, Nasutitermes triodiae,* and occasionally *Drepanotermes* spp. Saunders (1969) noted that the basal area around mounds (probably *Amitermes laurensis*) in north Queensland was often free of grass but supported "Townsville lucerne", a valuable legume in the pastures of this region. However, this is not a general phenomenon as in many areas of north Queensland we have observed grass growing around the base of mounds of this species. In certain semi-desert areas of northern Somali, Macfadyen (1950) found that large termite mounds (probably Macrotermitinae) appeared as a characteristic pattern of white dots on air-photographs. The pattern was due to bare areas around the base of mounds; these bare areas were estimated to be 20-40 m in diameter. In East Africa, Burtt (1942) noted that thickets which are confined to areas of soil washed from mounds (probably of Macrotermitinae) are composed of species normally found on hardpans. In Zambia (near Abercorn), Glover (1949) unpublished in Glover *et al.* (1964) found that the miniature hardpans at the base of mounds were almost bare, whereas in the Shinyanga district of Tanzania characteristic hardpan plants occurred around the base of mounds in *Commiphora-Acacia* scrub.

Thus it appears that the soil around the base of termite mounds is often bare or may be colonized by species of plants normally found on hardpans. It is not obvious from the literature why the area around some mounds remains bare while others appear to be readily colonized. The nature of the vegetation around the base of mounds depends, as already noted for the vegetation growing on the mounds themselves, on the general climate, the species of plants available for colonization, and the nature of the soil washed off the mounds; there is also the possibility that the soil contains substances which inhibit the growth of plants. The only detailed study of vegetation in the immediate vicinity of mounds is that of Glover *et al.* (1964) on the Loita plains in Kenya. In this area there is a distinct pattern of vegetation appearing as lines of rings or ellipses running at right angles to the contour. The rings on the interfluves are circles 6.5-10 m in diameter; those on the slope are ovate to elongate-ellipsoid with the narrowest end pointing downslope, being 6.5-10 m at their widest point and averaging 14 m in length. Each ring is associated with a mound of *Odontotermes* sp. and each ring consists of distinct communities of plants. Glover *et al.* (1964) suggested that this pattern was due to a response by plants to variations, on and around the mounds, in moisture and amounts of clay and salts washed off the mounds. Downslope from the mounds is a hard, compacted, impervious zone formed from clay washed off the mound; this hardpan supports a sparse, "short grass" vegetation. In contrast, the mounds themselves slow the movement of water flowing down the slope, with the result that there is greater penetration of water, and consequently more luxuriant vegetation ("tall grass" zone), immediately upslope and alongside the mounds.

CHAPTER 9

Agricultural Significance of Termites

The most significant effect of termites on man is the damage done to timber used in buildings and for other purposes, and some of these economically important species are soil-inhabitants. The activities of soil termites also impinge on man in various ways. Among their destructive effects are damage to underground cables and airfields (Ratcliffe *et al.,* 1952), earthen dams (Naudé, 1934), and irrigation ditches (Ghilarov, 1962). Among their beneficial effects are the use of termite mound material for making bricks (Drummond, 1888; Nazaroff, 1931) and pottery (Harris, 1961), for plastering walls and surfacing roads, pavements (Nazaroff, 1931) and tennis courts (Ratcliffe *et al.,* 1952); termite mound have also been used as ovens (Drummond, 1888). Termites themselves are used as food in certain parts of the world (Hegh, 1922) and in northern Australia the didgeridoo (or didjeridu), which has been said to be one of the oldest musical instruments in the world, is made from parts of gum trees hollowed out by termites. In addition "works of art" made from pieces of timber partly eaten by termites are currently on sale in Australia.

Harris (1954) stated that "the farmer in the tropics, unless living at an altitude sufficient to produce a temperate climate, has to compete with termites for the timberwork of his home and farm buildings as well as for his fences and such parts of his implements as may be made of wood, and upon all of which his success depends. While growing crops may not often be damaged, they become liable to be eaten by termites as soon as they ripen. On the other hand, it is a matter of speculation as to what a farm would be like without the scavenging activities of the subterranean termites, and the part they play in the breaking down of plant residues, returning the component parts to the soil. Soil fertility depends on the life which goes on beneath the surface, and in many parts of the tropics the termite appears to be an important part of this life, and therefore of some potential significance to soil fertility generally." With the exception of damage to buildings, fences, etc., which is beyond the scope of this book, the agricultural significance of termites can be considered under the following categories:

1. Damage to economically important plants

2. Acceleration of erosion
3. Use of mounds as a fertilizer or as a substrate for growing crops
4. Effects on the decomposition of organic matter
5. Effects on soil properties that influence plant growth
6. Control

I. Damage to Economically Important Plants

A. DAMAGE TO FORESTS

Termites are one of the most important insect pests in certain forests (Harris, 1955, 1961, 1966, 1969; Greaves, 1962b) and many of the most destructive species have some contact with the soil. For instance, the most injurious species in Australian forests, *Coptotermes acinaciformis*, is a soil inhabitant, building its nests either within trees or in mounds (Ratcliffe *et al.*, 1952; Gay and Calaby, 1970). The economic loss may be great as Greaves *et al.* (1967) estimated that in virgin *Eucalyptus pilularis* Sm. forest termites (*C. acinaciformis* and *C. frenchi*) were responsible for 92% of the total loss and in less mature forest the corresponding figure was 64%; the revenue from felled trees averaged A$149.00/ha but the loss in royalties due to defects averaged A$299.00/ha. In parts of Africa damage to indigenous trees is rare whereas introduced trees, particularly *Eucalyptus* spp., are often severely attacked; seedling trees appear to be particularly susceptible. In Brazil Fonseca (1950) reported attacks by *Syntermes* on *Eucalyptus* seedlings resulting in the loss of 70% of the plants.

B. DAMAGE TO ORCHARDS, PLANTATIONS, AND CROPS

Less significant, but often locally important, is the damage to orchards and crops. In tropical Africa the damage to crops may be severe (Bernard, 1964; MacGregor, 1950; Harris, 1954, 1961, 1969). Hill (1921) and Ratcliffe *et al.* (1952) reported damage to a wide variety of crops, fruit trees and ornamental trees in northern Australia, the majority of damage being attributed to *Mastotermes darwiniensis.* In southern Australia *Coptotermes acinaciformis* and *C. frenchi* cause damage to fruit trees. In Asia a wide range of crops is attacked and tea sustains particularly high losses (Chatterji *et al.*, 1958; Jepson, 1929; MacGregor, 1950; Newsam and Rao, 1958; Thakur *et al.*, 1958; UNESCO and Zoological Survey of India, 1962).

Harris (1954) also notes that there are many areas in the tropics where mulches would be of great value in the dry season, but the practice of mulching is not followed because termites consume the mulch too rapidly for it to be of any value.

C. DAMAGE TO PASTURES

Grass-eating termites are often numerous in tropical and sub-tropical grasslands grazed by stock. Occasionally, spectacular effects of their activity resulting in almost complete denudation and leading to accelerated erosion have been reported. These incidents have been well documented in South Africa (Naudé, 1934; Coaton, 1951, 1954; Anon., 1960; Hartwig, 1955, 1966) where the species responsible for damage are largely harvester termites of the sub-family Hodotermitinae, but certain Nasutitermitinae (e.g. *Trinervitermes* spp.) and Macrotermitinae have also been implicated. Hodotermitinae do not appear to cause much damage to virgin veld (Coaton, 1954). Denudation by these species follows an increase in numbers to "saturation level" which is usually a consequence of overgrazing (see p. 85), and prevention is largely a problem of stock management. Apparently certain areas in Zululand have had their carrying capacity decreased by 25% annually due to harvester termites (Anon., 1960) before control measures were applied. In semi-arid regions of Central Asia (Bilova, 1949; Luppova, 1958) the hodotermitid *Anacanthotermes ahngerianus* is a pest of pastures with a dense cover of grass, and the bare areas around the nests of this species may occupy 20% of the surface. In Australia instances of denudation are rare (Ratcliffe *et al.*, 1952). One instance has been documented by Watson and Gay (1970) in south-west Queensland, where denudation was caused by *Drepanotermes rubriceps* and *D. perniger*. A succession of favourable seasons had promoted prolific growth of native grasses and consequently the termites built up to dense populations. Denudation occurred during the ensuing dry period and denuded areas included some on which no stock had been grazed. Instances of "sick" grassland in southern Australia (Ratcliffe *et al.*, 1952) have been associated with, and attributed to, large populations of subterranean termites (*Amitermes neogermanus* probably being the species involved).

The large populations of grass-eating termites in northern Australia occur on native pastures where grazing is extensive rather than intensive and it has been suggested (Ratcliffe *et al.*, 1952) that they occur only on land of poor quality. This is possibly a circular argument although it is supported by the fact that in the Rupununi savanna of Guyana, Goodland (1965) found an exact and inverse relationship between the occurrence of termite mounds and the level of soil nutrients. He found that the termitaria were richer in nutrients than the surrounding soils. This was due to the incorporation of plant residues into the mound (see p. 118), which accounted for all of the difference between the level of nutrients in the termitaria and surrounding soils, but not for all of the difference between the latter and the soils where termites (i.e. termite mounds) were absent. Where the level of nutrients exceeded 280 kg/ha there were no termite mounds. In contrast to these observations is MacGregor's (1950) report that in Somalia "ant-hills" are numerous where grazing is good. Whether or not there is a relationship between the abundance of termitaria and the grazing-quality of the land it is certain that grass-eating termites remove considerable quantities of vegetation which could possibly be utilized by grazing animals. We (Wood and Lee, in press) have shown that competition among colonies of a grass- and debris-eating termite (*Amitermes laurensis*) is greater on native pastures heavily grazed by stock than on ungrazed or lightly grazed pastures. Thus as stocking rates increase, either by the use of fertilizers, irrigation, better quality grasses, or by the introduction of legumes into the pasture, competition among termites is also likely to increase. However, we do not know whether or not the termites are selective in their choice of grasses, nor do we know what proportion of the grass that they eat would normally be consumed by stock; Gay (1961) suggested that they mainly stored dead material which would be unattractive to stock. Saunders (1969) reported that on Cape Yorke Peninsula and the subcoastal areas of north Queensland there was no shortage of pasture but that in the low-rainfall (less than 635 mm per year) inland areas termites could render land of low cattle-carrying capacity almost valueless. After detailed studies of the grazing habits of kangaroos, Frith and Calaby (1969) concluded that in many areas there was little competition for food between kangaroos and other grazing animals. They suggested that kangaroos and stock were compatible in most pastoral regions under extensive systems of grazing. However, one cannot say, on the basis of present knowledge, whether or not grass-feeding termites can be ranked with kangaroos as low-level competitors to be tolerated and possibly "managed", or whether, like the rabbit, they should be more or less exterminated. In addition, any attempts to manage (or exterminate) termite populations must take into account their effects on the soil itself.

II. Acceleration of Erosion

Harris (1949a, b) considered that termites promoted loss of soil by erosion in the following ways:

(1) By removing the plant cover with resultant exposure of surface soil to erosive forces.

(2) By digesting or removing organic matter which would otherwise be incorporated into the soil and thus making the soil more susceptible to erosion.

(3) By bringing to the surface soil which, due to its reduced content of organic matter, had less resistance to erosion by water and wind.

The first point is well illustrated by the denudation of the South African veld by grass-feeding harvester termites (Hodotermitinae). Denudation leads to accelerated erosion as the encroaching Karoo (scrub) does not protect the soil, whereas the grass it replaces binds the soil very efficiently (Coaton, 1954; Anon., 1960). The end result is the silting up of lakes and transformation of veld into wasteland. Accelerated erosion, following denudation of grass-cover by *Drepanotermes,* in south-west Queensland has been noted by Watson and Gay (1970).

The second point is very difficult to assess as one does not know what would happen to the organic matter (plant debris) in the absence of termites. Possibly it would accumulate undecomposed and become a fire hazard.

The third point was noted by Drummond (1888) who described how termite mounds and above-ground earthen runways were eroded by rain and wind on the 1500 m high plateau between Lakes Nyasa and Tanganyika and the debris carried away in streams and rivers. He concluded by remarking on how Herodotus had described Egypt as the "gift of the Nile", but that "... had he lived today he might have carried his vision farther back still and referred some of it to the labours of the humble termites in the forest slopes about Victoria Nyanza". On ancient landscapes the erosion of soil brought above the ground by termites is sometimes an important soil-forming process. This subject has already been discussed in some detail (p. 153). However, the observations of Nye (1954) and Williams (1968) are of agricultural significance in that in the absence of the erosion of soil from termitaria, the surface soil, instead of being a gravel-free, loamy sand, would have been predominantly stony.

Isolated instances of erosion resulting from excess drainage of water through subterranean galleries of termites have been reported by Naudé (1934) in the Transvaal and Ghilarov (1962) near Samarkand. In the latter case the whole of the water in irrigation ditches passed into the subterranean passages constructed by termites, resulting in erosion of subsoil and consequent collapse of the ground surface.

III. Use of Mounds for Growing Crops

The relative fertility of termite mounds and the adjacent soil has, as we have already noted (p. 107), received much attention. The results are often conflicting due largely to the differences between soils and between the habits of different species of termites and, unfortunately, in some published work neither soils nor termites have been identified. Nevertheless, it is worth considering some aspects of the practice, which is fairly widespread in parts of Africa and Asia, of growing crops on termite mounds or on land where termite mounds have been levelled.

Large termite mounds (species not identified) are common on grey soils near Soekamandi in Java. Doop (1938) reported that sisal grew better on the mounds than on the intervening flat land and that levelling of the mounds increased productivity on the intervening areas. Hesse (1955) also reported better growth of sisal on large mounds of various species of Macrotermitinae (*Macrotermes falciger, M. subhyalinus* and *M. natalensis*) in East Africa and attributed this partly to the response of sisal, a calciphile, to the high content of calcium carbonate in the mounds, and partly to the better drainage and better soil structure of the mounds. In some cases the latter factors appeared to be the most important as the surrounding soils are often heavy, compact and subject to waterlogging. Pendleton (1941, 1942) reported conflicting results from Thailand. In the flat lowlands rice is the principal crop but various typical "upland" crops, such as native cotton, tobacco, sugar cane and chillies, are planted and grow well on termitaria scattered throughout the paddy fields. Sometimes the termite mounds are levelled and in certain areas, particularly where there are supposedly "better" soils, there is greater growth of tobacco on the levelled termitaria than on the intervening land, whereas in other areas growth is retarded on the levelled termitaria. Joachim and Kandiah (1940) reported similarly conflicting opinions on the growth of crops on areas where mounds had been levelled although, in general, many crops in the "chena" (shifting cultivation) lands of Ceylon grew better on termite mounds (built by *Odontotermes redemanni*) than on the surrounding land. Nye (1955) reported that annual crops, such as maize, grew relatively poorly on levelled or collapsed mounds of *Macrotermes bellicosus* in Nigeria.

A slightly different problem is presented by the large mounds of certain Macrotermitinae in Africa. In areas where they are particularly abundant these mounds present a serious obstacle to cultivation. Meyer (1960) investigated an area in the central Congo basin where these mounds (all were abandoned and dated from a drier period in the Quaternary) numbered 4-7/ha and occupied 30% of the ground surface (see p. 44). The massive, central part of these mounds is constructed from subsoil, which is very infertile, and indiscriminate levelling of the mounds, without preserving the surrounding topsoil, results in large, sterile patches of ground. However, crops could be successfully grown if the outer layer of the mound was scraped off and the central portion buried or dumped elsewhere.

Obviously the growth of crops on termite mounds, or on areas where mounds have been levelled, depends on the properties of the crops, the mounds, and the soils, and in no single situation have all these factors been adequately analysed. There is a further aspect, not mentioned in the literature, which could be of general significance. We have shown (p. 149) that the organic fraction (that is the carton-like material which is composed largely of termite excrement) of mounds of *Nasutitermes exitiosus* inhibits microbial activity. The inhibitory substances have not been identified and it is not known whether or not the mounds of other species of termites contain these substances. However, if the occurrence of toxic substances in termite excreta is a general phenomenon then, in addition to being found in termitaria, these substances will occur in the galleries of subterranean termites which are particularly abundant in many areas in the tropics and also in semi-arid areas outside the tropics (for example in "mallee" country in southern Australia). Certain instances of "soil toxicity" could possibly be related to the accumulation in the soil of inhibitory substances from the nest-systems of termites.

Termite mounds also have other incidental uses in agriculture. Tobacco farmers around Mareeba in northern Queensland collect the carton material from mounds of *Coptotermes acinaciformis* and use the slowly-burning material to sterilize their seed-beds (Ratcliffe *et al.*, 1952). In parts of central Asia nitrate solonchaks are used by the population as nitrogenous fertilizers. In some areas the high nitrogen content of these soils may be related to termite activity, as Kozlova (1951) calculated that on certain takyr soils the nitrate reserve in termite mounds (probably *Anacanthotermes ahngerianus*; see also p. 109) amounted to 208 kg/ha. Hesse (1955) noted that in many areas of East Africa termite mounds are used as salt-licks by cattle and game animals.

IV. Effects on the Decomposition of Organic Matter

The role of soil animals in decomposing organic matter and incorporating organic matter into the soil has been the subject of a number of investigations in recent years. It has been shown that soil animals are important agents in the comminution of leaf litter in deciduous woodlands in Europe and North America (Edwards and Heath, 1963; Crossley and Witkamp, 1964; Drift, 1963; Kurcheva, 1960), tropical forests in Africa (Madge, 1965), and sclerophyll *Eucalyptus* forests in Australia (Wood, 1971). The groups of animals having the greatest influence on the rate of decomposition of leaf litter appear to be earthworms (Lumbricidae in Europe and North America, other families in the tropics and southern hemisphere), relatively large arthropods such as millipedes and larvae of various insects, and in some cases enchytraeid worms. Wood-eating termites, where they are present, are important agents in decomposing woody litter, such as branches, logs and tree stumps, and in regions where they are absent decomposition is achieved largely by a vast array of insects (see Kuhnelt, 1961), notably various beetles and their larvae. There is little information available on the role of soil animals in the decomposition of grass litter. Curry (1969) showed that the rate of decomposition of grass in a pasture in Eire was scarcely affected by the fauna, whereas Rhee (1963) demonstrated that earthworms (Lumbricidae) consumed significant amounts of grass-litter. One would think that grass-, litter- and humus-feeding termites would significantly influence the rate of decomposition of organic matter in certain grasslands, such as tropical and sub-tropical savannas, where they are often very abundant, but there is no information available on the subject. Occasionally the dung of grazing animals is a significant source of organic matter and its decomposition is strongly influenced by soil fauna, notably various Coleoptera (Bornemissza, 1960; Gillard, 1967) and, in some cases, termites (Ferrar and Watson, 1970).

In agricultural environments, particularly those where there is intensive cultivation and application of fertilizers, the contribution of soil animals to the circulation of organic matter and nutrients is of little significance. However, under less intensive systems of management, particularly where there is little or no cultivation of the soil, the decomposition of organic matter by soil animals is of some importance and there are spectacular instances of the beneficial effects of accelerated litter breakdown following the introduction of earthworms (Rhee, 1963; Stockdill, 1966) and the accumulation of litter following the elimination of earthworms (Raw, 1962).

As the role of termites in the cycling of organic matter and nutrients has received little attention it is not surprising that there is little information available on their significance from this point of view, under agricultural conditions. Under extensive systems of management, such as forestry, termites can make a significant contribution to the decomposition of organic matter, although assessments of whether this is beneficial or deleterious have yet to be made. Maldague's (1964) investigations of a termite population (dominated by a humivorous species, *Cubitermes fungifaber*) in a forest site in the Congo indicated that approximately half the annual litter fall was consumed by termites, although the errors in his calculations (see p. 91 and p. 134) reduce this figure to approximately one tenth or less. Our own work with *Nasutitermes exitiosus* in dry sclerophyll forest indicates that this species consumes 16-17% of total annual fall of woody litter, and residues of digestion are withheld from the plant/soil system for many years (see p. 132). Hopkins (1966), working in Nigeria, concluded that the rate of decay of wood was largely dependent on the activities of termites. He distributed pieces of wood in three habitats; a moist deciduous forest, a derived savanna, and a moist evergreen forest. The percentage of samples attacked by termites in these three areas was 34%, 33%, and 2% respectively. A 50% loss in weight of the samples in the first two sites occurred after 2-8 months but had not been achieved at all in the last of these sites after 15 months. MacGregor (1950) noted that the decomposition of fellings and leaf-litter in forests by termites may be beneficial

Use has been made in some areas of the rapidity with which wood is attacked by termites. In the Sudan, Dinka tribesmen follow the practice of felling trees and shrubs and stacking the timber to a depth of about 0.5 m. After a few months the branchwood is destroyed by termites and the subsequent release of nutrients into the soil boosts the fertility of poor or depleted land (Burnett, 1948). Harris (1955) reported that this practice, as opposed to burning, in Malawi had a pronounced beneficial effect on soil fertility

V. Effects on Soil Properties that Influence Plant Growth

Excluding "above-ground" factors, growth of plants depends on the availability of water and nutrients in the soil, and the ability of the plant roots to exploit these resources. Termites affect nutrient availability by transporting soil and organic matter to mounds and other structures, from which they are redistributed by erosion and decomposition. They affect root growth through their influences on soil structure, pore space, permeability, water-holding capacity, aggregation and stability of aggregates (see pp. 100-107).

A. EFFECTS ON AVAILABILITY OF NUTRIENTS

The termite colony is very largely a self-enclosed system, particularly in those species with a well-developed, concentrated nest-system. Nutrients can be returned to the ecosystem in three ways:

(a) By predation.
(b) By accession of the bodies of alates and other castes.
(c) By decomposition of epigeal structures (mounds, covered runways, etc.).

Predation, quantitatively, is an unknown factor (see p. 82).

Ghilarov (1962) noted that after mass flights of termites in Central Asia depressions in the soil surface became covered with the wings of termites. From the figures of Ratcliffe et al. (1952), Bouillon and Mathot (1964), Bouillon (1970) and Sands (1965b) on annual production of alates from individual colonies, and the figures of Wood and Lee (in press), Bouillon and Mathot (1964), Bouillon (1970) and Sands (1965a) on the abundance of occupied mounds, we have calculated (on the basis of a nitrogen content of 10% in the termite body) the total amount of nitrogen leaving the colony annually in the bodies of alates to be: 1.4-7.0 mg/m^2 for *Nasutitermes exitiosus* in dry sclerophyll forest in southern Australia, 4.0 mg/m^2 for *Cubitermes exiguus* in savanna in the Congo and 7.0 mg/m^2 for *Trinervitermes geminatus* in savanna in Nigeria. The vast majority of alates perish before being able to establish a colony and possibly in areas of low rainfall, where there is little leaching of soluble salts, the bodies of termites make a significant contribution to the accession of nitrogen.

From our discussion of the chemical effects of termites on soils (p. 107) it is apparent that at least some termite mounds and other structures contain, relative to the surrounding soil, more carbon, nitrogen, calcium, slightly more potassium, and more exchangeable calcium, magnesium, and potassium. With the exception of the large concentrations of calcium in some mounds of Macrotermitinae these elements are derived ultimately from food brought into the mound by the termites. Eventual re-distribution of these elements by erosion and decomposition enriches the surrounding soils; we have shown that the rate of turnover may be relatively rapid (5-10 years) or exceedingly slow (up to 100 years). The question is: how does this compare, qualitatively and quantitatively, with what would happen in the absence of termites? We do not know, and to our knowledge no attempt has been made to solve this question. It is possible that the nutrients in trees, logs, and other woody material may be withheld from circulation longer in the absence than in the presence of wood-eating termites. On the other hand, nutrients in grass and litter may be returned to the soil more quickly in the absence of termites, by virtue of the activities of other soil organisms or other agencies, such as fire. The effects of "humus-feeding" termites and termites without a concentrated nest-system may bear more resemblance to the effects of other soil animals (insects, earthworms, etc.). Possibly humus-feeding termites, which are very abundant in parts of Africa and South America but may be absent from Australia (see p. 16), contribute to the low content of organic matter in many African soils. They feed on soil rich in organic matter and, if their digestive processes are as efficient as those of wood-, litter- and grass-eating termites (see p. 125), their excreta probably has a low content of organic matter and nutrients. These are only suppositions but, in the absence of any evidence on this subject, could at least be useful in suggesting future lines of research.

In this connection it is worth noting that information is available on the contribution of some groups of soil animals to nutrient cycling. Satchell (1963) estimated that the nitrogen turnover (excreted nitrogen and return of nitrogen in dead tissue) of *Lumbricus terrestris* L. in deciduous woodland in northern England was 100 kg/ha/year, which is equal to the annual accession of nitrogen in the litter fall, although litter is not the only source of nitrogen for earthworms. This return of nitrogen to the ecosystem was several times larger than the annual retention of nitrogen by trees. Few, if any, species in these habitats are as significant as *L. terrestris*; for instance Bocock (1963) found that the millipede *Glomeris marginata* (Villers) consumed 1.7-10% of the total annual litter fall of deciduous woodland.

B. EFFECTS ON SOIL STRUCTURE

Although there have been few specific studies on the effects of termites on soil structure (see p. 104) we know that their subterranean galleries accelerate the infiltration and penetration of water and increase porosity; on the other hand, the formation of hardpans around certain mounds (see p. 166) has the opposite effect. On pale grey soils in the Golodnaya Steppe of Central Asia plants apparently grow better on areas where there are termites and Ghilarov (1962) attributed this to the beneficial effects of termites on soil structure. These observations in themselves cannot be taken as evidence of the beneficial effects of termites on soil structure as differences in nutrient status (particularly nitrogen, see pp. 108, 174) between areas where termites are present and areas where they are absent are also likely to affect the growth of plants. It is likely, however, that there is a beneficial effect on structure, particularly in heavy-textured soils, as Hopp and Slater (1948) showed experimentally that the burrowing activities of ants (*Tetramorium caespitosum* L.) resulted in a two-fold increase in yield of vegetation.

Stockdill (1966) showed that the yield of certain pastures in New Zealand was greatly increased by the introduction of lumbricid earthworms. He attributed this increase in productivity partly to improvement in soil structure, but other factors were also involved (see p. 182). It is not clear how significant are the improvements to soil structure compared with other factors, but Hopp and Slater (1948) showed that improvements to structure are probably the most significant factor in the response of plants to earthworm activity. In many semi-arid or seasonally semi-arid areas, particularly in the tropics, earthworms are scarce and termites are one of the dominant groups of soil animals. We know that a few of these species are pests but we cannot make even an educated guess as to the overall effects of the vast majority of the termite fauna on plant productivity.

VI. Control

A detailed treatment of this subject is outside the scope of this book, but we will briefly indicate the control methods used under a variety of circumstances.

A. CONTROL IN FORESTS

Wilkinson (1965) distinguished between termites having a restricted range (i.e. colonies confined to a single tree) and those having a free range (i.e. colonies capable of attacking several trees). In the first group are the Kalotermitidae and Termopsinae, the control of which centres largely around "tree hygiene", such as the clearing of dead wood both on the tree and on the forest floor. Termites with colonies not confined to a single tree and having the ability to infest several trees by way of runways within the soil or on the soil surface, often require treating with insecticides. Species such as *Coptotermes acinaciformis* and *C. frenchi* nesting within the trunks of mature trees (*Eucalyptus* spp.) can be killed by blowing arsenic trioxide dust into the nursery through an auger hole bored in the tree (Greaves *et al.*, 1967). In plantations, seedlings can be protected by mechanical cultivation and by using dieldrin in the planting holes (Sands, 1960b, 1962), and MacGregor (1950) reported that in some areas of Uganda control was achieved by removing queens from the nests.

B. CONTROL IN ORCHARDS, PLANTATIONS AND CROPS

As noted above, control of Kalotermitidae and Termopsinae is largely a matter of "tree hygiene". Prevention of attacks by Kalotermitidae on fruit trees, grape vines, tea bushes, rubber, coconuts and other plants is achieved by clearing dead timber, burning badly damaged plants and treating cavities, pruning scars and other injuries to the tree with insecticides (Andrews, 1924; Ferrero, 1959; Jepson, 1929; Richards, 1917; Thompson, 1933; Wolfenberger, 1958).

Hill (1921) investigated various methods of chemical control in northern Australia, principally directed against the more or less omnivorous *Mastotermes darwiniensis* which attacks plants via the soil.

(1) Soil fumigation with carbon disulphide gave only temporary control and was expensive.

(2) Soil treatment with insecticides (lead arsenate and mercuric chloride) was effective and this method has been widely used since by application of insecticides either in planting holes around the base of the plants, or by broadcasting. Various insecticides have been successfully employed including BHC (Newsam and Rao, 1958), DDT (Chatterji *et al.*, 1958), aldrin and dieldrin (Thakur *et al.*, 1958) and arsenic trioxide (Fonseca, 1950).

(3) Trials with poisoned baits (bran moistened with arsenical solutions) were inconclusive, although Hill suggested that the method might be satisfactory for controlling *Mastotermes darwiniensis,* and in fact satisfactory control of this species in sugar cane was reported by Bates (1926) following the use of poisoned bait and clearing of timber around the cane fields. Poisoned baits are used with success in South Africa (Naudé, 1934; Coaton, 1950).

(4) Fumigation of hollow trunks and roots with fumes of arsenic and sulphur effectively prevented further damage but was more expensive than injection of insecticides.

(5) A suspension of lead arsenate in water gave effective control following injection into the hollow trunks of citrus, mango, and other trees, although Thompson (1933) found that injection of paris-green into citrus trees (to control Kalotermitidae) rendered the fruit more acid.

Cultural and management practices have also beeen frequently employed to combat termites in orchards, plantations and various crops. The clearing of timber around cane fields in Australia to prevent attack by *Mastotermes* has already been noted. MacGregor (1950) has reported that in Somalia damage to crops is not serious if the soil is well cultivated, and in general, cultivation would appear to be effective mainly by destroying subterranean gallery-systems. Attacks by termites on cotton have been countered by close spacing of the seedlings (Pearson and Maxwell-Darling, 1958), fallowing (Crowther and Barlow, 1943), and by growing different varieties (Harris, 1954). Where practicable, the addition of well-rotted compost may be advantageous as Harris (1954) noted that in East African gardens the risk of termite damage to growing crops could be markedly reduced if the humus content of the soil was maintained at a high level. The emphasis here would be on well-composted material, as the addition of raw plant debris (e.g. as in mulches) would attract the species of termites likely to attack growing plants.

Destruction of the termite colony itself has been practised for a long time, in the case of those species that build conspicuous mounds, by breaking open the nest and removing the queen (Naudé, 1934; MacGregor, 1950; Hartwig, 1966). The method is generally ineffective (Coaton, 1950) as the queen may be replaced, there may be several queens in the nest only one of which is destroyed, or the damage may be caused by other species of termites. A more certain method of killing the colony is by poisoning. Fumigation with substances such as carbon disulphide, benzene hexachloride, and a 3 : 1 mixture of burning arsenic trioxide and sulphur (Hartwig, 1966), or the introduction of arsenic trioxide dust (Holdaway and Hill, 1936) or aldrin (Sands, 1962) into the nursery chambers, are all effective. The latter method is probably more certain in that the poison is disseminated throughout the colony by termites themselves during the process (trophallaxis) of mutual licking, grooming, and exchange of nutrients.

It is only in South Africa that the depredations of termites in pastures have been considered sufficiently injurious to merit the adoption of extensive control measures. Successful control is achieved by baiting (Coaton, 1954), using chaffed hay poisoned with sodium fluosilicate. The major disadvantages appear to be a shortage of hay in certain areas and the dangers to livestock and other animals from the sodium fluosilicate.

We have noted the abundance and wide distribution of grass and grass- and litter-feeding termites in various parts of the world, particularly in northern Australia (p. 74 and p. 86), and have indicated (p. 171) that, with a few exceptions, so little is known about their habits that we do not know whether their presence is harmful or beneficial. Generally speaking they are most numerous on land that, currently, is of low value and thus control measures must be inexpensive. For instance, injurious populations of *Drepanotermes* in southern Queensland (Watson and Gay, 1970; see also p. 170 and p. 172) occurred on land worth A$5.00/ha. Control was attempted by "contour ripping" which resulted in the flooding of colonies after rain, and by piping dieldrin into furrows on a 20 metre grid. These methods gave a significant reduction in numbers but not an effective control. It would appear that on land of this type control measures, if they are deemed necessary, will largely revolve around management practices. However, for their successful adoption, such procedures require a good knowledge of the ecology of the termites and, in general, this information is lacking.

CHAPTER 10

Some Ecological Comparisons

Our primary aim has been to assess the role of termites as soil animals. In conclusion, we shall attempt to compare their influence on the soil with that of some other soil animals, especially earthworms, for which data are available, and to assess their significance in the ecosystem.

I. Comparison of Termites with Other Soil Animals

A. EARTHWORMS

Termites have long been regarded as the analogues in tropical soils of earthworms in the soils of temperate regions (Drummond, 1886, and many others subsequently). There is some truth in the analogy, in that both groups are often found in great numbers, dominating the soil fauna, both make burrows that are prominent features of soil profiles, and both physically re-sort soil horizons. However, there are considerable differences between the two groups of animals in their effects on soils.

1. *Populations*

Populations of lumbricid earthworms in temperate regions range from extremely low ($<1/m^2$ and $<1 g/m^2$) in acid, moorland soils (Svendsen, 1957), through intermediate densities approaching $200/m^2$ (up to $100 g/m^2$) in woodlands (Bornebusch, 1930; Edwards and Heath, 1963) and pastures (Kollmannsperger, 1934), to maximum densities exceeding $450/m^2$ ($200 g/m^2$ or more) in some grasslands (Raw, 1959; Stöckli, 1949; Waters, 1955). There is less information on other groups of earthworms. Madge (1965) estimated the population (probably all Eudrilidae) in Nigerian tropical forest as $34/m^2$ ($10 g/m^2$), Wood (1971) estimated densities of $49/m^2$ to $105/m^2$ ($17 g/m^2$ to $41 g/m^2$) for Megascolecidae in montane soils in the Snowy Mountains, Australia, and Lee (1959) estimated densities of $75/m^2$ to $100/m^2$ for Megascolecidae in soils of New Zealand lowland tussock grasslands.

Comparisons of metabolic activity of populations of termites, earthworms, and some other groups of soil animals are discussed on p. 93, and it is concluded that the metabolism of termites in tropical soils is probably of the same order as that of the groups defined by Macfadyen (1963) as "large herbivores" and "large decomposers" (the latter group includes earthworms) of soil-inhabiting invertebrates in temperate woodlands.

2. Physical Effects on Soils

The principal physical effects of earthworms on soils result from their burrowing, ingestion of soil and organic matter, and deposition of casts on the soil surface or beneath the surface. In soils with large earthworm populations their burrows may account for up to 67% of the total air space (Satchell, 1958), although Stockdill (1966) reported a reduction of macro-porosity in New Zealand pastures with large populations of *Allolobophora caliginosa* (Sav.). Satchell concluded that where earthworm populations are large they enhance soil aeration, drainage and water absorption, and under some circumstances limit soil erosion by reducing run-off. Despite the reduction in macro-porosity, Stockdill found increases in field capacity, available moisture, and infiltration rates in soils with large populations of *A. caliginosa* compared with soils without *A. caliginosa*. He attributed these increases to improvement in soil structure, due to the casts of the earthworms. Satchell (1958) reviewed the evidence for stability of worm-cast aggregates, and concluded that worm casts contain stable aggregates and enhance the crumb structure of fertile soils. The stability of the aggregates may result from (i) mechanical reinforcement of mineral soil by incorporation of ingested plant remains with the ingested soil; (ii) polysaccharide gums produced by the earthworms' intestinal bacteria; (iii) calcium humate, which is a powerful stabilizing agent, produced in the worm's intestine from ingested decomposing organic matter; (iv) mucoid substances excreted by bacterial colonies in the casts, or (v) inhibition of bacterial growth in casts due to antibiotics secreted by actinomycetes, which increase in numbers during the passage of soil through the intestine.

The physical effects of termites on soils are rather different. "Humus-feeding" termites habitually ingest mineral soil (p. 16), and in this respect resemble earthworms. They use an intimate mixture of excreted mineral and organic materials, together with soil transported in the mouth parts, for construction of their termitaria. Other termites ingest only organic matter, but select, excavate and carry mineral soil particles, which are cemented together to construct nests or mounds. Their subterranean galleries, apart from those in termitaria, are access channels connecting the termitarium to sources of food, water or materials for construction. No data exist on the total space occupied by subterranean galleries. There is little evidence in Australia that galleries are often sufficiently numerous to have much effect on porosity, except in termitaria themselves, but in Africa and Asia, where subterranean Macrotermitinae and various "humus-feeding" termites are often very abundant, there may be a considerable effect on total pore space and the nature and distribution of pores. Re-sorted soil used for construction is often packed so that little pore space remains (p. 30), and cemented so that it inhibits infiltration of water. Gallery linings frequently consist of repacked mineral soil, and are often cemented with faecal material. Soil is moved to the surface by species that construct mounds or earth sheetings over food sources, and by those that pack soil in disused feeding galleries in logs, etc. (p. 155). The soil is often derived from deep soil horizons, and it is eventually eroded and spread on the soil surface, so tending to invert soil profiles (p. 152). The amount of soil so moved is less, probably by at least one order of magnitude, than that deposited on the surface as casts by large populations of lumbricid earthworms, but these earthworms have their burrows mainly in the A horizon and do not move large quantities of soil from deep horizons to the surface.

3. Chemical Effects on Soils

The common misconception that earthworms feed on soil has led to many comparisons between the composition of worm casts and surrounding soils, and to the conclusion that digestion of soil by earthworms results in increases in content of plant nutrients. Earthworms do ingest soil, but their energy is derived mainly from digestion of plant tissue, which is collected from the soil surface or selected from the soil, and their casts consist of a mixture of soil and plant debris. Satchell (1958) concluded that increases in base-exchange capacity, total exchangeable bases, total and exchangeable calcium, exchangeable potassium and magnesium, available phosphorus, and organic matter in worm casts relative to surrounding soils all result from incorporation of organic matter in the casts. He quoted experiments of Nye (1955), in which the total nutrient content of soil in pots where earthworms had been active for four months did not differ from that of soil in pots without earthworms. Changes in chemical composition of soil that has been worked by termites are similar and are also attributable to the incorporation of organic matter (see Chapter 5). Earthworms do not concentrate organic matter in central nests or mounds, as many termites do, but incorporate it into the soil more or less *in situ.*

Satchell (1963) examined the effects of *Lumbricus terrestris* L. on the turnover of nitrogen in the soils of woodland in northern England. He concluded that turnover by this species was of the order of 100 kg/ha of nitrogen per year. Estimates of litter fall and its nitrogen content showed that the amount cycled by the earthworms was at least equivalent to the supply from litter. Laverack (1963) quoted analyses by Heidermanns (1937), and Abdel-Fattah (1957), showing that 85-100% of the nitrogen excreted as urine by *L. terrestris* is in the form of ammonia or urea, both of which are readily available to soil micro-organisms. Nitrogen excreted by termites is probably mainly in the form of uric acid or urates (Moore, 1969), and much of it is incorporated in mounds or nests, where it is not readily available to soil micro-organisms.

4. Effects on Organic Matter

The ability of earthworms to digest the principal components of plant tissue is much less than that of termites. A little of the cellulose from ingested plant tissue is probably digested by many species of earthworms, but it can not be their principal source of energy, as it is for termites. Laverack (1963) listed the enzymes lichenase, protease, cellulase, chitinase, amylase, lipase, and perhaps invertase that have been recorded from the gut of earthworms. It has been suggested that the cellulase and chitinase might be produced by symbiotic micro-organisms, but Laverack concluded that these enzymes are probably produced by the earthworms themselves. Earthworms do not usually ingest plant tissue until it has been partially decomposed by micro-organisms, and some species may derive most of their energy from digestion of microbial or fungal tissue. Their principal effect on the plant tissue is probably comminution, which results in the exposure of a larger surface as a substrate for microbial decomposition. In contrast, many termites feed on sound wood, grass, or other undecomposed plant tissue; the ingested food is intensely degraded, and the end products excreted by some species (e.g. *Nasutitermes exitiosus*) are similar to the residual humic substances of soils, and not only contain little material that is readily available to micro-organisms but may actually depress microbial activity (Chapter 6).

5. Effects on Profile Morphology

Earthworms, when present in large numbers, greatly affect the morphology of soil profiles by (i) incorporating organic matter from the surface into superficial soil horizons; (ii) formation of stable aggregates; (iii) burying stones under layers of fine material cast at the surface; (iv) making burrows, often penetrating to deep soil horizons, which are subsequently in-filled with A horizon material washed down by percolating water; (v) possibly to some extent counteracting the process of podzolization by comminuting and mixing mineral and organic matter to produce colloidal materials (Powers and Bollen, 1935, in Satchell, 1958).

Termites affect soil profiles (see Chapter 7) by (i) transporting fine materials from deep soil horizons to the surface and using them for construction, thus tending to invert soil profiles; (ii) removing organic matter from wide areas and storing it in central nests or mounds; (iii) cementing superficial soil horizons; (iv) building mounds, which in some cases become semi-permanent features of the landscape and affect run-off and water infiltration; (v) making deep burrows, which, like those of earthworms, are subsequently in-filled with A horizon material washed down by percolating water; (vi) constructing numerous ramifying tunnels in the upper soil horizons.

Probably the most important difference between the effects of earthworms and termites on soil profiles is in their influence on the distribution of organic matter. Soil scientists in temperate regions have distinguished two basic humus forms—*mull*, in which plant debris is well-decomposed and intimately mixed with mineral soil in the A horizon, and there is little surface accumulation of litter, and *mor*, in which plant debris forms a surface layer of undecomposed and partly decomposed litter, sharply distinguished from underlying, predominantly mineral soil horizons. There are many intermediate forms (see Kubiena, 1955). *Mull* is usually associated with the presence of large populations of earthworms, which are probably largely responsible for litter incorporation, and *mor* with absence or paucity of earthworms and other litter-incorporating animals, such as diplopods and some insect larvae. Where termites are very numerous (except perhaps where the dominant species are humus-feeders) there appears to be neither *mull* nor *mor*, but a virtual absence of litter accumulation or of widespread incorporation of organic matter in the soil. This is likely to be most obvious in areas where the termite fauna is dominated by Macrotermitinae, as the termite-fungus association appears to utilize plant tissue more or less completely (p. 144). Unfortunately there have been no comprehensive studies of humus forms of soils where the fauna is dominated by termites.

6. Effects on Plant Growth

There are many reports of stimulation of plant growth and a few of damage to plants by earthworms. Stockdill (1966) has provided the only well authenticated evidence of stimulation of growth. He introduced *Allolobophora caliginosa* into soils supporting pastures of rye grass and clover, near Hindon, in New Zealand, and recorded increases of 72.6% in pasture yield compared with similar areas where *A. caliginosa* was not introduced. He attributed the stimulation of pasture growth to the earthworms' incorporating animal dung and dead plant tissue into the soil, thus improving soil structure, increasing available moisture (by up to 69% at 0-10 cm depth) and water infiltration rate (by >100%), increasing the content of exchangeable bases at depths down to 24 cm, incorporating DDT, applied for control of the pasture pest *Costelytra zealandica* (White) (Coleoptera; Melolonthinae), into the root zone of the pasture, and possibly by the secretion of plant growth substances (as was demonstrated by R. L. Nielson).

Effects of termites on plant growth are reviewed in Chapter 9. In general their effects are deleterious, and may lead to suppression of species that are favoured as food or, in extreme cases, to denudation of pastures. In addition, termitaria often profoundly affect the composition of the vegetation.

B. OTHER SOIL ANIMALS

There is comparatively little authenticated information of effects of soil animals, apart from earthworms, on soil formation and plant growth.

Nielsen (1963) investigated the range of carbohydrases possessed by 30 species of soil and litter invertebrates, including Oligochaeta, Isopoda, Diplopoda, Chilopoda, Insecta, and Gastropoda. Most species had the enzymes necessary for the hydrolysis of virtually all naturally occurring di- and trisaccharides, and also some sugars that they must rarely encounter. Among the polysaccharides, soluble starch and glycogen were hydrolyzed by all species. Cellulase was reported from earthworms, snails, slugs, and possibly from enchytraeid worms, diplopods, and tipulid larvae; its activity appeared to be low except in snails and slugs, which, unlike other groups, had active pectinase and xylanase. Nielsen concluded that, of the animals tested, probably only snails and slugs can decompose significant quantities of plant structural polysaccharides. He considered that the initial hydrolysis of such materials was primarily a function of the soil microflora, and that the chief importance of soil and litter invertebrates must be sought in their effect upon stimulation of the chemical activity of the microflora by comminution of plant litter.

The difference between the situation described by Nielsen and that where termites are dominant soil animals is obvious. Many termites are primary decomposers of plant tissue, while others are secondary decomposers. The significance of their contribution to the cycling of organic matter in the ecosystem is discussed below.

II. Significance of Termites in the Ecosystem

The food of termites (p. 5) includes a wide range of plant materials such as living wood, dead wood in various stages of decomposition, herbaceous plants and grasses, plant debris, fungi, dung and soil rich in organic matter (humus). Investigations in Africa (see Tables 8 and 10, p. 73 and p. 79 respectively; Emerson, 1949; Harris, 1963; Kemp, 1955) have shown that all, or the majority, of these feeding-groups may be found in certain habitats. In such areas a large proportion of the energy resource of the ecosystem is potentially available to termites. In this respect termites differ markedly from other soil animals, the majority of which are saprophagous, feeding on micro-organisms (fungi, etc.), humus and decomposing plant debris; only a minority feed on freshly fallen plant debris or on the tissues of living plants.

The most realistic means of assessing the significance of herbivores and decomposers in the ecosystem is by accounting for their food consumption and assimilation, respiration, and production (total material laid down as tissue and reproductive products; Macfadyen, 1967). All these factors can be quantified in terms of energy and, although no single ecosystem has been completely documented, some of the more significant contributions in this field have been summarized by Wiegert and Evans (1967). There have been few estimates of food consumption and assimilation by termites (p. 131), only one reliable estimate of respiration (p. 91), and we know of no estimates of production. In addition, some termites reingest their own excretory products and the majority use them for nest construction, and this too must be accounted for. Thus the impact of termites on the flow of energy through an ecosystem cannot be assessed at the present time. However, the following comparisons indicate that termites, where they are abundant, are likely to be one of the more important groups of organisms.

We have already (p. 93) compared the biomass and respiration of termites with that of soil animals in temperate woodland. There are no comparable figures for soil animals in the tropics, although the biomass of earthworms (10 g/m^2 in a Nigerian forest, Madge, 1965; $0.06\text{-}4.55 \text{ g/m}^2$ in various habitats in Uganda, Block and Banage, 1968) appears to be much lower than in many habitats in temperate regions (p. 181). Gillon and Gillon (1967) estimated the biomass of epigeal macro-arthropods (excluding ants and termites) in tropical savanna in the Ivory Coast at 1.3 g/m^2, which appears low in comparison with the biomass of single species of termites (Table 31) and our suggestion (p. 91) that the total biomass of termites may exceed 50 g/m^2. We have already noted (pp. 85, 170) that termites feeding on herbaceous plants and grasses may compete for food with herbivorous mammals. The biomass of termites and grazing animals in Africa and Australia are compared in Table 31. The figures for biomass of grazing mammals in Africa are not likely to be exceeded in natural habitats as the biomass of African herbivores appears to be considerably greater than in other parts of the world (e.g. kangaroos in Australia, Frith and Calaby, 1970—see Table 31; bison and other wild ungulates in North America ($2.4\text{-}3.5 \text{ g/m}^2$), Petrides 1956). The termites listed in Table 31 are humivores (*Cubitermes* spp.) or feed on dead wood (*Nasutitermes exitiosus*), but the abundance (up to $2600/\text{m}^2$) of the grass-harvesting *Trinervitermes geminatus* in Nigeria (Sands, 1965a, b; see also Tables 10 and 17) indicates that its biomass may exceed 10 g/m^2, which is similar to the highest recorded biomass of grazing mammals.

The only reliable estimate of termite respiration is for *Cubitermes exiguus* (Hébrant, 1964, 1967; Bouillon, 1970; see also Tables 15, p. 92, and 31) in steppe savanna in the Congo. The metabolism of $9.0\text{-}17.4 \text{ kcal/m}^2/\text{year}$ is of the same order of magnitude as that of the Uganda kob (*Adenota kob thomasi*

TABLE 31

Comparison of the Biomasses of Termites and Mammalian Herbivores in Africa and Australia

Species	Habitat	Biomass (g/m^2)	Author and reference
Termites			
Cubitermes fungifaber + unidentified spp.	Rain forest, Congo	11.0	Maldague (1964)
Cubitermes exiguus	Steppe savanna, Congo	1.3–1.9	Bouillon (1970)
Nasutitermes exitiosus	Dry sclerophyll forest, Australia	3.0	Lee and Wood (in press)
Mammalian herbivores			
Uganda kob	Savanna, Uganda	2.2	Beuchner and Golley (1967)
Wild ungulates (22 spp.)	Wooded savanna, Tanzania	12.3–17.5*	Lamprey (1964)
Wild ungulates + cattle	Open plains, Kenya	5.2–12.6*	Foster and Coe (1968)
Wild ungulates (17 spp.)	Bush savanna, Rhodesia	4.4*	Dasmann (1962)
Red kangaroo	Semi-arid woodland, Australia	0.013–0.100†	Frith and Calaby (1970)

*From Vos (1969).
†Calculated on the basis of mean weight of one kangaroo being 30 kg.

Neumann) of 61.7 kcal/m²/year (Beuchner and Golley, 1967) and the African elephant (*Loxodonta africana* Blumenbach) of 23.0 kcal/m²/year (Petrides and Swank, 1965), but greatly exceeds that of the red kangaroo (*Megaleia rufa* Desm.) of 0.13-0.99 kcal/m²/year (see Table 31 for biomass; S.M.R. of marsupials = 48.6 kcal/kg$^{3/4}$/day-T. G. Dawson, personal communication). Wiegert and Evans (1967) calculated from Lamprey's (1964) data (biomass given in Table 31) that the mean annual respiration of all large grazing mammals in the Tarangire Game Reserve (Tanzania) was 155 kcal/m². We suggested (p. 91) that the mean annual respiration of the total termite population may exceed 100 kcal/m² in certain habitats.

Engelmann (1966) examined the relationship between maintenance metabolism (= annual population respiration) and net productivity (= annual population production) for a wide range of animals and concluded that the animals fell into two groups, poikilotherms and homiotherms. This relationship has been examined in greater detail, and the distinction between the two groups confirmed, by McNeill and Lawton (1970). Poikilothermic animals are more efficient producers than homiothermic animals, that is for a given annual population respiration they have a greater annual population production. Engelmann (1966) noted that this apparent disadvantage of homiotherms was possibly offset by the fact that their efficiency of digestion and assimilation (approximately 70%) was greater than that (approximately 30%) of poikilotherms. Termite populations have not been considered from this point of view and, unfortunately, there is no information on their population production. However, unlike most poikilotherms, they have an extremely efficient digestive system (see p. 125) and if, like other poikilotherms, they are efficient producers they could have a significant influence on the rate and direction of energy flow in many ecosystems, even those, such as the African savannas, where large mammals appear to be dominant. A further important consideration is that termites tend to maintain a closed society in which dead and injured individuals are consumed by the termites themselves, and in which waste products are incorporated into termitaria. Eventually, the energy locked up in termite populations and their termitaria must be dissipated, and in this respect predation on termites and the decomposition of termitaria are of significance.

Macfadyen (1963, 1964) constructed a balance sheet for the total annual flow of energy through a temperate meadow supporting domestic cattle. Of the total energy captured by plant photosynthesis, less than one seventh is respired by the plants, two sevenths are consumed by herbivores and four sevenths are exploited by the "decomposer industry" after the plants have died. There are no comparable figures for tropical grasslands where termites are often very abundant and where they influence the flow of energy at both the herbivore and decomposer level. In such areas the relative respiration of herbivores and decomposers, and thus the fate of plant tissues (primary production), may be strongly influenced by the relative abundance of herbivorous and saprophagous termites.

Sampling Termite Populations

The fact that no estimate of the total termite population of any soil has ever been made is an indication of the difficulties involved in quantitative sampling of these animals. The nests of termites may be subterranean, on the ground surface, in fallen logs or tree stumps, inside standing trees (both living and dead) or attached to the sides of branches or trunks of trees. The numbers of termites in the nest fluctuate not only in relation to the season but also diurnally. A few termites (Kalotermitidae and Termopsinae) which nest in logs or trees never have any contact with the soil, although they cannot be disregarded as "soil termites" as their activities in decomposing wood impinge on the soil organic cycle. In addition to termites foraging out from arboreal, above-ground or subterranean nests, soil termites include numerous species which do not build distinct nests but live in small colonies in underground galleries often associated with stones, grass tussocks or accumulations of litter, or as inquilines in the nests of other termites.

Generally the quantitative sampling of soil animals has no need to take account of diurnal fluctuations. With termites this is an important factor in sampling populations in mounds, subterranean galleries and feeding sites, such as branches, logs and grass tussocks. Although diurnal variations should be taken into account, the problems of sampling are more concerned with the necessary number, size and distribution of sampling units. These problems are related to the abundance and spatial distribution of the termites themselves. Generally the distribution of termites is markedly discontinuous, ranging from small aggregations in soil to extremely large aggregations in nests and sources of food, such as tree stumps and logs.

I. Sampling of Soil- and Litter-inhabiting Termites

There is a great deal of published information on sampling soil- and litter-inhabiting invertebrates such as mites, various insects, myriapods, and earthworms (see Macfadyen, 1962). Samples are usually taken by means of special soil-corers the *size* of which depends on the abundance of the particular group being sampled, the object being to obtain, for the purposes of statistical accuracy, tens or hundreds of individuals per core rather than thousands or numbers less than ten. The *number* of samples taken depends on the spatial distribution of the animals concerned, highly aggregated populations generally requiring more samples for a given statistical accuracy than randomly distributed populations. The *placement* of samples is usually determined by some system, such as transects or stratified random sampling, that avoids biased distribution of the samples on the part of the operator.

The density of subterranean termite populations in any particular habitat has never been estimated reliably. Harris (1963) examined core samples 75 cm² in area and 15 cm deep and found termites in the great majority of cores, the mean number per core being 138. This is probably the best available estimate of subterranean termite populations, but its value is reduced by the fact that the mean density is virtually meaningless, in view of the fact that a wide variety of habitats was covered. However, it illustrates the point that where subterranean termites are abundant this size of sample is probably adequate. Other workers have used core samples to estimate the populations of soil animals in general, and of these the surveys of Salt (1952) and Strickland (1944, 1945) contain some useful information on subterranean termites. Salt (1952) took core samples 81 cm² in area and 15 cm deep. Termites occurred in 6 out of the 12 cores taken, the numbers per core varying from 0 to 38 with a mean of 11.3. Strickland (1944) used core samples 81 cm² in area but did not indicate anything more than the mean density. In a later investigation (Strickland, 1945), each of his samples consisted of 5 cores, each 58 cm² in area and 7.5 cm deep. He found termites in 10 out of 13 samples, the numbers per sample varying from 0 to 593 with a mean of 81. Clearly, in the sites studied by Salt and Strickland, accurate estimation of density would require larger cores (to avoid the high percentage of zero counts) and many more cores per site.

In these surveys the flotation extraction technique (Salt *et al.*, 1948) was used to obtain termites from the cores of soil. Maldague (1964) used a simple Tullgren funnel (see Haarlov, 1947) to extract termites from soil and litter, but gave no indication of the size of sample or the variation in numbers between samples. Small core samples 20 cm² in area and 4 cm deep have been used by the authors to sample micro-arthropod populations (mites, collembola, etc.) in Australia. The animals are extracted in modified air-conditioned Tullgren funnels. A wide variety of habitats has been covered in southern Australia from desert sand dunes to rain forest and alpine habitats. In semi-arid habitats termites were found in just under 10% of the cores (over 200 cores taken) while their occurrence in other habitats was negligible. Obviously termites are relatively rarer in southern Australia than in the tropical or sub-tropical regions in Africa and estimation of their density probably required samples at least 500 cm² in area.

Estimation of relative density, for the purpose of comparing different species within habitats or comparing habitats as a whole, raises less problems than estimates of absolute density. For instance small cores (20 cm² area), such as the ones taken by us in southern Australia, can provide information on the frequency of occurrence of termites in different habitats. In order to compare the relative density of different species within and between habitats in Northern Nigeria, Sands (1965a) dug pits 1.68 m² in area and 0.91 m deep. A total of 50 pits were dug in each of three areas and subterranean termites were recorded as "occurrences", that is, each separately distinguishable chamber or tunnel containing live termites was scored once. Few species had a frequency of occurrence of more than 1.0 per pit and for many species the frequency was less than 0.1; total frequencies were 7.6 to 10.8 per pit, but as the soil was hand sorted it is not certain whether or not this general low frequency of occurrence reflects a low population density or the well-known inaccuracies of hand sorting. Kemp (1955) adopted a similar method for comparing the termite fauna of a wide variety of habitats in north-eastern Tanzania. Her trenches were 5 m² in area and 1 m deep; the soil was presumably hand sorted and the mean number of occurrences of termites varied from 0 to about 7.

Estimates based on evidence of activity, although non-quantitative, provide useful information on differences between species within habitats, as well as overall differences between habitats. These methods usually sample a certain proportion of the population only. Relative intensity of foraging activity can be estimated by using baits of susceptible timber or other suitable substrate (Coaton, 1947; Kemp, 1955) or by direct observations of foraging individuals (Andrews and Middleton, 1911; Brian, 1965). Pit-fall traps, although widely used to estimate activity of surface-active arthropods such as certain ants, beetles, and spiders (Southwood, 1966), could possibly be used to estimate the activity of certain termites but to our knowledge this has never been attempted.

II. Sampling of Nest- and Mound-building Termites

The sampling of large, relatively static aggregations poses quite different problems which will be discussed here with particular reference to termite mounds. There are two aspects to this problem, estimating the density of mounds per unit area and estimating the number of termites per mound.

The sampling of arboreal nests, whether inside or attached to the outside of the tree, depends largely on methods suitable for sampling the trees themselves (Greaves et al., 1965, 1967; Greaves and Florence, 1966). The colonies of species, such as Coptotermes acinaciformis and C. frenchi in southern Australia, which nest inside the trunks of trees, can be detected by measuring temperatures in holes bored in the trees (Greaves, 1964), as temperatures in the nursery are higher (up to 20°C higher in winter) than in the uninfested wood.

Subterranean nests are more difficult to sample satisfactorily unless their presence is indicated by characteristic openings at the soil surface. They could possibly be detected by various sound-amplifying devices (Snyder, 1952) and, when the opportunity permits, they can be observed directly during the course of large scale earth-moving projects (Hartwig, 1966).

A. ESTIMATING THE DENSITY OF MOUNDS

1. *Quadrats or direct counting*

In grassland or sparsely wooded country it is possible to mark out quadrats and count the mounds in each quadrat. Sands (1965a) used 10 quadrats of area 405 m² to estimate the abundance of mounds of *Trinervitermes geminatus* in northern Nigeria, and Bouillon and Mathot (1964) used 6 to 25 quadrats of area 100 m² to estimate the abundance of mounds of *Cubitermes exiguus* and *C. sankurensis* in the Congo. Marking out large quadrats is tedious and is virtually impossible in areas with a high density of trees and shrubs. More often mounds have been counted in the whole of the particular area being investigated or a sufficiently large portion of it. Bodot (1967b) counted mounds in plots of 1 ha in the Ivory Coast, Maldague (1964) used an area of 1200 m² in Congo rain forest, and we (Wood and Lee, in press) used areas of 0.3 ha to 2.0 ha in Australia.

The most suitable size of quadrats is determined by the density of the mounds; the higher the density the smaller the size of quadrat that will give a reliable estimate. Small mounds at high densities (several hundred per ha) are more amenable to being counted in quadrats than are larger mounds which, although more readily seen and therefore requiring less intensive searching of an area, often occur at low densities (less than 10/ha).

Line transects or belt transects, which are really elongate quadrats, could be a useful method of estimating the abundance of mounds, particularly in areas where laying out quadrats or covering large areas of ground is impracticable. Hartwig (1966) counted the number of subterranean nests of *Odontotermes latericius* in trenches 0.61 m wide by 15.9 km long, dug during the course of drainage excavations in South Africa; we know of no other instance where sampling of line transects has been used.

2. *Measurements of distance between "nearest neighbours"*

If mounds are distributed at random their density can be estimated from the following expression (Clark and Evans, 1954);

$$m = \frac{1}{4\bar{r}^2}$$

where m = density per unit area; $\bar{r}$ = mean distance between nearest neighbours. However, in the few cases where this method has been adopted for studying ant nests (Waloff and Blackith, 1962) and termite mounds (Sands, 1965a; Wood and Lee, in press; see also Chapter 4), the distribution of mounds was found to be non-random. Thus the method appears to be of little use in estimating density, but if the density is known it can provide useful information on spatial relationships and competition between colonies.

3. Aerial photography

Large termite mounds in sparsely wooded country can often be detected on aerial photographs. The large mounds of *Nasutitermes triodiae* in northern Australia can be seen on 1 : 15 500 aerial photographs, but for accurate counting we found that enlargements up to 1 : 2500 were required. The distribution of termite mounds is often associated with local variations in topography, geology, and vegetation, and if mounds can be detected on aerial photographs, they can be useful indicators for aerial surveying (Macfadyen, 1950). The most obvious examples are the large mounds of Macrotermitinae in Africa which often have a characteristic vegetation growing on them (see p. 162). The difference in appearance between scrub-covered mounds and the surrounding savanna grassland in an area of the Congo was sufficiently obvious on aerial photographs (scale 1 : 25 000) to enable Bouillon and Kidieri (1964) to relate the distribution of mounds of *Macrotermes subhyalinus* to features of the landscape, and these authors suggested that aerial photography would also be applicable to studying the distribution and abundance of mounds of *Macrotermes bellicosus* and some species of *Trinervitermes* and *Cubitermes* in areas of savanna or steppe.

In addition to supporting a distinct vegetation, some termite mounds influence the pattern of vegetation around them (see p. 166) and this pattern is sometimes visible on aerial photographs, as was demonstrated by Glover *et al.* (1964) in their study of vegetation patterns on the Loita plains of Kenya. Aerial photography can provide information on the density and distribution of mounds in relation to gross features of the landscape that cannot readily be obtained by ground surveys alone. However, its use should be supported by ground reconnaissance, and its usefulness is limited to large mounds in treeless or sparsely timbered country.

B. ESTIMATING THE POPULATION IN MOUNDS

1. Counting the whole, or a proportion, of the population

The methods used fall into two groups; those where the whole mound is sampled and the total population, or an estimated proportion, is counted, and those where a sample is taken from the mound and the termites counted in the sample. Whole mound samples were used by Holdaway *et al.* (1935), Gay and Greaves (1940), Maldague (1964), Bouillon and Mathot (1964) and Gay and Wetherly (1970). In the case of *Nasutitermes exitiosus* in southern Australia (Holdaway *et al.,* 1935) the time of day and the time of year significantly affect the number of termites in the mound, there being a higher proportion of the population in the mound (that is fewer foraging) during winter and in the early morning during summer. Greaves (1967) applied this knowledge in order to estimate the population of *Coptotermes acinaciformis* and *C. frenchi* in nests inside the trunks of living trees. By cooling the tree above and below the nursery with dry ice, the termites were concentrated in the nursery, following which the portion of the tree containing the nursery was removed. The second method was used by Hartwig (1956) and Sands (1965b). The latter author took core samples (volume 200 cm³) by swinging a weighted club with a sharpened tubular side arm into the base of mounds of *Trinervitermes geminatus* (Fig. 30) and by this means samples were obtained rapidly before the termites had time to respond to the disturbance. The reliability of the method depends on the assumption that the concentration of termites in the sample core is the same as that in the rest of the mound, or at least in the inhabited part of the mound.

   The separation of termites from mound material has been achieved by flotation methods, which extract all individuals whether living, dead, or damaged, or by a method which removes only healthy, living individuals. Flotation was used by Maldague (1964), who extracted termites from whole mounds and estimated the population by counting individuals in aliquot sub-samples, and by Sands (1965b). Holdaway *et al.* (1935), Gay and Greaves (1940), and Greaves (1967) used the method of Gay *et al.* (1955) to extract

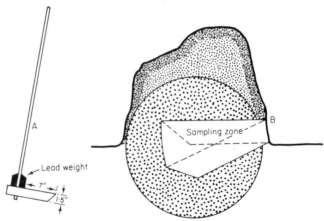

Fig. 30. Method of obtaining core samples from mounds of *Trinervitermes geminatus.* (Reproduced with permission from Sands, 1965b.)

healthy, living termites from broken-up mound material. The number of termites recovered was determined from weighed aliquot sub-samples. The percentage of dead or damaged termites remaining was estimated by eye, and while this may seem crude and subject to inaccuracies the authors claimed that experienced workers arrived at similar estimates.

2. *Mark-recapture methods*

Mark-recapture methods were used by Brian *et al.* (1965) to estimate the populations of ants (*Tetramorium caespitum* Latreille) by incorporating phosphorus -32 into the tissues and, after releasing the marked individuals, sampling the population under slates placed on the nests. As far as we know this technique has not been applied to termite populations. A comprehensive review of marking techniques and methods for analysing the results is given by Southwood (1966), and Brian (1965) has noted some of the problems involved in applying this technique to social insects.

GLOSSARY

List of Termite Names and Authorities for Species

Authorities for names in this list were derived from Hill (1942), Snyder (1949), Bouillon (1964a), Bouillon and Mathot (1965), Sands (1965c), Gay (1968), and Ruelle (1970).

Ahamitermes			*A. minimus*	Light
Allodontotermes			*A. modicus*	Hill
A. giffardi	Silvestri		*A. neogermanus*	Hill
Allognathotermes			*A. obtusidens*	Mjöberg
A. hypogeus	Silvestri		*A. parvus*	Hill
Amitermes			*A. perarmatus*	(Silvestri)
A. abruptus	Gay		*A. unidentatus*	(Wasmann)
A. agrilis	Gay		*A. vitiosus*	Hill
A. boreus	Gay		*A. westraliensis*	Hill
A. colonus	Hill		*A. xylophagus*	Hill
A. darwini	Hill		*Anacanthotermes*	
A. dentosus	Hill		*A. ahngerianus*	(Jacobson)
A. deplanatus	Gay		*A. ochraceus*	(Burmeister)
A. eucalypti	Hill		*A. turkestanicus*	(Jacobson)
A. evuncifer	Silvestri		*Ancistrotermes*	
A. excellens	Silvestri		*A. cavithorax*	(Sjöstedt)
A. exilis	Hill		*A. crucifer*	(Sjöstedt)
A. germanus	(Hill)		*A. guineensis*	(Silvestri)
A. gracilis	Gay		*Anoplotermes*	
A. hartmeyeri	(Silvestri)		*A. pacificus*	Fr. Müller
A. hastatus	(Haviland)		*Apicotermes*	
A. herbertensis	Mjöberg		*A. gurgulifex*	Emerson
A. heterognathus	Silvestri		*A. occultus*	Silvestri
A. lanceolatus	Gay		*Armitermes*	
A. latidens	Mjöberg		*A. holmgreni*	Snyder
A. lativentris	Mjöberg		*Australitermes*	
A. laurensis	Mjöberg		*Basidentitermes*	Silvestri
A. meridionalis	(Froggatt)		*potens*	

Bifiditermes
 B. durbanensis (Haviland)
 Cavitermes (Emerson)
 tuberosus
 Cephalotermes (Sjöstedt)
 rectangularis
Ceratokalotermes
 Constrictotermes (Holmgren)
 cavifrons
Coptotermes
 C. acinaciformis (Froggatt)
 C. brunneus Gay
 C. crassus Snyder
 C. formosanus Shiraki
 C. frenchi Hill
 C. lacteus (Froggatt)
 C. niger Snyder
Crepititermes
 C. verruculosus (Emerson)
Cryptotermes
 C. brevis (Walker)
 C. havilandi (Sjöstedt)
Cubitermes
 C. bilobatus (Haviland)
 C. exiguus Mathot
 C. fungifaber (Sjöstedt)
 C. sankurensis Wasmann
 C. severus Silvestri
 C. subarquatus Sjöstedt
 C. ugandensis Fuller
 C. umbratus Williams
Drepanotermes
 D. perniger (Froggatt)
 D. rubriceps (Froggatt)
Eburnitermes
 Eremotermes nanus Harris
 Euchilotermes Silvestri
 tensus
Euhamitermes
Eurytermes
Firmitermes
 Globitermes (Haviland)
 sulphureus

Grallatotermes (Desneux)
 grallator
Glyptotermes
Heterotermes
 H. ferox (Froggatt)
 H. indicola (Wasmann)
 H. paradoxus Hill
 intermedius
 H. paradoxus (Froggatt)
 paradoxus
 H. tenuis (Hagen)
Hodotermes
 H. mossambicus (Hagen)
 Hoplognathotermes Silvestri
 subterraneus
Hospitalitermes
Incolitermes
Kalotermes
 K. flavicollis (Fabricius)
 K. minor Hagen
 K. tabogae Snyder
Labiotermes
 L. labralis (Holmgren)
Macrosubulitermes
Macrotermes
 M. bellicosus (Smeathman)
 M. falciger (Gerstäcker)
 M. natalensis (Haviland)
 M. subhyalinus (Rambur)
Mastotermes
 M. darwiniensis Froggatt
Microcerotermes
 M. arboreus Emerson
 M. cameroni Snyder
 M. cavus Hill
 M. distinctus Silvestri
 M. edentatus Wasmann
 M. implacidus Hill
 M. nervosus Hill
 M. newmani Hill
 M. parvulus (Sjöstedt)
 M. parvus (Haviland)
 M. serratus (Froggatt)

M. turneri	(Froggatt)	*O. sudanensis*	Sjöstedt
Microhodotermes		*Ophiotermes*	
Microtermes		*Orthognathotermes*	
M. subhyalinus	Silvestri	*Paracapritermes*	
Mimeutermes	Silvestri	*Parrhinotermes*	
sorex		*Pericapritermes*	
Nasutitermes		*P. urgens*	Silvestri
N. beckeri	Prashad and	*Porotermes*	
	Sen-Sarma	*P. adamsoni*	(Froggatt)
N. corniger	(Motschulsky)	*Procubitermes*	
N. ekunduensis	(Sjöstedt)	*P. niapuensis*	(Emerson)
N. ephratae	(Holmgren)	*Promirotermes*	
N. eucalypti	(Mjöberg)	*Psammotermes*	
N. exitiosus	(Hill)	*P. hybostoma*	Desneux
N. fumigatus	(Brauer)	*Pseudacanthotermes*	
N. graveolus	(Hill)	*P. militaris*	(Hagen)
N. guyanae	(Holmgren)	*P. spiniger*	(Sjöstedt)
N. kimberleyensis	(Mjöberg)	*Pseudhamitermes*	
N. latifrons	(Sjöstedt)	*Protocapritermes*	
N. longipennis	(Hill)	*Reticulitermes*	
N. magnus	(Froggatt)	*R. flavipes*	(Kollar)
N. nigriceps	(Haldeman)	*R. hesperus*	Banks
N. rippertii	(Rambur)	*R. lucifugus*	(Rossi)
N. surinamensis	(Holmgren)	*R. lucifugus* var.	de Feyteaud
N. torresi	(Hill)	*santonensis*	
N. triodiae	(Froggatt)	*R. tibialis*	Banks
Neocapritermes	(Emerson)	*Rhinotermes*	
angusticeps		*Schedorhinotermes*	
Neotermes		*S. intermedius*	(Brauer)
N. holmgreni	Banks	*S. intermedius*	(Hill)
N. tectonae	(Dammerman)	*actuosus*	
Occasitermes		*S. intermedius*	(Hill)
Occulitermes		*seclusus*	
Odontotermes		*Speculitermes*	
O. badius	(Haviland)	*S. silvestrii*	(Emerson)
O. latericius	(Haviland)	*Sphaerotermes*	(Sjöstedt)
O. magdalenae	Grassé and	*sphaerothorax*	
	Noirot	*Stolotermes*	
O. obesus	(Rambur)	*Subulitermes*	
O. obscuriceps	(Wasmann)	*Syntermes*	
O. redemanni	(Wasmann)	*Tenuirostritermes*	(Desneux)
O. snyderi	(Emerson)	*tenuirostris*	

Termes		*T. trinervius*	(Rambur)
T. hispaniolae	(Banks)	*T. trinervoides*	(Sjöstedt)
T. panamaensis	(Snyder)	*Tumulitermes*	
T. sunteri	(Hill)	*T. comatus*	(Hill)
Thoracotermes		*T. dalbiensis*	(Hill)
T. brevinotus	Silvestri	*T. hastilis*	(Froggatt)
Trinervitermes		*T. pastinator*	(Hill)
T. ebenerianus	Sjöstedt	*T. tumuli*	(Froggatt)
T. geminatus	(Wasmann)	*Zootermopsis*	
T. occidentalis	(Sjöstedt)	*Z. angusticollis*	(Hagen)
T. oeconomus	(Trägårth)	*Z. nevadensis*	(Hagen)
T. togoensis	(Sjöstedt)		

References

Abdel-Fattah, R. F. (1957). On the excretory substances in the urine and body fluids of earthworms. *Bull. Coll. Arts Sci. Baghdad 2*, 141-161.

Adamson, A. M. (1943). Termites and the fertility of soils. *Trop. Agric. Trin. 20(6)*, 107-112.

Alibert, J. (1965). Mue et trophallaxie proctodéale chez *Calotermes flavicollis. C. r. hebd. Séanc. Acad. sci. Paris 261*, 3207-3210.

Allee, W. C., Emerson, A. E., Park, O., Park, T. and Schmidt, K. P. (1949). "Principles of Animal Ecology". W. B. Saunders Co., Philadelphia and London.

Andrewartha, H. G. and Birch, L. C. (1954). "The Distribution and Abundance of Animals". Univ. Chicago Press, Chicago.

Andrews, E. A. (1911). Observations on termites in Jamaica. *J. Anim. Behav. 1*, 193-228.

Andrews, E. A. (1924). Termites. *Q. Jl Indian Tea Ass. 4*, 118-125.

Andrews, E. A. and Middleton, A. R. (1911). Rhythmic activity in termite communities. *Johns Hopkins Univ. Circ. n.s. 2*, 26-34.

Anonymous. (1960). Destruction of grazing by harvester termites. *Fmg S. Afr. 35*, 6-9.

Araujo, R. L. (1970). Termites of the Neotropical Region. *In* "Biology of Termites" (K. Krishna and F. M. Weesner, eds), Vol. 2, pp. 527-576. Academic Press, N.Y. and London.

Bachelier, G. (1963). Les Termites. *In* "La Vie Animale dans les Sols", pp. 201-206. O.R.S.T.O.M., Paris.

Bates, G. (1926). Cane pest combat and control. Giant white ants *Mastotermes darwiniensis* Frogg. *Qd agric. J. 25*, 4-5.

Beaumont, J. (1889). Observations on the termites or white ants of the isthmus of Panama. *Trans. N.Y. Acad. Sci. 8*, 85-114.

Beaumont, J. (1890). Observations on the termites or white ants of the isthmus of Panama. *Trans. N.Y. Acad. Sci. 9*, 157-180.

Becker, G. and Seifert, K. (1962). Ueber die chemische Zussamensetzung des Nest- und Galeriemateriels von Termiten. *Insectes soc. 9*, 273-287.

Beckwith, T. D. and Rose, E. J. (1929). Cellulose digestion by organisms from the termite gut. *Proc. Soc. exp. Biol. Med. 27*, 4-6.

Bernard, F. (1954). Role des insectes sociaux dans les terrains du Sahara. *In* "Biology of Deserts" (J. Cloudsley-Thompson, ed.), pp. 104-111. Inst. of Biology, London.

Bernard, J. (1964). Les termites et l'agriculture. *Bull. Éc. natn. supér, Agric. Tunis 3*, 83-95.

Beuchner, H. K. and Golley, F. B. (1967). Preliminary estimation of energy flow in Uganda kob (*Adenota kob thomasi* Neumann). *In* "Secondary Productivity of Terrestrial Ecosystems" (K. Petrusewicz, ed.), pp. 243-254. Institute of Ecology, Polish Acad. Sci., Warsaw.

Bilova, T. (1949). "O faune nasekomyh Ust'-Urta i ee vrednyh predstaviteljah." Ust'-Urt (Karakalinskij), ego priroda i hozjajstvo. Taskent.

Block, W. and Banage, W. B. (1968). Population density and biomass of earthworms in some Uganda soils. *Rev. Écol. Biol. Sol. 5,* 515-521.

Bocock, K. L. (1963). The digestion and assimilation of food by *Glomeris. In* "Soil Organisms" (J. Doeksen and J. van der Drift, eds), pp. 85-91. North Holland, Amsterdam.

Bodenheimer, F. S. (1937). Population problems of social insects. *Biol. Rev. 12,* 393-430.

Bodot, P. (1961). La destruction des termitières de *Bellicositermes natalensis* par une fourmi *Dorylus (Typhlopone) dentifrons* Wasmann. *C. r. hebd. Séanc. Acad. sci. Paris 253,* 3053.

Bodot, P. (1964). Études écologiques et biologiques des termites dans les savanes de Basse Côte d'Ivoire. *In* "Études sur les Termites Africains" (A. Bouillon, ed.), pp. 251-262. Leopoldville Univ., Leopoldville.

Bodot, P. (1967a). Étude écologique des termites des savanes de Basse Côte d'Ivoire. *Insectes soc. 14,* 229-258.

Bodot, P. (1967b). Cycles saisonniers d'activité collective des termites des savanes de Basse Côte d'Ivoire. *Insectes soc. 14,* 359-388.

Bodot, P. (1969). Composition des colonies de termites: ses fluctuations au cours du temps. *Insectes soc. 16,* 39-54.

Bont, A. F. de (1964). Termites et densité d'oiseaux. *In* "Études sur les Termites Africains" (A. Bouillon, ed.), pp. 273-283. Leopoldville Univ., Leopoldville.

Bornebusch, C. H. (1930). The fauna of the forest soil. *Forst. ForsVaes. Danm. 11,* 1-224.

Bornemissza, G. F. (1960). Could dung-eating insects improve our pastures? *J. Aust. Inst. agric. Sci. 26,* 54-56.

Bouillon, A. (1964a). Préférences en matière de sol chez *Cubitermes exiguus* Mathot et role de guide joué par un *Microtermes* associé. *In* "Études sur les Termites Africains" (A. Bouillon, ed.), pp. 285-294. Leopoldville Univ., Leopoldville.

Bouillon, A. (ed.) (1964b). "Etudes sur les Termites Africains". Leopoldville Univ., Leopoldville.

Bouillon, A. (1970). Termites of the Ethiopian Region. *In* "Biology of Termites" (K. Krishna and F. M. Weesner, eds), Vol. 2, pp. 153-280. Academic Press, N.Y. and London.

Bouillon, A. and Kidieri, S. (1964). Répartition des termitières de *Bellicositermes bellicosus rex* Grassé et Noirot dans l'Ubangi, d'après les photos aériennes. Corrélations écologiques qu'elle révèle. *In* "Études sur les Termites Africains" (A. Bouillon, ed.), pp. 373-376. Leopoldville Univ., Leopoldville.

Bouillon, A. and Mathot, G. (1964). Observations sur l'écologie et le nid de *Cubitermes exiguus* Mathot. Description de nymphes-soldats et d'un pseudimago. *In* "Études sur les Termites Africains" (A. Bouillon, ed.), pp. 215-230. Leopoldville Univ., Leopoldville.

Bouillon, A. and Mathot, G. (1965). Quel est ce termite africain? *Zooleo* No. 1, 115 pp. Leopoldville Univ., Leopoldville.

Boyer, P. (1948). Sur les matériaux composant la termitière géante de *Bellicositermes rex. C. r. hebd. Séanc. Acad. sci. Paris 227,* 488-490.

Boyer, P. (1955). Premières études pédologiques et bactériologiques des termitières. *C. r. hebd. Séanc. Acad. sci. Paris 240,* 569-571.

Boyer, P. (1956a). Action des termites constructeurs sur certains sols d'Afrique Tropicale. *Proc. 6th Int. Congr. Soil Sci., Paris, 1956 Vol. 3,* 95-103.

Boyer, P. (1956b). Rélations entre la flore intestinale de *Bellicositermes natalensis* et celle du sol. *Proc. 6th Int. Congr. Soil. Sci., Paris, 1956 Vol. 3,* 111-113.

Boyer, P. (1956c). Étude pédologique de la répartition et du dosage des bases totales dans les matériaux de la termitière de *Bellicositermes natalensis* (Hav.). *C. r. hebd. Séanc. Acad. sci. Paris 242,* 801-803.

Boyer, P. (1958). Influence des remaniements par le termite et de l'érosion sur l'évolution pédogenétique de la termitière épigée de *Bellicositermes rex. C. r. hebd. Séanc. Acad. sci. Paris 247,* 749-751.

Boyer, P. (1959). De l'influence des termites de la zone intertropicale sur la configuration de certains sols. *Rev. Géomorph. dyn. 10,* 41-44.

Brian, M. V. (1965). "Social Insect Populations" 135 pp. Academic Press, N.Y. and London.

Brian, M. V., Hibble, J., and Stradling, D. J. (1965). Ant pattern and density in a southern English heath. *J. Anim. Ecol. 34,* 545-555.

Brooks, M. A. (1963). Symbiosis and aposymbiosis in arthropods. *Symp. Soc. gen. Microbiol. 13,* 200-231.

Buchanan, F. (1807). "A Journey from Malabar through the Countries of Mysore, Canara and Malabar", Vol. 2, pp. 432-460. East India Company, London.

Burbidge, N. T. (1960). The phytogeography of the Australian region. *Aust. J. Bot. 8,* 75-212.

Burnett, J. R. (1948). Crop production. *In* "Agriculture in the Sudan" (J. D. Tothill, ed.). Oxford Univ. Press, Oxford.

Burtt, B. D. (1942). Some East African vegetation communities. *J. Ecol. 30,* 65-146.

Butler, J. H. A. and Ladd, J. N. (1969). The effect of methylation of humic acids on their influence on proteolytic enzyme activity. *Aust. J. Soil Res. 7,* 263-268.

Calaby, J. H. (1960). Observations on the banded ant-eater *Myrmecobius f. fasciatus* Waterhouse (Marsupialia), with particular reference to its food habits. *Proc. zool. Soc. Lond. 135,* 183-207.

Calaby, J. H. and Gay, F. J. (1956). The distribution and biology of the genus *Coptotermes* (Isoptera) in Western Australia. *Aust. J. Zool. 4,* 19-39.

Calaby, J. H. and Gay, F. J. (1959). Aspects of the distribution and ecology of Australian termites. *In* "Biogeography and Ecology in Australia" (A. Keast, R. L. Crocker and C. S. Christian, eds), pp. 211-223. Junk, The Hague.

Chatterji, S ., Sarup, P., and Chopra, S. C. (1958). Effect of some modern organic insecticides on termite damage to wheat crops. *Proc. natn Acad. Sci. India B28,* 399-405.

Cheema, P. S., Das, S. R., Dayal, H. M., Koshi, T., Maheshwari, K. L., Nigam, S. S. and Ranganathan, S. K. (1960). Temperature and humidity in the fungus garden of the mound-building termite *Odontotermes obesus* (Rambur). *In* "Termites in the Humid Tropics", New Delhi Symposium, pp. 145-149. UNESCO, Paris.

Chevalier, A. (1949). Points de vue nouveaux sur les sols d'Afrique tropicale, sur leur dégradation et leur conservation. *Bull. agric. Congo belge 40,* 1057-1092.

Clark, P. J. and Evans, F. C. (1954). Distance to nearest neighbours as a measure of spatial relationships in populations. *Ecology 35,* 445-453.

Cleveland, L. R. (1923). Correlation between the food and morphology of termites and the presence of intestinal protozoa. *Am. J. Hyg. 3*, 444-461.

Cleveland, L. R. (1924). The physiological and symbiotic relationships between the intestinal protozoa of termites and their host, with special reference to *Reticulitermes flavipes* Kollar. *Biol. Bull. mar. biol. Lab., Woods Hole 46*, 177-225.

Cleveland, L. R. (1926). Symbiosis among animals with special reference to termites and their intestinal flagellates. *Q. Rev. Biol. 1*, 51-60.

Cleveland, L. R. and Grimstone, A. V. (1964). The fine structure of the flagellate *Mixotricha paradoxa* and its associated microorganisms. *Proc. R. Soc. B159*, 668-686.

Coaton, W. G. H. (1947). The Pienaars river complex of wood-eating termites. *J. ent. Soc. sth Afr. 9*, 130-177.

Coaton, W. G. H. (1950). Termites and their control in cultivated areas in South Africa. *Union S. Afr. Dept Agric. For. Bull. 305*, 1-28.

Coaton, W. G. H. (1951). The snouted harvester termite; natural mortality as an aid to chemical control. *Fmg S. Afr. 26*, 263-267.

Coaton, W. G. H. (1954). Veld reclamation and harvester termite control. *Fmg S. Afr. 29*, 243-248.

Coaton, W. G. H. (1958). The Hodotermitid harvester termites of South Africa. *Union S. Afr. Dept Agric. Bull. 375*.

Cohen, W. E. (1933). An analysis of termite (*Eutermes exitiosus*) mound material. *J. Coun. sci. ind. Res. Aust. 6*, 166-169.

Coleman, G. S. (1963). The growth and metabolism of rumen ciliate protozoa. *Symp. Soc. gen. Microbiol. 13*, 298-324.

Collins, M. S. (1969). Water relations in termites. *In* "Biology of Termites" (K. Krishna and F. M. Weesner, eds), Vol. 1, pp. 433-458. Academic Press, N.Y. and London.

Conrad, G. (1959). Importance et rôle des termites dans les formations pédologiques fossiles du Quarternaire de la région de Béni-Abbès. *C. r. hebd. Séanc. Acad. sci. Paris 249*, 2089-2091.

Cook, S. F. (1932). The respiratory gas exchange in *Termopsis nevadensis*. *Biol. Bull. mar. biol. Lab., Woods Hole 63*, 246-257.

Cook, S. F. (1943). Nonsymbiotic utilization of carbohydrates by the termite, *Zootermopsis angusticollis*. *Physiol. Zoöl. 16*, 123-128.

Cook, S. F. and Scott, K. G. (1933). The nutritional requirements of *Zootermopsis (Termopsis) angusticollis*. *J. cell. comp. Physiol. 4*, 95-110.

Corbett, G. H. and Miller, N. C. E. (1936). The termite *Microtermes pallidus* Hav., in relation to tea in Malaya. *Scient. Ser. Dep. Agric. Straits Settl. F.M.S. 17*, 1-12.

Cowles, R. B. (1930). The life history of *Varanus niloticus* (Lin.) as observed in Natal, South Africa. *J. Ent. Zool. 22*. 1-31.

Crossley, D. A. and Witkamp, M. (1964). Forest soil mites and mineral cycling. *Acarologia 6*, 137-146.

Crowther, F. and Barlow, H. W. B. (1943). Tap-root damage of cotton, ascribed to termites, in the Sudan Gezira. *Emp. J. exp. Agric. 11*, 99-112.

Curry, J. P. (1969). The decomposition of organic matter in soil. Part I. The role of the fauna in decaying grassland herbage. *Soil Biol. Biochem. 1*, 253-258.

Dasmann, R. F. (1962). Game ranching in African land-use planning. *Bull. epizoot. Dis. Afr. 10*, 13-17.

Day, M. F. (1938). Preliminary observations on the gaseous environment of *Eutermes exitiosus* Hill (Isoptera). *J. Coun. sci. ind. Res. Aust. 11*, 317-327.

Deligne, J. (1966). Charactères adaptifs au régime alimentaire dans la mandibule des Termites (Insectes, Isoptères). *C. r. hebd. Séanc. Acad. sci. Paris 263*, 1323-1325.

Desneux, J. (1948). Les nidifications souterrains des *Apicotermes*. Termites de l'Afrique tropicale. *Revue Zool. Bot. afr. 41*, 1-54.

Desneux, J. (1952). Les constructions hypogées des *Apicotermes*. Termites de l'Afrique tropicale. *Annls Mus. r. Congo belge Ser. 8vo, Sci. Zool. 17*, 7-99.

Dickman, A. (1931). Studies on the intestinal flora of termites with reference to their ability to digest cellulose. *Biol. Bull. mar. biol. Lab., Woods Hole 61*, 85-92.

Doop, J. E. A. den (1938). The utilization of sisal waste in Java and Sumatra-Part II. *E. Afr. agric. J. 4*, 89-99.

Drift, J. van der (1951). Analysis of the animal community of a beech forest floor. *Tijdschr. Ent. 94*, 1-68.

Drift, J. van der (1963). The disappearance of litter in mull and mor in connection with weather conditions and the activity of the macrofauna. *In* "Soil Organisms" (J. Doeksen and J. van der Drift, eds), pp. 125-133. North Holland, Amsterdam.

Drummond, H. (1886). On the termite as the tropical analogue of the earth-worm. *Proc. R. Soc. Edinb. 13*, 137-146.

Drummond, H. (1888). "Tropical Africa", Chapter 6 "The White Ant. A Theory". London.

Ebeling, W. and Pence, R. J. (1957). Relation of particle size to the penetration of subterranean termites through barriers of sand or cinders. *J. econ. Ent. 50*, 690-692.

Edwards, C. A. and Heath, G. W. (1963). The role of soil animals in breakdown of leaf material. *In* "Soil Organisms" (J. Doeksen and J. van der Drift, eds), pp. 76-83. North Holland, Amsterdam.

Emerson, A. E. (1938). Termite nests—a study of the phylogeny of behaviour. *Ecol. Monogr. 8*, 247-284.

Emerson, A. E. (1945). The neotropical genus *Syntermes* (Isoptera: Termitidae). *Bull. Am. Mus. nat. Hist. 83*, 427-471.

Emerson, A. E. (1949). Termite studies in the Belgian Congo. *Rapp. a. Inst. scient. Afr. cent. 2*, 149-159.

Emerson, A. E. (1955). Geographical origins and dispersions of termite genera. *Fieldiana, Zool. 37*, 465-521.

Emerson, A. E. (1956). Regenerative behaviour and social homeostasis of termites. *Ecology 37*, 248-258.

Engelmann, M. D. (1966). Energetics, terrestrial field studies, and animal productivity. *Adv. ecol. Res. 3*, 73-115.

Erhart, H. (1951a). Sur l'importance des phénomènes biologiques dans la formation des cuirasses ferrugineuses en zone tropicale. *C. r. hebd. Séanc. Acad. sci. Paris 233*, 804-806.

Erhart, H. (1951b). Sur le rôle des cuirasses termitiques dans la géographie des régions tropicales. *C. r. hebd. Séanc. Acad. sci. Paris. 233*, 966-968.

Erhart, H. (1953). Sur les cuirasses termitiques fossiles dans la Vallée du Niari et dans le Massif du Chaillu (Moyen Congo, A.E.F.). *C. r. hebd. Séanc. Acad. sci. Paris 237*, 431-433.

Ferrar, P. and Watson, J. A. L. (1970). Termites associated with dung in Australia. *J. Aust. ent. Soc., 9*, 100-102.

Ferrero, F. (1959). Les termites et leurs dégâts sur vignes dans le région de Banyuls. *Phytoma 11(108)*, 30-31.

Fölster, H. (1964). Die Pedi-Sedimente der Sudsudanesischen Pediplane. Herkunft und Bodenbildung. *Pédologie 14,* 68-84.

Fonseca, J. P. da (1950). On the chemical control of underground termites. *Archos Inst. biol., S. Paulo 19,* 57-84.

Foster, J. B. and Coe, M. J. (1968). The biomass of game animals in Nairobi National Park, 1960-66. *J. zool. Res. 155,* 413-425.

Fries, R. E. (1921). Zur Kenntnis der Vegetation der Termitenhugel in Nord-Rhodesia. *In* "Wissenschaftliche Ergebnisse der Schwedischen Rhodesia-Kongo Expedition 1911-12". Band I, Botanische Untersuchungen, pp. 30-39. Stockholm.

Fripiat, J. J., Gastuche, M. C., Vielvoye, L. and Sys, C. (1957). Les argiles des sols de la région d'Elisabethville. *Pédologie 7,* 12-18.

Frith, H. J. and Calaby, J. H. (1969). "Kangaroos". F. W. Cheshire, Melbourne.

Fuller, C. (1915). Observations on some South African termites. *Ann. Natal Mus. 3(2),* 329-505.

Fuller, C. (1918). Notes on white ants. *Bull. S. Afr. biol Soc. 1,* 16-20.

Fyfe, R. V. and Gay, F. J. (1938). The humidity of the atmosphere and the moisture conditions within mounds of *Eutermes exitiosus* Hill. *Coun. sci. ind. Res. Aust. Pamphlet 82,* 22 pp.

Gay, F. J. (1961). The control of termites in Australia. *Symposia Genetica et Biol. It. 11,* 47-60.

Gay, F. J. (1968). A contribution to the systematics of the genus *Amitermes* (Isoptera: Termitidae) in Australia. *Aust. J. Zool. 16,* 405-457.

Gay, F. J. and Calaby, J. H. (1970). Termites from the Australian Region. *In* "Biology of Termites" (K.Krishna and F. M. Weesner, eds), Vol. 2, pp. 393-448. Academic Press, N.Y. and London.

Gay, F. J. and Greaves, T. (1940). The population of a mound colony of *Coptotermes lacteus* (Frogg.). *J. Coun. sci. ind. Res. Aust. 13,* 145-149.

Gay, F. J., Greaves, T., Holdaway, F. G. and Wetherly, A. H. (1955). Standard laboratory cultures of termites for evaluating the resistance of timber, timber preservatives, and other materials to termite attack. *Bull. Commonw. scient. ind. Res. Org. 277,* 60 pp. Melbourne.

Gay, F. J. and Wetherly, A. H. (1970). The population of a large mound of *Nasutitermes exitiosus* (Hill) (Isoptera: Termitidae). *J. Aust. ent. Soc. 9,* 27-30.

Gerasimov, I. P. (1962). Latérites actuelles et sols latéritiques. *Bull. Inform. Acad. Sci. URSS, Sér. Géogr. 2.*

Ghilarov, M. S. (1962). Termites of the USSR, their distribution and importance. *In* "Termites in the Humid Tropics", New Delhi Symposium, pp. 131-135. UNESCO, Paris.

Gillard, P. (1967). Coprophagous beetles in pasture ecosystems. *J. Aust. Inst. agric. Sci. 33,* 30-34.

Gillon, Y. and Gillon, D. (1967). Méthodes d'estimation des nombres et biomasses d'Arthropodes en savane tropicale. *In* "Secondary Productivity of Terrestrial Ecosystems" (K. Petrusewicz, ed.), pp. 519-544. Institute of Ecology, Polish acad. Sci., Warsaw.

Glover, P. E. (1937). A contribution to the ecology of the high-veld flora. *S. Afr. J. Sci. 34,* 224-259.

Glover, P. E., Trump, E. C., and Wateridge, L. E. D. (1964). Termitaria and vegetation patterns on the Loita plains of Kenya. *J. Ecol. 52,* 365-377.

Gokhale, N. G., Sarma, S. N., Bhattacharyya, N. G. and Dutta, J. S. (1958).

Effect of termite activity on the chemical properties of tea soils. *Sci. Cult. 24,* 229.

Goodland, R. J. A. (1965). On termitaria in a savanna ecosystem. *Can. J. Zool. 43,* 641-650.

Grassé, P. P. (1937). Recherches sur la systématique et la biologie des termites de l'Afrique Occidentale Française. Première partie. Protermitidae, Mesotermitidae, Metatermitidae (Termitinae). *Annls Soc. ent. Fr. 106,* 1-100.

Grassé, P. P. (1939). Le reconstruction du nid et le travail collectif chez les termites supérieurs. *J. Psychol. norm. path. 36,* 370-396.

Grassé, P. P. (1949). Ordre des Isoptères ou Termites. *In* "Traité de Zoologie" Vol. 9 (P. P. Grassé, ed.), pp. 408-544. Masson, Paris.

Grassé, P. P. (1950). Termites et sols tropicaux. *Revue int. Bot. appl. Agric. trop. 1950,* 549-554.

Grassé, P. P. (1959a). La reconstruction du nid et les coordinations interindividuelles chez *Bellicositermes natalensis* et *Cubitermes* sp. La théorie de la stigmergie: Essai d'interpretation du comportement des termites constructeurs. *Insectes soc. 14,* 73-102.

Grassé, P. P. (1959b). Un nouveau type de symbiose: la meule alimentaire des termites champignonnistes. *Nature, Lond. 3293,* 385-389.

Grassé, P. P. and Joly, P. (1941). La teneur en matières organiques de quelques tertes de termitières. *Bull. Soc. zool. Fr. 66,* 57-62.

Grassé, P. P. and Noirot, C. (1948). La "climatisation" de la termitière par ses inhabitants et le transport de l'eau. *C. r. hebd. Séanc. Acad. sci Paris 227,* 869-871.

Grassé, P. P. and Noirot, C. (1951). La sociotomie: Migration et fragmentation de la termitière chez les *Anoplotermes* et les *Trinervitermes. Behaviour 3,* 146-166.

Grassé, P. P. and Noirot, C. (1957). La signification des meules à champignons des Macrotermitinae (Ins., Isoptères). *C. r. hebd. Séanc. Acad. sci. Paris 244,* 1845-1850.

Grassé, P. P. and Noirot, C. (1958a). La meule des termites champignonnistes et sa signification symbiotique. *Annls Sci. nat. Zool. (11)20,* 113-128.

Grassé, P. P. and Noirot, C. (1958b). La société de *Calotermes flavicollis* (Insectes, Isoptères), de sa fondation au premier essaimage. *C. r. hebd. Séanc. Acad. sci. Paris 246,* 1789-1795.

Grassé, P. P. and Noirot, C. (1959a). Rapports des termites avec les sols tropicaux. *Rev. Géomorph. dyn. 10,* 35-40.

Grassé, P. P. and Noirot, C. (1959b). L'évolution de la symbiose chez les Isoptères. *Experientia 15,* 365-372.

Grassé, P. P. and Noirot, C. (1961). Nouvelles recherches sur la systématique et l'éthologie des termites champignonnistes du genre *Bellicositermes* Emerson. *Insectes soc. 8,* 311-359.

Greaves, T. (1962a). Studies of the foraging galleries and the invasion of living trees by *Coptotermes acinaciformis* and *C. brunneus* (Isoptera). *Aust. J. Zool. 10,* 630-651.

Greaves, T. (1962b). Termites in Australian forests. *Proc. 11th Int. Congr. Ent., Vienna, 1960,* pp. 238-240.

Greaves, T. (1964). Temperature studies of termite colonies in living trees. *Aust. J. Zool. 12,* 250-262.

Greaves, T. (1967). Experiments to determine the populations of tree-dwelling colonies of termites (*Coptotermes acinaciformis* (Froggatt) and *C. frenchi* Hill). *Tech. Pap. Div. Ent. C.S.I.R.O. Aust. 7*, 19-33.

Greaves, T., Armstrong, G. J., McInnes, R. S. and Dowse, J. E. (1967). Timber losses caused by termites, decay, and fire in two coastal forests in New South Wales. *Tech, Pap. Div. Ent. C.S.I.R.O. Aust. 7*, 2-18.

Greaves, T. and Florence, R. G. (1966). Incidence of termites in blackbutt regrowth. *Aust. For. 30*, 153-161.

Greaves, T., McInnes, R. S. and Dowse, J. E. (1965). Timber losses caused by termites, decay and fire in an alpine forest in New South Wales. *Aust. For. 29*, 161-174.

Griffith, G. ap (1938). A note on termite hills. *E. Afr. agric. J. 4*, 70-71.

Griffith, G. ap (1953). Vesicular laterite. *Nature, Lond. 171*, 530.

Haarlov, N. (1947). A new modification of the Tullgren apparatus. *J. Anim. Ecol. 16*, 115-121.

Harris, W. V. (1949a). Quelques aspects agricoles du problème des Termites en Afrique orientale. *Revue int. Bot. appl. Agric. trop. 1949*, 506-513.

Harris, W. V. (1949b). Some aspects of the termite problem. *E. Afr. agric. J. 14*, 151-155.

Harris, W. V. (1954). Termites and tropical agriculture. *Trop. Agric. Trin. 31*, 11-18.

Harris, W. V. (1955). Termites and the soil. *In* "Soil Zoology" (D. K. McE. Kevan, ed.), pp. 62-72. Butterworths, London.

Harris, W. V. (1956). Termite mound building. *Insectes soc. 3*, 261-265.

Harris, W. V. (1961). "Termites: their recognition and control". Longmans Green & Co., London.

Harris, W. V. (1963). "Exploration du Parc National de la Garamba", Part 42. Isoptera, 43 pp. Imprim. Hayez, Brussels.

Harris, W. V. (1966). The role of termites in tropical forestry. *Insectes soc. 8*, 255-266.

Harris, W. V. (1969). "Termites as pests of crops and trees". Commonwealth Institute of Entomology, London.

Harris, W. V. (1970). Termites of the Palaearctic Region. *In* "Biology of Termites" (K. Krishna and F. M. Weesner, eds), Vol. 2, pp. 295-313. Academic Press, N.Y. and London.

Hartwig, E. K. (1955). Control of snouted harvester termites *Fmg S. Afr. 30*, 361-366.

Hartwig, E. K. (1956). The determination of the population distribution in *Trinervitermes* nests as a basis for control measures. *Boll. Lab. Zool. gen. agr. R. Scuola Agric. Portici 33*, 629-639.

Hartwig, E. K. (1966). The nest and control of *Odontotermes latericius* (Haviland) (Termitidae: Isoptera). *S. Afr. J. agric. Sci. 9*, 407-418.

Hébrant, F. (1964). Mesures de la consommation d'oxygène chez *Cubitermes exiguus* Mathot (Isoptera, Termitinae). *In* "Études sur les Termites Africains" (A. Bouillon, ed.), pp. 153-171. Leopoldville Univ., Leopoldville.

Hébrant, F. (1967). Étude de l'influence du poids des individus, et de l'humidité du de milieu sur la consommation d'oxygène d'ouvriers de *Cubitermes exiguus* Mathot (Isoptera, Termitinae). *C. r. 5th Congr. U.I.E.I.S., Toulouse, 1965*, pp. 107-115.

Hébrant, F. (1970). Circadian rhythms of respiratory metabolism in whole colonies of the termite, *Cubitermes exiguus. J. Insect Physiol. 16*, 1229-1235.

Hegh, E. (1922). "Les Termites". Brussels.

Heidermanns, C. (1937). Uber die Harnstoffbildung beim Regenwurm. *Zool. Jb., Allgem. Zool. Physiol. Tiere 58*, 57-68.

Hendee, E. C. (1934). The association of termites and fungi. *In* "Termites and Termite Control" (C. A. Kofoid, ed.). 2nd edition, pp. 105-116. Univ. California Press.

Hesse, P. R. (1955). A chemical and physical study of the soils of termite mounds in East Africa. *J. Ecol. 43*, 449-461.

Hesse, P. R. (1957). Fungus combs in termite mounds. *E. Afr. agric. J. 23*, 104-105.

Hill, G. F. (1921). The white ant pest in Northern Australia. *Bull. advis. Coun. Sci. Ind., Melb. 21*, 1-26.

Hill, G. F. (1922a). Descriptions and biology of some North Australian termites. *Proc. Linn. Soc. N.S.W. 47*, 142-160.

Hill, G. F. (1922b). On some Australian termites of the genera *Drepanotermes, Hamitermes* and *Leucotermes. Bull. ent. Res. 12*, 363-399.

Hill, G. F. (1935). Australian *Hamitermes* (Isoptera), with descriptions of new species and hitherto undescribed castes. *Coun. sci. ind. Res. Aust. Pamphlet 52*, 13-32.

Hill, G. F. (1942). "Termites (Isoptera) from the Australian Region". Aust. Counc. Sci. Ind. Res., Melbourne.

Holdaway, F. G. (1933). The composition of different regions of mounds of *Eutermes exitiosus* Hill. *J. Coun. sci. ind. Res. Aust. 6*, 160-165.

Holdaway, F. G. and Gay, F. J. (1948). Temperature studies of the habitat of *Eutermes exitiosus* with special reference to the temperatures within the mound. *Aust. J. scient. Res. B1*, 464-493.

Holdaway, F. G., Gay, F. J. and Greaves, T. (1935). The termite population of a mound colony of *Eutermes exitiosus* Hill. *J. Coun. sci. ind. Res. Aust. 8*, 42-46.

Holdaway, F. G. and Hill, G. F. (1936). The control of mound colonies of *Eutermes exitiosus* Hill. *J. Coun. sci. ind. Res. Aust. 9*, 135-136.

Honigberg, B. M. (1970). Protozoa associated with termites and their role in digestion. *In* "Biology of Termites" (K. Krishna and F. M. Weesner, eds), Vol. 2, pp. 1-36. Academic Press, N.Y. and London.

Hopkins, B. (1966). Vegetation of the Olokemeji Forest Reserve, Nigeria. IV. The litter and soil with special reference to their seasonal changes. *J. Ecol. 54*, 687-703.

Hopp, H. and Slater, C. S. (1948). Influence of earthworms on soil productivity. *Soil Sci. 66*, 421-428.

Hungate, R. E. (1936). Studies on the nutrition of *Zootermopsis*. I. The role of bacteria and molds in cellulose decomposition. *Zentbl. Bakt. ParasitKde 94*, 240–249.

Hungate, R. E. (1938). Studies on the nutrition of *Zootermopsis*. II. The relative importance of the termite and the protozoa in wood digestion. *Ecology 19*, 1-25.

Hungate, R. E. (1939). Experiments on the nutrition of *Zootermopsis*. III. The anaerobic carbohydrate dissimilation by the intestinal protozoa. *Ecology 20*, 230-245.

Hungate, R. E. (1943). Quantitative analyses on the cellulose fermentation by termite protozoa. *Ann. ent. Soc. Am. 36*, 730-739.

Hungate, R. E. (1946a) The symbiotic utilization of cellulose. *J. Elisha Mitchell scient. Soc. 62*, 9-24.

Hungate, R. E. (1946b). Studies on cellulose fermentation. II. An anaerobic cellulose decomposing actinomycete, *Micromonospora propionici* n.sp. *J. Bact. 51*, 51-56.

Hungate, R. E. (1955). Mutualistic intestinal protozoa. *Biochem. Physiol. Protozoa 2*, 159-199.

Hungate, R. E. (1963). Symbiotic associations: the rumen bacteria. *Symp. Soc. gen. Microbiol. 13*, 266-297.

Hutton, J. T. (1955). A method of particle size analysis of soils. *Divl Rep. Div. Soils C.S.I.R.O. Aust. 11/55*.

Jepson, F. P. (1929). The control of *Calotermes* in living plants. *Bull. Dep. Agric. Ceylon 86*, 1-11.

Joachim, A. W. R. and Kandiah, S. (1940). Studies on Ceylon soils. XIV. A comparison of soils from termite mounds and adjacent land. *Trop. Agric. Mag. Ceylon agric. Soc. 95*, 333-338.

Joachim, A. W. R. and Pandittesekera, D. G. (1948). Soil fertility studies. IV. Investigations on crumb structure and stability of local soils. *Trop. Agric. Mag. Ceylon agric. Soc. 104*, 119-129.

Jones, E. W. (1956). Ecological studies in the rain forest of South Nigeria. IV. *J. Ecol. 44*, 83-117.

Kaiser, P. (1953). *Anoplotermes pacificus*, eine mit Pflanzenwurzeln vergesellschaftet lebende Termite. *Mitt. zool. Mus. Hamb. 52*, 77-92.

Kalmbach, E. R. (1943). "The armadillo, its relation to agriculture and game". Game, Fish and Oyster Commission, Austin, Texas.

Kalshoven, L. G. E. (1930). De biologie van de Djatitermiet (*Kalotermes tectonae* Damm.) in Verband met Zijn Bestrijding. *Meded. Inst. PlZiekt., Buitenz. 76*, 1-154.

Kalshoven, L. G. E. (1936). Onze Kennis van de Javaansche Termiten. *Hand. ned.-indisch. natuurw. Congr. 7*, 427-435.

Kalshoven, L. G. E. (1941). Invloed van de locale macroscopische fauna en met name van de termieten, op de vruchlboacheid van dem bodem. *Tectona 34*, 568-582.

Kalshoven, L. G. E. (1958). Observations on the black termites, *Hospitalitermes* spp., of Java and Sumatra. *Insectes soc. 5*, 9-30.

Kalshoven, L. G. E. (1959). Observations on the nests of initial colonies of *Neotermes tectonae* (Damm.) in teak trees. *Insectes soc. 6*, 231-242.

Kemp, P. B. (1955). The termites of north-eastern Tanganyika: their distribution and biology. *Bull. ent. Res. 46*, 113-135.

Kirby, H. (1941). Protozoa and other animals. *In* "Protozoa in Biological Research" (N. Calkins and F. M. Summers, eds), pp. 890-1008. Columbia Univ. Press, N.Y.

Kistner, D. H. (1969). The biology of termitophiles. *In* "Biology of Termites" (K. Krishna and F. M. Weesner, eds), Vol. 1, pp. 525-557. Academic Press, N.Y. and London.

Knight, P. (1939). "Problems of Insect Study". Edwards, Ann Arbor, Michigan.

Kofoid, C. A. (1934). "Termites and Termite Control" (C. A. Kofoid, ed.), 2nd edition. Univ. California Press.

Kollmannsperger, F. (1934). Die Oligochaeten des Bellinchen-Gebietes, eine ökologische, ethologische und tiergeographische Untersuchung. Inaugural Dissertation, Berlin. pp. 1-115.

Kozlova, A. V. (1951). Accumulation of nitrates in termite mounds in Turkmenia.*Pochvovedenie 1951(10)*, 626-631.
Krishna, K. (1969). Introduction. *In* "Biology of Termites" (K. Krishna and F. M. Weesner, eds), Vol. 1, pp. 1-17. Academic Press, N.Y. and London.
Krishna, K. and Weesner, F. M. (1969). "Biology of Termites" (K. Krishna and F. M. Weesner, eds), Vol. 1. Academic Press, N.Y. and London.
Krishna, K. and Weesner, F. M. (1970). "Biology of Termites" (K. Krishna and F. M. Weesner, eds), Vol. 2. Academic Press, N.Y. and London.
Kubiena, W. (1938). "Micropedology". Collegiate Press, Ames, Iowa.
Kubiena, W. (1948). "Entwicklungslehre des Bodens". Springer, Vienna.
Kubiena, W. (1955). Animal activity in soils as a decisive factor in establishment of humus forms. *In* "Soil Zoology" (D. K. McE. Kevan, ed.), pp. 73-82. Butterworths, London.
Kuhnelt, W. (1961). "Soil Biology" (English translation by N. Walker). Faber and Faber, London.
Kurcheva, G. F. (1960). The role of invertebrates in the decomposition of oak litter. *Pedology 4*, 16-23.
Ladd, J. N. and Butler, J. H. A. (1969). Inhibition and stimulation of proteolytic enzyme activities by soil humic acids. *Aust. J. Soil Res. 7*, 253-261.
Lake, P. (1890). The geology of South Malabar, between the Beypore and Ponnani Rivers. *Mem. geol. Surv. India 24*, 201-246.
Lamprey, H. P. (1964). Estimation of the large mammal densities, biomass and energy exchange in the Tarangire Game Reserve and the Masai Steppe in Tanganyika. *E. Afr. Wildl. J. 2*, 1-47.
Laverack, M. S. (1963). "The Physiology of Earthworms". Int Ser. Monogr. Pure and Appl. Biol. no. 15. Pergamon Press, Oxford.
Lee, K. E. (1959). The earthworm fauna of New Zealand. *Bull. N.Z. Dep. sci. ind. Res. 130*, 1-486.
Lee, K. E. and Wood, T. G. (1968). Preliminary studies of the role of *Nasutitermes exitiosus* (Hill) in the cycling of organic matter in a yellow podzolic soil under dry sclerophyll forest in South Australia. *Trans. 9th Int. Congr. Soil Sci., Adelaide, 1968, 2*, 11-18.
Lee, K. E. and Wood, T. G. (in press). Physical and chemical effects on soils of some Australian termites, and their pedological significance. *Pedobiologia*.
Leenheer, L. de, d'Hoore, J. and Sys, K. (1952). Cartographie et caractérisation pédologique de la catena de Yangambi. Les Termitières. *Publ. Inst. natn. Ét. agron. Congo belge, Ser. scient. 55*, 53-54.
Leopold, B. (1952). Studies on lignin. XIV. The composition of Douglas fir wood digested by the West Indian dry-wood termite (*Cryptotermes brevis* Walker). *Svensk Papp-Tidn. 5*, 784-786.
Light, S. F. and Weesner, F. M. (1955). The incipient colony of *Tenuirostritermes tenuirostris* (Desneux). *Insectes soc. 2*, 135-146.
Loos, R. (1964). A sensitive anemometer and its use for the measurement of air currents in the nests of *Macrotermes natalensis* (Haviland). *In* "Etudes sur les Termites Africains" (A. Bouillon, ed.), pp. 363-372. Leopoldville Univ., Leopoldville.
Luppova, A. N. (1958). Termity Turkmenii. *Tr. Inst. Zool. Parazitol. Akad. Nauk Turkm. SSR 2*, 81-144.
Lüscher, M. (1951a). Significance of "fungus gardens" in termite nests. *Nature, Lond. 167*, 34-35.

Lüscher, M. (1951b). Beobachtungen über die Kolonie-gründung bei verschiedenen afrikanischen Termitenarten. *Acta trop. 8*, 36-43.

Lüscher, M. (1955). Der Sauerstoffverbauch bei Termiten und die Ventilation des Nestes bei *Macrotermes natalensis* (Haviland). *Acta trop. 12*, 287-307.

Macfadyen, A. (1962). Soil arthropod sampling. *Adv. ecol. Res. 1*, 1-34.

Macfadyen, A. (1963). The contribution of the microfauna to total soil metabolism, *In* "Soil Organisms" (J. Doeksen and J. van der Drift, eds), pp. 3-16. North Holland, Amsterdam.

Macfadyen, A. (1964). Energy flow in ecosystems and its exploitation by grazing. *In* "Grazing in Terrestrial and Marine Environments" (D. J. Crisp, ed.), pp. 3-20. Blackwell, Oxford.

Macfadyen, A. (1967). Methods of investigation of productivity of invertebrates in terrestrial ecosystems. *In* "Secondary Productivity of Terrestrial Ecosystems" (K. Petrusewicz, ed.), pp. 383-412. Institute of Ecology, Polish Acad. Sci., Warsaw.

Macfadyen, W. A. (1950). Vegetation patterns in the semi-desert plains of British Somaliland. *Geogrl J. 116*, 199-211.

MacGregor, W. D. (1950). Termites, soil and vegetation. *For. Abstr. 12*, 3-8.

Madge, D. S. (1965). Leaf fall and litter disappearance in a tropical forest. *Pedobiologia 5*, 273-288.

Maignien, R. (1966). "Review of Research on Laterites". UNESCO, Paris.

Maldague, M. E. (1959). Analyses de sols et matériaux de termitières du Congo Belge. *Insectes soc. 6*, 343-359.

Maldague, M. E. (1964). Importance des populations de termites dans les sols équatoriaux. *Trans. 8th Int. Congr. Soil Sci., Bucharest, 1964, 3*, 743-751.

Martyn, E. B. (1931). A botanical survey of the Rupununi Development Company's ranch at Waranama, Berbice River. *Agric. J. Br. Guiana 4*, 18-25.

Mathur, R. N. (1962). Enemies of termites (white ants). *In* "Termites in the Humid Tropics", New Delhi Symposium, pp. 137-139. UNESCO, Paris.

McMahan, E. A. (1969). Feeding relationships and radioisotope techniques. *In* "Biology of Termites" (K. Krishna and F. M. Weesner eds), Vol. 1, pp. 387-406. Academic Press, N.Y. and London.

McNeill, S. and Lawton, J. H. (1970). Annual production and respiration in animal populations. *Nature, Lond. 225*, 472-474.

Meiklejohn, J. (1965). Microbiological studies on large termite mounds. *Rhod. Zamb. Mal. J. agric. Res. 3*, 67-79.

Meyer, J. A. (1960). Résultats agronomiques d'un essai de nivellement des termitières réalisé dans la Cuvette centrale Congolaise. *Bull. agric. Congo belge 51*, 1047-1059.

Milne, A. (1961). Definition of competition among animals. *Symp. Soc. exp. Biol. 15*, 40-61.

Milne, G. (1947). A soil reconnaissance journey through parts of Tanganyika Territory. December 1935 to February 1936. *J. Ecol. 35*, 192-264.

Misra, J. N. and Ranganathan, V. (1954). Digestion of cellulose by the mound building termite *Termes (Cyclotermes) obesus* (Rambur). *Proc. Indian Acad. Sci. 39*, 100-113.

Mitchell, F. J. (1965). Australian geckos assigned to the genus *Gehyra* Gray. *Senckenberg. biol. 46*, 287-319.

Moore, B. P. (1965). Pheromones and insect control. *Aust. J. Sci. 28*, 243-245.

Moore, B. P. (1969). Biochemical studies in termites. *In* "Biology of Termites"

(K. Krishna and F. M. Weesner, eds), Vol. 1, pp. 407-432. Academic Press, N.Y. and London.

Morison, C. G. T., Hoyle, A. C. and Hope-Simpson, J. F. (1948). Tropical soil-vegetation catenas and mosaics. A study in the south-western part of the Anglo-Egyptian Sudan. *J. Ecol.* 36, 1-84.

Murray, J. M. (1938). An investigation of the interrelationships of the vegetation, soils and termites. *S. Afr. J. Sci.* 35, 288-297.

Myers, J. G. (1936). Savannah and forest vegetation of the interior Guiana plateau. *J. Ecol.* 24, 162-184.

Naudé, T. J. (1934). Termites in relation to veld destruction and erosion. *S. Afr. Dep. Agric. Plant Industr. Ser.* 2, *Bull. 134*, 1-20.

Nazaroff, P. S. (1931). Note on the spongy ironstone of Angola. *Geol. Mag.* 68, 443-446.

Nel, J. J. C. (1968). Aggressive behaviour of the harvester termites *Hodotermes mossambicus* (Hagen) and *Trinervitermes trinervoides* (Sjöstedt). *Insectes soc.* 15, 145-156.

Newsam, A. and Rao, B. S. (1958). Control of *Coptotermes curvignathus* Holmgren with chlorinated hydrocarbons. *J. Rubb. Res. Inst. Malaya* 15, 209-215.

Nielsen, C. O. (1963). Carbohydrases in soil and litter invertebrates. *Oikos 13*, 200-215.

Noirot, C. (1959). Remarques sur l'écologie des termites. *Annls soc. r. zool. Belg.* 89, 151-168.

Noirot, C. (1961). L'évolution de la faune de Termites des savanes côtiers de Côte-d'Ivoire. *Proc. 11th Int. Congr. Ent., Vienna, 1960, 1*, 658-659.

Noirot, C. (1969). Formation of castes in the higher termites. *In* "Biology of Termites" (K. Krishna and F. M. Weesner eds), Vol. 1, pp. 311-350. Academic Press, N.Y. and London.

Noirot, C. (1970). The nests of termites. *In* "Biology of Termites" (K. Krishna and F. M. Weesner eds), Vol. 2, pp. 73-125. Academic Press, N.Y. and London.

Noirot, C. and Noirot-Timothée, C. (1967). L'epithelium absorbant de la panse d'un termite supérieur. Ultrastructures et rapport avec la symbiose bactérienne. *Annls. Soc. ent. Fr.* 3, 577-592.

Noirot, C. and Noirot-Timothée, C. (1969). The digestive system. *In* "Biology of Termites" (K. Krishna and F. M. Weesner eds), Vol. 1, pp. 49-88. Academic Press, N.Y. and London.

Northcote, K. H. (1965). A factual key for the recognition of Australian soils. 2nd edition. *Divl Rep. Div. Soils C.S.I.R.O. Aust.* 2/65.

Nutting, W. L. (1969). Flight and colony foundation. *In* "Biology of Termites" (K. Krishna and F. M. Weesner, eds), Vol. 1, pp. 233-282. Academic Press, N.Y. and London.

Nye, P. H. (1954). Some soil-forming processes in the humid tropics. I. A field study of a catena in the West African forest. *J. Soil Sci.* 5, 7-21.

Nye, P. H. (1955). Some soil-forming processes in the humid tropics. IV. The action of the soil fauna. *J. Soil Sci.* 6, 73-83.

Ollier, C. D. (1959). A two-cycle theory of tropical pedology. *J. Soil Sci. 10*, 137-148.

Oshima, M. (1919). Formosan termites and methods of preventing their damage. *Philipp. J. Sci.* 15, 319-383.

Pathak, A. N. and Lehri, L. K. (1959). Studies on termite nests. I. Chemical, physical and biological characteristics of a termitarium in relation to its surroundings. *J. Indian Soc. Soil Sci. 7*, 87-90.

Park, T. (1954). Experimental studies in interspecific competition. 2. Temperature, humidity and competition in two species of *Tribolium*. *Physiol. Zoöl. 27*, 177-238.

Paulian, R. (1970). The termites of Madagascar. In "Biology of Termites" (K. Krishna and F. M. Weesner, eds), Vol. 2, pp. 281-294. Academic Press, N.Y. and London.

Pearson, E. O. and Maxwell-Darling, R. C. (1958). "The Insect Pests of Cotton in Tropical Africa". Empire Cotton Growing Corp. and Commonwealth Inst. Entomology.

Pendleton, R. L. (1941). Some results of termite activity in Thailand soils. *Thai Sci. Bull. 3(2)*, 29-53.

Pendleton, R. L. (1942). Importance of termites in modifying certain Thailand soils. *J. Am. Soc. Agron. 34*, 340-344.

Petrides, G. A. (1956). Big game densities and range carrying capacities in East Africa. *Trans. N. Am. Wildl. Conf. 21*, 525-537.

Petrides, G. A. and Swank, W. G. (1965). Estimating the productivity and energy relations of an African elephant population. *Proc. 9th Int. Grassld Congr., Sao Paulo, 1964*, pp. 831-841.

Pierantoni, U. (1935). La simbiosi fisiologica nei termitidi xilofagi e nei loro flagellati intestinali. *Arch. zool. Ital. 22*, 135-171.

Ploey, J. de (1964). Nappes de gravats et couvertures argilo-sableuses au Bas-Congo; leur génèse et l'action des termites. In "Études sur les Termites Africains" (A. Bouillon, ed.), pp. 399-414. Leopoldville Univ., Leopoldville.

Pochon, J., Barjac, H. de, and Roche, A. (1959). Recherches sur la digestion de la cellulose chez le termite *Sphaerotermes sphaerothorax*. *Annls Inst. Pasteur 96*, 352-355.

Powers, W. L. and Bollen, W. B. (1935). The chemical and biological nature of certain forest soils. *Soil Sci. 40*, 321-329.

Rao, K. P. (1960). Occurrence of enzymes for protein digestion in the termite *Heterotermes indicola*. In "Termites in the Humid Tropics", New Delhi Symposium, pp. 71-72. UNESCO, Paris.

Ratcliffe, F. N., Gay, F. J. and Greaves, T. (1952). "Australian Termites". C.S.I.R.O. Aust., Melbourne.

Ratcliffe, F. N. and Greaves, T. (1940). The subterranean foraging galleries of *Coptotermes lacteus* (Frogg.). *J. Coun. sci. ind. Res. Aust. 13*, 150-161.

Raw, F. (1959). Estimating earthworm populations using formaline. *Nature, Lond. 184*, 1661-1662.

Raw, F. (1962). Studies of earthworm populations in orchards. I. Leaf burial in apple orchards. *Ann. appl. Biol. 50*, 389-404.

Reynoldson, T. B. (1955). Observations on the earthworms of North Wales. *NWest Nat. 3*, 291-304.

Rhee, J. A. van (1963). Earthworm activities and the breakdown of organic matter in agricultural soils. In "Soil Organisms" (J. Doeksen and J. van der Drift, eds), pp. 55-59. North Holland, Amsterdam.

Richards, P. B. (1917). The history and present position of white ant treatment in Malaya. *Agric. Bull. F.M.S. 5*, 338-348.

Robinson, J. B. D. (1958). Some chemical characteristics of "termite soils" in Kenya coffee fields. *J. Soil Sci. 9*, 58-65.

Roonwall, M. L. (1970). Termites of the Oriental Region. *In* "Biology of Termites" (K. Krishna and F. M. Weesner, eds), Vol. 2, pp. 315-391. Academic Press, N.Y. and London.

Rudman, P. and Gay, F. J. (1963). The causes of natural durability in timber. X. The deterrent properties of some three-ringed carbocyclic and heterocyclic substances to the subterranean termite *Nasutitermes exitiosus* (Hill). *Holzforschung 17*, 21-25.

Rudman, P. and Gay, F. J. (1967a). The causes of natural durability in timber. XX. The cause of variation in the termite resistance of jarrah (*Eucalyptus marginata* ɔm.). *Holzforschung 21*, 21-23.

Rudman, P. and Gay, F. J. (1967b). The causes of natural durability in timber. XXI. The anti-termitic activity of some fatty acids, esters and alcohols. *Holzforschung 21*, 24-26.

Ruelle, J. E. (1964). L'architecture du nid de *Macrotermes natalensis* et son sens fonctionnel. *In* "Études sur les Termites Africains" (A. Bouillon, ed.), pp. 327-362. Leopoldville Univ., Leopoldville.

Ruelle, J. E. (1970). A revision of the termites of the genus *Macrotermes* from the Ethiopian region (Isoptera: Termitidae). *Bull. Br. Mus. nat. Hist. Entomol. 24(9)*, 365-444.

Salt, G. (1952). The arthropod population of the soil in some East African pastures. *Bull. ent. Res. 43*, 203-220.

Salt, G., Hollick, F. S., Raw, F. and Brian, M. V. (1948). The arthropod population of pasture soil. *J. Anim. Ecol. 17*, 180-201.

Sands, W. A. (1956). Some factors affecting the survival of *Odontotermes badius*. *Insectes soc. 3*, 531-536.

Sands, W. A. (1960a). The initiation of fungus comb construction in laboratory colonies of *Ancistrotermes guineensis* (Silvestri). *Insectes soc. 7*, 251-259.

Sands, W. A. (1960b). Termite control in West African afforestation. *Rep. 7th Commonw. ent. Conf.*, pp. 106-108.

Sands, W. A. (1961). Foraging behaviour and feeding habits in five species of *Trinervitermes* in West Africa. *Entomologia exp. appl. 4*, 277-288.

Sands, W. A. (1962). The evaluation of insecticides as soil and mound poisons against termites in agriculture and forestry in West Africa. *Bull. ent. Res. 53*, 179-192.

Sands, W. A. (1965a). Termite distribution in man-modified habitats in West Africa, with special reference to species segregation in the genus *Trinervitermes* (Isoptera, Termitidae, Nasutitermitinae). *J. Anim. Ecol. 34*, 557-571.

Sands, W. A. (1965b). Mound population movements and fluctuations in *Trinervitermes ebenerianus* Sjöstedt (Isoptera, Termitidae, Nasutitermitinae). *Insectes soc. 12*, 49-58.

Sands, W. A. (1965c). A revision of the termite subfamily Nasutitermitinae (Isoptera: Termitidae) from the Ethiopian region. *Bull. Br. Mus. nat. Hist., Entomol. Suppt 4*, 1-172.

Sands, W. A. (1965d). Alate development and colony foundation in five species of *Trinervitermes* (Isoptera, Nasutitermitinae) in Nigeria, West Africa. *Insectes soc. 12*, 117-130.

Sands, W. A. (1969). The association of termites and fungi. *In* "Biology of Termites" (K. Krishna and F. M. Weesner, eds), Vol. 1, pp. 495-524. Academic Press, N.Y. and London.

Satchell, J. E. (1958). Earthworm biology and soil fertility. *Soils Fertil. 21*, 209-219.

Satchell, J. E. (1963). Nitrogen turnover by a woodland population of *Lumbricus terrestris. In* "Soil Organisms" (J. Doeksen and J. van der Drift, eds), pp. 60-65. North Holland, Amsterdam.

Saunders, G. W. (1969). Termites on northern beef properties. *Qd agric. J. 95*, 31-36.

Saurin, E. and Roch, E. (1958). Observations sur des formations "latéritiques" au Cambodge et au Viet-Nam Sud. *C. r. hebd. Séanc. Acad. sci. Paris 247*, 358-360.

Schmidt, R. S. (1955). The evolutionary nest-building behaviour in *Apicotermes* (Isoptera). *Evolution, N.Y. 9*, 157-181.

Schmidt, R. S. (1958). The nest of *Apicotermes träghårdi* (Isoptera), new evidence in the evolution of nest building. *Behaviour 12*, 76-94.

Schubert, W. J. (1965). "Lignin Biochemistry". Academic Press, N.Y. and London.

Seifert, K. (1962a). Die chemische Veränderung der Holzzellwand-Komponenten unter dem Einfluss pflanzlicher und tierischer Schädlinge. 1. Mitteilung: Überblick über die bisher veroffentlichte Literatur. *Holzforschung 16*, 78-91.

Seifert, K. (1962b). Die chemische Veränderung der Holzzellwand-Komponenten unter dem Einfluss pflanzlicher und tierischer Schädlinge. 2. Mitteilung: Abbau von *Pinus sylvestris* L. durch *Coniophora cerebella* Pers. *Holzforschung 16*, 102-113.

Seifert, K. (1962c). Die chemische Veränderung der Holzzellwand-Komponenten unter dem Einfluss pflanzlicher und tierischer Schädlinge. 3. Mitteilung: Uber die Verdauung der Holzsubstanz durch die Larven des Hausbockkäfers (*Hylotrupes bajulus* L) und des Gewöhnlichen Nagekäfers (*Anobium punctatum* De Geer). *Holzforschung 16*, 148-154.

Seifert, K. (1962d). Die chemische Veränderung der Holzzellwand-Komponenten unter dem Einfluss tierischer und pflanzlicher Schädlinge. 4. Mitteilung: Die Verdauung von Kiefern- und Rotbuchenholz durch die Termite *Kalotermes flavicollis* Fabr. *Holzforschung 16*, 161-168.

Seifert, K. and Becker, G. (1965). Der chemische Abbau von Laub- und Nadelholzarten durch verschiedene Termiten. *Holzforschung 19*, 105-111.

Sen, A. (1944). The influence of feed upon the composition of termite soils. *Curr. Sci. 13*, 280-281.

Shrikhande, J. G. and Pathak, A. N. (1948). Earthworms and insects in relation to soil fertility. *Curr. Sci. 17*, 327-328.

Sillans, R. (1959). "Les Savannes de l'Afrique Centrale". Lechavelier, Paris.

Sivarajasingham, S., Alexander, L. T., Cady, J. G. and Cline, M. G. (1962). Laterite. *Adv. Agron. 14*, 1-60.

Skaife, S. H. (1955). "Dwellers in Darkness". Longmans Green, London.

Smeathman, H. (1781). Some account of the termites which are found in Africa and other hot climates. *Phil. Trans. R. Soc. 71*, 139-192.

Snyder, T. E. (1948). "Our Enemy the Termite". Comstock, N.Y.

Snyder, T. E. (1949). Catalog of the termites (Isoptera) of the world. *Smithson. misc. Collns 112*, 1-490.

Snyder, T. E. (1952). Detection of termites by microphones. *Pest Control 20(7)*, 33-34.

Snyder, T. E. (1956). "Annotated, Subject-heading Bibliography of Termites, 1350 B.C. to A.D. 1954". Smithsonian Institution, Washington.

Snyder, T. E. (1961). "Supplement to the Annotated, Subject-heading Bibliography of Termites, 1955 to 1960". Smithsonian Institution, Washington.

Snyder, T. E. (1968). "Second Supplement to the Annotated Subject-heading Bibliography of Termites, 1961-1965". Smithsonian Institution, Washington.

Southwood, T. R. E. (1966). "Ecological Methods with Particular Reference to the Study of Insect Populations". Methuen, London.

Stace, H. C. T., Hubble, G. D., Brewer, R., Northcote, K. H., Sleeman, J. R., Mulcahy, M. J. and Hallsworth, E. G. (1968). "A Handbook of Australian Soils". Rellim Press, Adelaide.

Stockdill, S. M. J. (1966). The effect of earthworms on pastures. *Proc. N.Z. ecol. Soc. 13,* 68-75.

Stöckli, A. (1949). Die ernährung der Pflanze in ihrer Abhängigkeit von der Kleinlebewelt des Bodens. *Z. Pfl.Enähr. Dung. 45,* 41-53.

Stoops, G. (1964). Application of some pedological methods to the analysis of termite mounds. *In* "Études sur les Termites Africains" (A. Bouillon, ed.), pp. 379-398. Leopoldville Univ., Leopoldville.

Stoops, G. (1968). Micromorphology of some characteristic soils of the Lower Congo (Kinshasa). *Pédologie 18,* 110-149.

Strickland, A. H. (1944). The arthropod fauna of some tropical soils. *Trop. Agric. Trin. 21,* 107-114.

Strickland, A. H. (1945). A survey of the arthropod soil and litter fauna of some forest reserves and cacao estates in Trinidad (British West Indies). *J. Anim. Ecol. 14,* 1-11.

Stuart, A. M. (1967). Alarm, defense and construction behaviour relationships in termites (Isoptera). *Science, N.Y. 156,* 1123-1125.

Stuart, A. M. (1969). Social behaviour and communication. *In* "Biology of Termites" (K. Krishna and F. M. Weesner eds), Vol. 1, pp. 193-232. Academic Press, N.Y. and London.

Stumper, R. (1923). Sur la composition chimique des nids de l'*Apicotermes occultus* Silv. *C. r. hebd. Séanc. Acad. sci. Paris 177,* 409-411.

Svendsen, J. A. (1957). The distribution of Lumbricidae in an area of Pennine moorland (Moor House Nature Reserve). *J. Anim. Ecol. 26,* 411-421.

Sys, C. (1955). The importance of termites in the formation of latosols. *Sols Afr. 3,* 392-395.

Taltasse, P. (1957). Les cabaças de jacaré et le role des termites. *Rev. Géomorph. dyn. 8,* 166-170.

Tessier, F. (1959a). La latérite du cap Manuel à Dakar et ses termitières fossiles. *C. r. hebd. Séanc. Acad. sci. Paris 248,* 3320-3322.

Tessier, F. (1959b). Termitières fossiles dans la latérite de Dakar (Sénégal). Remarques sur les structures latéritiques. *Annls Fac. Sci. Univ. Dakar 4,* 91-132.

Thakur, C., Prasad, A. R. and Singh, R. P. (1958). Use of aldrin and dieldrin against termites and their effects on soil fertility. *Indian J. Ent. 19,* 155-163.

Thomas, A. S. (1941). The vegetation of the Sese Islands, Uganda. *J. Ecol. 29,* 330-353.

Thompson, W. L. (1933). Termites as a pest of citrus trees. *Proc. Fla St. hort. Soc. 46,* 84-87.

Trager, W. (1932). A cellulase from the symbiotic intestinal flagellates of termites and of the roach, *Cryptocercus punctulatus. Biochem. J. 26,* 1762-1771.

Tricart, J. (1957). Observations sur le role ameublisseur des termites. *Rev. Géomorph. dyn. 8*, 170-172.

Troll, C. (1936). Termitensavannen. *In* "Landekundliche Forschrift Festschrift für Norbert Krebs", pp. 275-312. Englehorn, Stuttgart.

UNESCO and Zoological Survey of India (1962). Symposium on "Termites in the Humid Tropics". UNESCO, Paris.

Uttangi, J. C. and Joseph, K. J. (1962). Flagellate symbionts (Protozoa) of termites from India, *In* "Termites in the Humid Tropics", New Delhi Symposium, pp. 155-161. UNESCO, Paris.

Vos, A. de (1969). Ecological conditions affecting the production of wild herbivorous mammals on grasslands. *Adv. ecol. Res. 6*, 137-183.

Waloff, N. and Blackith, R. E. (1962). Growth and distribution of the mounds of *Lasius flavus* (Fabricius) (Hym.: Formicidae) in Silwood Park, Berkshire. *J. Anim. Ecol. 31*, 421-437.

Waters, R. S. (1955). Numbers and weights of earthworms under a highly productive pasture. *N.Z. Jl Sci. Technol. A 36*, 516-525.

Watson, J. A. L. and Gay, F. J. (1970). The role of grass-eating termites in the degradation of a mulga ecosystem. *Search, 1*, 43.

Watson, J. A. L. and Perry, D. H. (in prep.). The biology and Taxonomy of the genus *Drepanotermes* (Isoptera: Amitermitinae).

Watson, J. P. (1960). Some observations on soil horizons and insect activity in granite soils. *Proc. 1st Fed. Sci. Congr. Rhodesia and Nyasaland*, pp. 271-276.

Watson, J. P. (1962). The soil below a termite mound. *J. Soil Sci. 13*, 46-51.

Weesner, F. M. (1960). Evolution and biology of termites. *A. Rev. Ent. 5*, 153-170.

Wheeler, W. M. (1936). Ecological relations of ponerine and other ants to termites. *Proc. Am. Acad. Arts Sci. 71*, 159-243.

Wiegert, R. G. and Evans, F. C. (1967). Investigations of secondary productivity in grasslands. *In* "Secondary Productivity in Terrestrial Ecosystems" (A. Petrusewicz, ed.), pp. 499-518. Polish Acad. Sci., Warsaw.

Wild, H. (1952). The vegetation of southern Rhodesian termitaria. *Rhodesia agric. J. 49*, 280-292.

Wilkinson, W. (1965). The principles of termite control in forestry. *E. Afr. agric. For. J. 31*, 212-217.

Williams, E. C. (1941). An ecological study of the floor fauna of the Panama rain forest. *Bull. Chicago Acad. Sci. 6*, 63-124.

Williams, M. A. J. (1968). Termites and soil development near Brock's Creek, Northern Territory. *Aust. J. Sci. 31*, 153-154.

Williams, R. M. C. (1959). Colony development in *Cubitermes ugandaensis. Insectes soc. 6*, 292-304.

Williams, R. M. C. (1965). "Termite Infestation of Pines in British Honduras". Overseas Res. Publ. no. 11, H.M.S.O., London.

Williams, R. M. C. (1966). The East African termites of the genus *Cubitermes* (Isoptera: Termitidae). *Trans. R. ent. Soc. Lond. 118*, 73-118.

Wolfenberger, D. O. (1958). Insect pests of the avocado and their control. *Univ. Fla Agric. exper. Sta. Bull. 605*, 36-38.

Wood, J.G. and Williams, R. J. (1960). "Vegetation". *In* "The Australian Environment". C.S.I.R.O. Aust., Melbourne.

Wood, T. G. (1971). The effects of soil fauna on the decomposition of *Eucalyptus* leaf litter in the Snowy Mountains, Australia. *In* "IV Colloquium Pedobiologiae, C.R. 4ème Coll. Int. Zool. Sol." (Ed. I.N.R.A., Paris), *in press.*

Wood, T. G. and Lee, K. E. (in press). Abundance of mounds and competition among colonies of some Australian termite species. *Pedobiologia.*

Yakushev, V. M. (1968). Influence of termite activity on the development of laterite soil. *Soviet Soil Sci. 1968(1)*, 109-111.

Zeuthen, E. (1953). Oxygen uptake as related to body size in organisms. *Q. Rev. Biol. 28*, 1-12.

Author Index

Numbers in *italics* refer to pages on which references are listed at the end of the paper

Subject Index

A

Abundance, *see also* distribution, 68-91
  of mounds, 68-69, 71-80
  of subterranean termites, 70-71
Acacia
  as food, 7
  effects on distribution, 78, 79, 80, 89
  erosion, 165
  mounds, 166
Acer pseudoplatanus, as food, 137
Achrestogonimes, 5
Adenota kob thomasi, biomass and metabolism, 187-189
Ahamitermes
  composition of carton, 141
  food, 13, 18
  nest, 45
Alates, 3
Alimentary system, of workers, 18-19
  symbiotic organisms, 125-131
Alkali-soluble materials
  in carton, 138
  in faeces, 138
  in wood, 138
  molecular weight, 138
Allodontotermes, see also Allodontoterms giffardi
  abundance, 79, 88
Allodontotermes giffardi, abundance, 73
Allognathotermes, see also Allognathotermes hypogeus
  abundance, 79
Allognathotermes hypogeus,
  abundance, 73
Allolobophora caliginosa
  effects on plant growth, 185
  effects on soils, 182

Amitermes, see also various species
  composition of carton, 141
  construction material, 28
  food, 10, 13, 15, 126, 133
  geographical distribution, 21, 81
  habitat, 133
  mounds, vegetation, 165
  nests, 41, 57
  site selection, 90
Amitermes abruptus, food, 14
Amitermes agrilis, food, 14
Amitermes boreus, food, 14
Amitermes colonus, food, 14
Amitermes darwini, food, 14
Amitermes dentosus, food, 14
Amitermes deplanatus, food, 14
Amitermes eucalypti, food, 14
Amitermes evuncifer
  abundance, 79
  building behaviour, 99
  competition, 87
  food, 72
  mounds, numbers/ha, 73
  nest, 66
  nest, organic matter, 108
Amitermes excellens, nest, 66
Amitermes exilis, food, 14
Amitermes germanus, food, 14
Amitermes gracilis, food, 14
Amitermes hartmeyeri, food, 14
Amitermes hastatus
  atmosphere in mounds, 55
  colony size, 97
  food, 11
  foraging, 52
  longevity of colonies, 96, 159
Amitermes herbertensis, food, 14
Amitermes heterognathus, food, 14
Amitermes lanceolatus, food, 14
Amitermes latidens, food, 14